Continually Working

BLACK LIVES & LIBERATION

SERIES EDITORS

Brandon Byrd, *Vanderbilt University*
Zandria F. Robinson, *Georgetown University*
Christopher Cameron, *University of North Carolina, Charlotte*

BLACK LIVES MATTER. What began as a Twitter hashtag after the 2013 acquittal of George Zimmerman for the murder of Trayvon Martin has since become a widely recognized rallying cry for black being and resistance. The series aims are two-fold: 1) to explore social justice and activism by black individuals and communities throughout history to the present, including the Black Lives Matter movement and the evolving ways it is being articulated and practiced across the African Diaspora; and 2) to examine everyday life and culture, rectifying well-worn "histories" that have excluded or denied the contributions of black individuals and communities or recast them as entirely white endeavors. Projects draw from a range of disciplines in the humanities and social sciences and will first and foremost be informed by "peopled" analyses, focusing on everyday actors and community folks.

CONTINUALLY WORKING

Black Women, Community Intellectualism *and* Economic Justice *in* Postwar Milwaukee

Crystal Marie Moten

Smithsonian National Museum
of American History
Washington, DC

in association with
Vanderbilt University Press
Nashville, Tennessee

Portions of Chapter 3 have appeared in Crystal Moten, "'Kept Right on Fightin' . . .': African American Women's Economic Activism in Milwaukee, Wisconsin," *Journal of Civil and Human Rights* 2 no. 1 (Spring/Summer 2016): 33–51.

Portions of Chapter 5 have appeared in Crystal Moten, "We've Been Behind the Scenes": Fair Employment and Project Equality in 1970s Milwaukee," in *The Strange Careers of Jim Crow North: Segregation and Struggle Outside the South*, edited by Brian Purnell and Jeanne Theoharis with Komozi Woodard (New York University Press, 2019), 259–284.

Library of Congress Cataloging-in-Publication Data

Names: Moten, Crystal, 1982- author.
Title: Continually working : Black women, community intellectualism, and
    economic justice in postwar Milwaukee / Crystal Moten.
Description: Nashville, Tennessee: Vanderbilt University Press, [2023] |
    Series: Black lives and liberation | Includes bibliographical references
    and index.
Identifiers: LCCN 2022053775 (print) | LCCN 2022053776 (ebook) | ISBN
    9780826505576 (paperback) | ISBN 9780826505583 (hardcover) | ISBN
    9780826505590 (epub) | ISBN 9780826505606 (adobe pdf)
Subjects: LCSH: African American
    women—Employment—Wisconsin—Milwaukee—History—20th century. |
    African American women—Wisconsin—Milwaukee—Economic conditions—20th
    century. | African American women—Wisconsin—Milwaukee—History—20th
    century. | Discrimination in
    employment—Wisconsin—Milwaukee—History—20th century. | Milwaukee
    (Wis.)—History—20th century.
Classification: LCC HD6096.W6 M67 2023 (print) | LCC HD6096.W6 (ebook) |
    DDC 331.4/09775—dc23/eng/20230104
LC record available at https://lccn.loc.gov/2022053775
LC ebook record available at https://lccn.loc.gov/2022053776

FOR MOM

Contents

Acknowledgments

Even though it was not possible to directly speak with every woman in this book whose story I have told, I must begin with acknowledging the women whose ideas, actions, strategies, experiences, struggles, and triumphs made this book possible. All errors and mistakes are mine alone. Additionally, the best ideas are nurtured and strengthened by and within community. Over the time I have worked on this book, my ideas have been encouraged, sharpened, and taken flight because of the many communities, assigned and chosen, of which I had the privilege to be a part.

Some aspects of this book emerged from the first graduate seminar I took on Black women's activism with Christina Greene, professor in the Afro American studies department at the University of Wisconsin–Madison. The primary research required for this seminar introduced me to the archives. Professor Greene's profuse comments (and purple ink) on my work throughout my graduate career made me a better thinker and writer. As my primary advisor, Nan Enstad's continued guidance and support as I navigated graduate school and the professoriate have been invaluable. The same is true for William P. Jones, whose mentorship, friendship, and kindness has meant so much over the course of my career. Additional thanks to the late Jeanne Boydston, Francisco Serrano, Finn Enke, Sue Zaeske, and Cindy Cheng. Without the administrative help and good cheer of Leslie Abadie and Carrie Tobin, I might not have figured out or kept track of all the degree requirements I needed to successfully graduate. To them, I am grateful.

Fellow students in the departments of Afro-American studies and history remain lifelong friends and have journeyed with me as the ideas of this book developed over time. Thanks to Shannon Dee Williams, Matthew Blanton, Kate Mason, Sherry Johnson, Tanisha Ford, Eric Darnell Pritchard, Tiffany Florvil, and Assata Kokayi. A multitude of thanks to Charles Hughes, Jennifer Holland, Libby Tronnes, Andrew Case, Meredith Beck Mink, and Megan Raby—members of a writing group that read my work from proposal, to shitty first draft, to conference paper, and to chapter, many times over. Words cannot describe my debt of gratitude to the late Doria Dee Johnson, a dear friend and colleague. Doria started the history graduate program after me and we always joked that I was assigned to be her "formal" mentor. While I had a few years on her in terms of the pursuit of a history PhD, I learned so much from her about Black feminist theory, public history, and community engagement. Unfortunately, she passed away before the completion of this project. I sorely miss her, but I hope my work as a public historian honors her memory.

While the intellectual communities I found in the departments of Afro-American studies and history provided connection and camaraderie, my communities outside of the academy included Fountain of Life Family Worship Center as well as the Madison Alumnae Chapter of Delta Sigma Theta Sorority, Incorporated. These friends, mentors, spiritual advisors, and sorors always reminded me of who and whose I am, strengthening me, praying for me, feeding me, and providing me with opportunities to prioritize my health, my heart, and my spirit while on a tedious academic journey. Thanks to the Reverend Dr. Alexander Gee and Jackie Gee, as well as the FOL music team including Becca Grant, Alicia Cooper, Corey Saffold, Lena Archer, Cynthia Woodland, Kiah Calmese Walker, Anthony Ward, and LaVar Charleston. Thank you to the ladies of my FOL small group: Jennifer Taylor Edens, Molli Mitchell, De'Kendrea Stamps, Sherly Bellevue, Anglinia Washington, Nikki Ward, and Angela Cunningham. Thank you to the members of Madison Alumnae Chapter—Pearl Leonard Rock, Michelle DeBose, Tracey Williams, Tracey Caradine, Candace McDowell, Carlettra Stanford, Terri Strong, and Dana Warren—for your leadership and sisterhood. To L.I.T.E.R.A.L.: Turika Pulliam, Bonnie Williams, Danielle Berry, Raven McMillan, Christina Sempasa, Lucy Osakwe, Crystal Leach, Astra Iheukumere, Andrea Jones, Marian Jordan, Travelle Ellis, Carola Gaines, Uchenna Oraedu, Courtney Robinson, and Karla Renee Williams. All my love.

I am thankful to the UW Graduate School for the Advanced Opportunity Fellowship that funded portions of my time in graduate school, but I am also tremendously grateful for the jobs I held with the UW PEOPLE Program, in Residence Life, at the Business Library, and at the Oscar Rennebohm Library at Edgewood College. These jobs increased my professional skill sets, and along the way, I met some fabulous people. Thanks to Joselyn Diaz-Valdes, Binnu Hill, and Emilie Hofacker, as well as Jackie Scola-Bernstein, Larry Davis, and my twin, Tim Frederickson. Gratitude to Sylvia Contreras, Nathan Dowd, and Jonathon Bloy.

A Consortium for Faculty Diversity postdoctoral fellowship aided in my transition from graduate student to professor and I am grateful for this program. My CFD fellowship year at Dickinson College gave me the opportunity to develop my research agenda and craft new classes. Through the CFD fellowship, I met and became lifelong friends with Marisol LeBrón and Jennifer Kelly. Thanks to colleagues in the Department of History: Karl Qualls, Jeremy Ball, Marcelo Borges, and Regina Sweeney. I am grateful for the generous friendship of Emily Pawley and Roger Turner, who have read my work, shared their home and family with me, and fed me delicious food on holidays and mundane days all the same. Gratitude to Lynn Johnson and Patricia Moonsammy, as well as Jerry Philogene, Susan Rose, Amy Farrell, Jennifer Musial, Sarah Niebler, Sarah Kersh, Poulomi Saha, Linda Brindeau, and Maria Bruno. I would also like to add a special thanks to Amaury Sosa for a conversation we shared that helped me solidify the subtitle of the book. Cross campus thanks goes to my friends who worked in Landes House, including Melissa Garcia, Donna Hughes, Paula Lima Jones, and Vincent Stephens. Abundant gratitude to Bronté and Cynthia Burleigh-Jones, whom I met while at Dickinson and whose deep friendship has sustained me throughout my professional journey. Finally, special thanks to the students at Dickinson College including those who took my classes or with whom I directly worked or mentored.

Additional Dickinson College funding allowed me the opportunity to consult new archives to deepen the research for this book, but it was a National Endowment for the Humanities Faculty Seminar, convened by Jeanne Theoharis and Komozi Woodard during the summer of 2015, that profoundly shaped my research trajectory and this book. The NEH seminar brought together scholars who specialized in Black freedom studies outside of the south. During our convening we discussed major themes and issues in the subfield and presented our work. I shared a book proposal for this manuscript, and the feedback I received proved invaluable. In addition to the intellectual dialogue, camaraderie, and lifelong friendships developed among participants in this seminar, a group of us formed the Freedom North NE Writing Collective. The members of this collective, including Say Burgin, Kris Burrell, Peter Levy, and Laura Warren Hill, have read every word of this manuscript, several times over. They have been with me every step of the way, giving me feedback, asking me probing questions, and helping me sharpen my analysis. In the final stages of this book, Kris Burrell and Say Burgin's support and encouragement helped push me and this project forward.

A Mellon Foundation / Associated Colleges of the Midwest Faculty Fellowship, as well as funding for research and professional development from Macalester College, also helped advance this project. During my tenure as a Mellon Faculty Fellow, I had the pleasure to develop friendships with Prentiss Dantzler, Stephanie Jones, and Charisse Burden-Stelly—scholars whose work I tremendously admire.

At Macalester College, colleagues in the history department provided invaluable support for this project. Katrina Phillips and Jess Pearson, along with Amy Elkins from the English department, read and provided feedback on an early draft chapter. Linda Sturtz, Karin Velez, Chris Wells, Ernie Capello, Amy Sullivan, Rebecca Wingo, Yue-Him Tam, Tiffany Gleason, and Herta Pitman provided invaluable support and encouragement as department colleagues, for which I am grateful. Outside of the history department, friends and colleagues made my time at Macalester joyous: Duchess Harris, Lizeth

Gutierrez, Karín Aguilar-San Juan, Bill Hart, Harry Waters Jr., Brian Lozenski, Adrienne Christiansen, Hana Dinku, Karla Benson Rutten, Joan Maze, Coco Du, Marian Aden, Donna Maeda, Donna Lee, Chris MacDonald-Dennis, Joan Ostrove, Devavani Chatterjea, and Louisa Bradtmiller. Althea Sircar's friendship, forged during our first year on campus, has meant so much to me and I thank God for her continued presence in my life. Outside of Macalester, friends at Sanctuary Covenant Church nurtured me and became a home away from home. Thanks to pastors Dennis Edwards, Edrin Williams, and Rose Lee-Norman. Also, thanks to the Praise and Worship Team, including Joseph Garnier, Doreen Esule, and Zipporah Sharon Bahn.

A conversation about Roxane Gay's *Hunger* at Peace Coffee Shop in Minneapolis seeded the idea for *The Drip*, a podcast where academics of color sit around and discuss great books. Over our brews, Anita Chikkatur, Adriana Estill, Todd Lawrence, and I bonded over our love of great literature. When I left Minnesota to take a new job in Washington, DC, they still let me participate. Thanks friends!

It is amazing that I finished this book at all, especially because as I was wrapping up the book, I pivoted professionally, taking a new job as curator of African American history at the Smithsonian National Museum of American History in Washington, DC. As I was finding my feet in a new professional environment, the COVID-19 pandemic halted much of my orientation to the museum field. Then the murder of George Floyd broke my heart and made me question if this book mattered at all. The reinvigoration of the modern Black Freedom Struggle inspired me to pick up my pen. Through it all, colleagues at the museum have been supportive and encouraging. Thanks to Kathy Franz, Amanda Moniz, Sam Vong, Paula Johnson, Paul Johnston, Ashley Rose Young, Theresa McCulla, Hal Wallace, Peter Liebhold, Kelsey Wiggins, Hillery York, Nancy Bercaw, Valeska Hilbig, and Carrie Kotcho. Enduring gratitude to the members of the African American History Curatorial Collective including Fath Davis Ruffins, Modupe Labode, Tsione Wolde-Michael, Krystal Klingenberg, and Tony Perry. While working at the American History Museum, I have had the immense privilege of teaching in the American University Public History program, and I am grateful to the students I taught in the fall 2020 public history seminar and the fall 2021 and summer 2022 Black digital history seminars: you inspire me and give me hope for our profession and for our nation.

I would be remiss if I did not thank Katelyn Knox and Alison Van DeVenter. I enrolled in Katelyn's book bootcamp program and it helped me solidify the book's main contributions, while also helping me create a revision roadmap that saw me to completion. Katelyn and Alison's feedback meant all the difference. Special thanks to the librarians, archivists, collections assistants, and other institutional staff that helped me when I visited their repositories, especially those at the Wisconsin Historical Society, the Milwaukee Public Library, the Milwaukee County Historical Society, and Marquette University Special Collections and Archives.

Finally, to my family: your love has sustained me. Wherever I have gone, you've been with me, believing in me and rooting for me. Thanks to my biggest cheerleaders: my mom, Brenda Moten, and sister, Shamaeca Clark-Pierce. Gratitude to my aunt Azella Collins and uncle Andre Moten: without your unfailing support I would not be where I am today. To Yvonne Collins Moore: the first doctor I knew and my role model; I still look up to you. And to Timi: your steadfast faith and determination inspire me daily, as does your ability to delicately balance work and pleasure, so that we can enjoy the life we've created together. My thanks are unending.

Prologue

I come from a family of doers. Of Black women who work long hours during the day at offices, hospitals, restaurants, mail facilities, and schools, Black women who leave those jobs and continue their work caring for their homes (sometimes single-handedly) and their communities. After work on evenings and weekends, they spend their time in the church, at the meeting house, in their cars, or on public transportation—on the way and leading the way to change and transformation of their own lives and of those in their family and community. These Black women would not consider themselves community organizers, and yet they participated, shaped, served, led, and gave without expecting credit, sometimes in ways that (they knew) would be impossible to trace. They were active and yet they often eschewed the label of activist. Little did they know they had a witness. Even before I had developed any type of analytical framework, I knew one thing for sure: the women in my family continually worked.

My witnessing of Black women's work began with what I saw with my grandmother, great aunts, mother, aunts, cousins, and sister, and it continued as I grew up. Two institutions reinforced the consciousness I was beginning to develop about the nature of Black women's work: my Black church and my Black elementary school—both in walking distance from my home on the South Side of Chicago. As early as I can remember, my mother took my sister and I to church, and it was Ingleside Whitfield United Methodist Church, coupled with my attendance at the Henry O. Tanner Elementary School, that shaped so much of my understanding of Black women's lives and labors. Here in these religious and educational spaces, which they both were, I saw Black working women in action.

The first 11 a.m. service we attended at Ingleside Whitfield left me amazed. I could not believe my eyes. Here, for the first time, I saw a Black woman in the pulpit and she wasn't reading announcements or scripture. She was preaching. This was not Women's Day; it was a regular, mundane Sunday. I mark it as a turning point in my life. Witnessing the Reverend Danita R. Anderson, Sunday after Sunday, in that pulpit, and then interacting with her in the church, in the fellowship hall, in confirmation class, in her office, and outside the church confirmed something I already knew about Black women's determination and commitment to community change—it was deep and continuous. The day I met Reverend Anderson I did not know anything about her, but I would come to learn that she was a leader in the United Methodist Church; she participated in a denominational organization, Black Methodists for Church Renewal (BMCR); and she was active in the local chapter of her sorority, Delta Sigma Theta. While I did not initially know these things about her, what I saw was an opening, a possibility, and a path. For a while I thought I might become a pastor too, but I think what witnessing her work showed me was that I did not have to follow one path, but I could create my own.

The year my mom, sister, and I began attending Ingleside Whitfield coincided with the year I started at Henry O. Tanner Elementary School, my neighborhood school located at 7300 South Evans. While I had been taught by Black teachers before, I credit my sixth grade teacher, Mrs. Lezah Barnett, with creating a learning environment that watered and encouraged my love of Black history, literature, and culture. Always a reader, I had no problem with Mrs. Barnett's instruction: when we finished our tasks for the day, she encouraged us to pick and read from any volume of the red encyclopedia of African American history that piqued our interests. Thumbing through this text repeatedly during my free time, I learned the basics of African and African American history. Mrs. Barnett's learning environment promoted self-directed edification as well as communal learning.

Mrs. Barnett was proudly Afrocentric and connected to what I know now as the Black Arts Movement. She taught us about the holiday of Kwanzaa, and we learned the Nguzo Saba, reciting them together all year around, not just from December 26 to January 1, the official days of the holiday. Mrs. Barnett encouraged us to learn and memorize our favorite poems and offered our classroom as a recitation space. The day one of my sixth-grade friends recited "Ego-Tripping" by Nikki Giovanni began my lifelong love of Black poetry. I found and memorized my own poem, "Midway" by Naomi Long Madgett, a poem whose first line still moves me to this day: "I've come this far to freedom and I won't turn back . . ."

These experiences at home, at church, and at school (and the neighborhood library) put in place a firm foundation—one that would be tested as I began my formal pursuit of history, which initially was not on the path I set for myself. During my last year of college, I had a disciplinary crisis of sorts: I knew I wanted to go to graduate school, but at the last minute I decided my declared major—anthropology— was not the discipline for me. I had a problem with what I understood to be the hallmark of a good anthropologist: discovering and studying a remote, exotic place as a distanced outsider. I did not have many examples of alternative anthropological paths and I had not been exposed to US urban anthropology. During the same year of this intellectual crisis, I signed up for the first two history classes I had ever taken as an undergrad—an oral history seminar and a seminar on Black women's history. These two classes, both taught by the late historian Dr. Leslie Brown, sealed my intellectual fate. Two books, *The Montgomery Bus Boycott and the Women Who Started It*, by Joann Gibson Robinson, and *Words of Fire: An Anthology of African American Feminist Thought*, edited by Beverly Guy-Sheftall, resonated deeply with me. I was shaken and angry that as old as I was, I had never heard of Joann Gibson Robinson and the Women's Political Council; additionally, the Black feminist intellectual tradition laid out in *Words of Fire* reminded me of Mrs. Barnett. While enrolled in these classes I decided the discipline of history better suited me.

I entered graduate school with questions that I needed to answer to reconcile my personal witness with what I saw as missing in the historiographical record. What was the history of Black women's activism? In what ways did they contribute to improving the lives of their families and communities? How were they involved in movements for Black freedom and justice, specifically the twentieth century civil rights movement? How did geography affect Black women's activism? Why were historians only focusing on the South? What about the North? What about the Midwest? How did Black women activists understand and define leadership? I was confused because I knew a tradition of Black working women's activism existed—I had witnessed it—but where was it in the history books? Had I believed that there were no traces of Black working women's activism available for me to study, this book would not exist. But I went into the archive anxious and expectant. Black women had to be there; they just had to be, because the evidence of their past activism reverberated in my present life and in my hope for our future.

Many historians speak of the archives as their happy place—the place where they are the most confident and sure—but for me the archive was frustrating and not for the expected reasons. I entered the archives expecting to have to dig and dig to find extant traces of Black women's actions. However, what I encountered was the exact opposite—in every collection I explored, I tripped and stumbled over Black women's work. They were all over the twentieth century record. In some collections so apparent were their actions that I could only come to one conclusion: these women, their efforts, and their work had been intentionally excised, erased, deleted, discarded, and analyzed out of the story. I was outraged. Despite the limitations of the archive (which I discuss in the introduction), Black women were/are there/here.

My questions, expectations, and hope of what I could find in the archive shape how I approach archival research. I retraced the steps of previous researchers and looked at the collections that had formed the basis of their analyses, but I also uncovered additional collections and found connections between various types of sources. Sometimes this meant following one Black woman across a vast historical trail—connecting the dots of her work by looking for her across archival collections, oral history projects, government documents, newspaper articles, images, and passing references. Usually, following one Black woman's work revealed many, despite history's insistence on highlighting exceptional individuals.

And so what results on the pages of this book is the convergence of my personal history and my professional training as a historian. Both shape my perspective and my life's mission to uncover and make accessible the lives, experiences, and contributions of Black working women, past, present, and future. *Continually Working* fulfills a small part of this mission. My work as a curator at a history museum, with the responsibility of ensuring that the national collection includes the material culture of Black working women's lives, fulfills another small part of this mission.

While I cannot go back in time and change the actions of previous historians, archivists, and other keepers of history, I can do my part to make sure that people today and in the future have access to the texts, objects, and histories that can change their lives—as they did mine.

Introduction

Continually Working tells the stories of Black working women who resisted employment inequality in Milwaukee, Wisconsin, from the 1940s through the 1970s. The book focuses on Black working women in the struggle for fair and equal employment because these women's thoughts, voices, and actions have been marginalized in the historical record.[1] Leaving out their stories has resulted in an incomplete understanding of the past. Exploring their histories paints a fuller picture of the struggle for Black freedom and justice during the twentieth century, exposing the strategies that helped them move closer to economic justice, the ones that didn't, and the resistance they encountered along the way.

Black women fled the South during the second great migration, the chronological focus of this book, for many reasons.[2] Near the top of many migrants' list was better employment and higher wages. As they arrived in the urban Midwest, in Wisconsin's largest city, which had been heralded as a working class city where a worker could "quit one job in the morning and get another one in the afternoon," expectations were high.[3] Black working women quickly realized this would not be their experience and they would largely be relegated to the same types of jobs they had in the South, working in the domestic service industry—cooking, washing, scrubbing, or sweeping other people's homes, offices, and restaurants. "This is up north now," activist Sylvia Bell White proclaimed.[4] What she meant was that a racist, sexist, discriminatory labor market and workplace was the rule in Milwaukee, not an exception.

Black working women frequently compared their work experience in Milwaukee to the South and expressed frustration that employment opportunities were foreclosed in Milwaukee for similar reasons as in the South: racism and sexism. Therefore, this book refers to the concrete wall Black working women kept confronting as the *Jim Crow job system*.[5] I define the Jim Crow job system as the legal, social, and cultural structures that combine to exclude Black workers from accessing, participating in, and progressing in employment. Using the metaphor of a concrete wall is appropriate because of the materiality of concrete: impenetrable and immovable. In some industries, Black working women found it near impossible to gain a foothold. Not surprisingly, being locked out of quality employment paralleled being locked into residential segregation and unequal education. Using the term *Jim Crow* also makes it plain that Black workers saw similarities between the job-related racism and discrimination they experienced in the South and in the Midwest. While the geographical location of work had changed as well as, perhaps, the industry, Black workers still encountered virulent racism and discrimination from their bosses, coworkers, and the state—which supposedly monitored and regulated race-based employment discrimination. Using *Jim Crow job system* underscores that employment inequality was built into the structure of most workplaces, be they public or private.

Racism operated through bureaucracy and the intense focus on policy and procedure. Policies and procedures were supposedly race-blind, but they were not race-neutral, and they had disparate effects on Black working women's economic possibilities. Requirements for birth certificates and certification of education stood as barriers to entry in various industries, from manufacturing to beauty.[6] As well as manifesting as bureaucratic racism through policy and procedure, the nature of the Jim Crow job system did mean last hired, first fired, poorly paid and dirty work, like the South. In the urban Midwest, all of this was true, and there were also jobs that were considered "back of the house work."[7] Sometimes Black working women could get a job at a downtown store or restaurant or in a hospital. However, the positions offered to her were in the back, at the bottom, and out of sight. Positions like stock girls or dishwashers were hidden from view and required little interaction with the white public. In Milwaukee, Black women also worked as nursing assistants, a back-breaking job considered undesirable by white working women. Repeatedly Black working women butted up against the Jim Crow job system.

The Jim Crow job system manifested through bureaucratic racism, and it stole Black workers' time. Philosopher Charles Mills explores the racial implications of time by positing "white time."[8] Building on the works of historian George Lipsitz and political scientist Michael Hanchard, Mills defines white time as "a sociomental representation of temporality shaped by the interests and experience" of white people.[9] In the words of Black feminist theorist Brittney Cooper, "white people own time," and it is shaped by white supremacist ideas that exclude marginalized groups.[10] The concept of white time is useful in elucidating the Jim Crow job system. It creates time-consuming measures that erect barriers between Black people and the work they seek. White time also controls the pace of economic justice, with justice coming slow and based on the priorities of white people, which means that often justice does not come at all. Ample examples throughout this book reveal white time—from the delays created by the state's bureaucratic racism to waiting to hear back about a job application that was purposely misfiled. White time steals from Black workers and transfers time, money, and resources to white people.

Equally as important as laying out my definition of the Jim Crow job system is being clear about what I mean by "Black working woman," which I define as any Black woman who labors, but with some caveats. I highlight non-elite Black working women and Black women with a working-class agenda (which typically meant a focus on employment and labor conditions, as well as education, housing, and social services). Community organizers or beauticians whose income was not stable enough to thrust them into a class with higher earning potential are included. Manufacturing and clerical workers who were able to get their feet in the door but circumscribed to lowly paid, menial work with no possibilities for promotion by their race and gender are centered in this analysis. Partnered mothers who labored at home caring for their children and household figure into this analysis. Previously working single mothers who received aid from the state because the low wage work they could potentially get would rob them of the energy they needed to care for their children and meet their needs are also among the Black working women this study considers. Finally, Black women who desired quality work but were denied these opportunities are also considered here. The point is that I employ an expansive definition of Black working woman.

This book examines Black working women's efforts to dismantle the Jim Crow job system and is guided by the following set of questions: What were the range of activities that Black working women in Milwaukee engaged in to resist employment injustice in the private and public sectors during the post–World War II period? How did the concerted efforts of Black working women expose how the Jim Crow job system functioned in postwar Milwaukee? What visions of economic justice did Black working women develop and offer in response to employment injustice? What does Black working women's economic activism reveal about the nature of their intellectual activity? To answer these questions, I examined archival records of individuals and organizations related to social and racial justice; assessed documents from state government departments, divisions, and offices; read the personal narratives and histories of Black women found in oral histories, Black newspapers, and other published and unpublished sources; and consider labor statistics disseminated by local, state, and federal offices. Black working women engaged in various forms of activism—they complained and filed grievances with their employers, organized, advocated for alternative and vocational education, started their own businesses, critiqued and appealed to the state of Wisconsin, developed and supported economic and social welfare programs, protested, and wrote and published their ideas and analyses—to respond to employment injustice.

I re/read the archive with a keen eye for Black working women's thoughts and ideas, especially as they relate to the fight for good jobs and a fair workplace.[11] Open to finding Black working women's ideas in places including and beyond traditional intellectual texts, I found their ideas, as well as their intellectual influence, in unlikely, yet ordinary places—in meeting minutes, organizational memos and resolutions, correspondence, newsletters, grant applications, and reports, as well as in the traditional speeches, interviews, articles, and books. In my analysis, no one format takes precedence over the other—all offer equally important insights to reveal about what Black working women thought, their resulting actions, and vice versa.

Working on the twentieth century means that a paper trail does exist for many of the stories I tell in this book. However, as scholars Marisa Fuentes, LaShawn Harris, Sarah Haley, Saidiya Hartman, and others remind us, records created by the state, as well as by corporations or even white nonprofit organizations, enact violence in their silences, omissions, and ways of bringing Black working women into the picture.[12] Black working women often appear as subjects, or beneficiaries of services, punishment, or white benevolence. Rarely are they authors of the stories where they appear in public or organizational records. However, studying the twentieth century also means that Black women, especially in their later years, kept their own papers, created their own archives, participated in oral history interviews, and sometimes donated these records to archival repositories. Of course, socioeconomic class factored into which Black women kept and donated their records, making capturing the ideas of Black working women or poor Black women more difficult and necessitating reading across the grain to see them when they appear in the text. When I do encounter Black working women's words, ideas, and actions in the record, I am attentive to them. More often, this means that the everyday actions and thoughts of Black working women are not necessarily available. Instead, what we have are flashpoints, culminating moments that have been building and that get large enough to make it into the archival record. Recognizing these limitations, working with and through them, while difficult, yields tremendous gains. The result is one view into the worlds of Black working women and their efforts to enact social, political, and economic change in their communities.

Black working women's activism and critiques can function as a diagnostic tool, revealing the nature of employment-based structural inequality while also illuminating their own visions for economic freedom for Black people.[13] Despite their continued and varied economic activism over several decades, employment inequality remained structurally entrenched. This book restores Black women's struggle for fair and equal work as a crucial aspect of the mid-twentieth century Black freedom struggle. It expands the sites of labor activism, situating struggles for employment justice both within and beyond the workplace and labor union. Although Black working women were marginalized by a staggeringly powerful system, these women fought bravely and creatively with strategies that still resonate today.

Analyzing the strategies Black working women used in the fight against the Jim Crow job system provides an opportunity to simultaneously explore the community intellectualism—the group centered day-to-day intellectual activities and practices—that sustained and undergirded this activism.[14] As these women engaged in their activism, they came together around a set of grievances and critiques related to their specific work conditions (and in some instances, lack of work opportunities)—the Jim Crow job system. Their intellectual practices supported their economic activism and centered women workers. This centering, in turn, made possible multiple ways of producing and disseminating the group's ideas. Unmediated by a single charismatic voice, their community intellectualism highlighted the various experiences, voices, and narratives within the group, which sometimes conflicted. This intellectual labor culminated in the development of context-specific solutions. In other words, community intellectualism reveals that the group takes precedence over the exceptional individual, process supersedes personalities, and the mundane matters more than the media-driven.

The focus on the group distinguishes this study from others that examine the intellectual thought of grassroots organizers, specifically those who write about organic intellectuals, as conceived of by Antonio Gramsci.[15] Gramsci's formulation is useful because it theorizes the relationship between organizers, social groups, and their ideas, specifically how ideas are activated and mediated at the grassroots level, and who does this intellectual work. Still, in its application the concept privileges the charismatic individual leader, usually male. Historically, gender inequality has obstructed the ways women could assert their ideas, especially in public, and I agree with feminist theorist Aimee Carrillo Rowe's claim that the organic intellectual "category remains vexed in ways that exceed Gramsci's Marxist theorization."[16] Specifically, Rowe asserts, "while Gramsci productively signals the ideological force [one's] 'connection' to home communities exerts over knowledge production, his account doesn't provide an intersectional lens to untangle how multiple, cross-cutting connectivities become vexed through [one's] labor as intellectuals."[17] Applying the concept outside of Gramsci's Italian, working-class Marxist context can be problematic because Gramsci neither centered nor directly addressed racial or gender inequality.[18] Many of the studies that take up the theory of organic intellectuals are biographical in nature, exploring the life of an individual who synthesized and popularized the ideas of his group or community, while also working for social change.[19] In these studies, the story of the exceptional leader is highlighted and prioritized. This book's focus on the community makes Gramsci's formulation insufficient.[20]

Moreover, the activists in this study have an intellectual gene- alogy rooted in the knowledge-making traditions of Black women. Eighteenth- and nineteenth-century Black women struggled to make their ideas heard and some of them succeeded. Phillis Wheatley Peters, Maria Stewart, Sojourner Truth, and Mary Ann Shadd Cary wrote poetry, published memoirs, penned articles, established newspapers, or traveled the country spreading their ideas about racial and gender justice.[21] By the early twentieth century, Anna Julia Cooper, Mary Church Terrell, Ida B. Wells, Charlotte Hawkins Brown, and Nannie Helen Burroughs had started organizations and schools, and worked on local and national levels for Black free- dom and justice.[22]

In considering specifically ideas related to economic justice, we can see Black women were thinking and organizing around these issues as well, including wrestling with Black people's role in the labor market, the necessity of Black entrepreneurship for racial uplift, and what role education should play in economic development. Eliza Potter, a nineteenth-century Black hairdresser, wrote about her work and profession in a memoir, *A Hairdresser's Experience in High Life*.[23] While Maggie Lena Walker, the first Black woman bank president, did not formally publish a book about her ideas regarding economic justice, as historian Elsa Barkley Brown has noted, her actions and life's work—which centered Black working women—articulated her ideas and theory.[24] Walker employed a majority Black working women staff in the St. Luke Penny Savings Bank and donated generously to causes spearheaded and led by Black women, such as the National Training School for Women and Girls founded by Black Baptist leader Nannie Helen Burroughs in Washington, DC, in 1908. Burroughs thought it important to provide educational opportunities to women who might not have the opportunity to go to school. Holding classes in the evening, as well as incorporating Black history into the curriculum, Burroughs knew that education and employment went hand in hand.[25] Well-known entrepreneur and Black beauty-industry mogul Madam C. J. Walker also expressed her ideas about Black economic development through her business endeavors, which enabled her to practice her "gospel of giving," a legacy that informs Black philanthropy to this day.[26] There are ample examples of Black women's thinking and organizing around Black economic development, even though historians have not necessarily focused on the topic. *Continually Working* prioritizes an examination of Black women's intellectual traditions, specifically their ideas related to Black economic development and employment, which have, of course, changed over time.

Centering Black, Midwestern, Working Women in the Twentieth Century Black Freedom Struggle

Continually Working puts Black, Midwestern, working women at the center of the story for twentieth-century struggles for Black freedom, which is long overdue. This book enters into conversation with several historical studies that focus on civil rights activism outside the South, economic justice, Black women's activism, and African American intellectual history.

In studies of Black life in the urban Midwest, scholars give disproportionate attention to Chicago and Detroit, and often these cities have stood in for what it means to be Black in the Midwest, both historically and historiographically. Stories of Black folks in these large urban metropolitan areas overshadow the lives of those in cities like Milwaukee and simply erases the experiences of Black rural Midwesterners.[27] Of course, places like Milwaukee cannot be separated from their geographical, Midwestern context, but Black urbanites in Chicago and Detroit experienced a different Midwestern context depending on the social and political economy of their specific location. We need more local stories to complicate what we know about Black people's lives and experiences in this region.[28] Additionally, in terms of Milwaukee's size and the strength of its industrial economy, the city continually ranked among the top Midwestern cities. Historian Joe Trotter's sustained analysis of the city substantiates this important point, and his book *Black Milwaukee: The Making of an Urban Industrial Proletariat, 1915–1945* is still the foremost text on the working class history of Black Milwaukeeans.[29] Trotter's work laid the foundation for *Continually Working*, and this book builds on Trotter's contributions by continuing the story into the post–World War II period and shifting the focus, specifically, to Black working women, an analysis that was missing from Trotter's early work.[30]

Within the last twenty years, historians have opened new avenues of research on twentieth-century Black freedom struggles. While the mid-century struggle for Black rights in the South has been the focus of many studies, recently historians have also been working to consider civil rights movements outside of the South. These studies underscore the importance of local stories for understanding the nature of the Black Freedom Struggle. *Freedom North: Black Freedom Struggle outside of the South, 1940–1980* reveals the nature of the freedom struggle in cities like Boston, Brooklyn, Detroit, Oakland, and others.[31] This collection of essays illustrates how activists in cities outside of the South waged local battles against injustice, disrupting the idea that activism outside of the South happened because of the Southern civil rights movement. Northern, Midwestern, and Western Black activists mobilized during World War II, engaged in local struggles against school segregation, and sowed the seeds for Black nationalism. Building on these ideas, Jeanne Theoharis, Brian Purnell, and Komozi Woodard published *The Strange Careers of Jim Crow North: Segregation and Struggle Outside of the South*, which emphatically argues that Jim Crow is a national cancer, not a disease relegated to the South.[32]

While histories of Milwaukee's postwar Black freedom struggle highlight Milwaukeeans' struggles for educational equality and fair housing, they do not focus solely on Black Milwaukeean's attempts to dismantle the Jim Crow job system. Jack Dougherty's *More Than One Struggle: The Evolution of Black School Reform in Milwaukee* tells the story of the fight for quality education through school reform.[33] Dougherty begins the book by considering Black teacher employment in the 1930s and 1940s, laying out the difficulties Black teachers faced in the city, but the story shifts to school desegregation as Dougherty analyzes the impact of *Brown v. Board of Education* on the Milwaukee public school system in the 1950s and after. Examining fair housing, the virulent backlash that accompanied Black activism, and Milwaukee activists' strategic use of their own homegrown civil rights and Black power rhetoric, Patrick Jones's effectively shows how Milwaukee was the "Selma of the North."[34] Dougherty's and Jones's groundbreaking works on Milwaukee civil rights history illuminate that there is so much more to the story.

Continually Working focuses on Black women's fight for good jobs, not because this was the only aspect of the Black freedom struggle they engaged in, but because histories of labor activism and economic development tend to be written from a masculinist frame and are located in the union, the shop floor, or the board room. This is especially true in the industrial Midwest, where Black male workers proved mostly successful in their quest for manufacturing employment.[35] Because of this imbalance in the historiography, while some stories of Black women's union activism are included in this book, this does not drive the narrative or analysis. In one of the few recent studies that center Black working women, *Gateway to Equality*, Keona Ervin situates her work in Border South studies and argues for the distinctiveness of Black women's economic activism in Missouri, which straddled the North and South.[36] In Saint Louis, Black working women became gainfully employed in textile and food processing industries, gaining status as industrial workers and the ability to organize formally within the labor movement between the 1930s and the 1960s. During the same time period, most Black working women in Milwaukee could not claim this status, and as a result did not organize around these occupations as Black women did in Saint Louis, making their organizing more difficult and focused on other commonalities. Stories of economic justice as they relate to business ownership tend to emphasize the contributions of Black male entrepreneurs, except for the few recent studies that examine Black beauty work or Black women in finance.[37] Michael Ezra's edited collection *The Economic Civil Rights Movement* illustrates the necessity of considering the economic component of Black folk's struggle for freedom and justice and demonstrates that no story is complete without this analysis.[38]

When considering Black women's fight for economic justice, examining their engagement with the state—whether asserting their rights, demanding protection, or making claims for social services—composes a central part of the story, especially because of the state's role in administering economic policy and procedure. *Continually Working* narrates a myriad of battles between Black working women, from beauticians to welfare mothers, against the state, uncovering how the state's bureaucratic racism undermined these women's efforts to pursue and secure economic justice. In revealing Black working women's interactions with the state, *Continually Working* is in conversation with studies like Lisa Levenstein's *A Movement without Marches* and Rhonda Y. Williams's *The Politics of Public Housing*.[39] Both of these studies uncover the political awakening and subsequent activism of poor Black women during the twentieth century by examining Black women's interactions with public institutions such as public housing departments, schools, hospitals, the legal system, and welfare departments. *Continually Working*'s consideration of the 1970s Milwaukee welfare rights movement connects it to historical studies that have examined the national welfare rights movement, which coalesced as a result of local struggles across the country.[40]

It might be audacious to assert that Black working women should be considered intellectuals, but that is exactly one of the claims this book makes. While the field of US intellectual history has seriously neglected Black working women's intellectual thought, some historians have made the point that Black women have ideas worth considering and that their activism is infused with these ideas.[41] This work starts from a position that Black working women are thinkers and uncovers some of their varied and at times conflicting ideas. Histories of the Black freedom struggle that focus on economics and politics seldom cast Black working women as central figures and even more rarely characterize them as thinkers or grapple with their ideas about economic justice. *Continually Working* starts from this standpoint because of the groundwork laid in books like *Toward an Intellectual History of Black Women*, which argues that Black women have an intellectual history worth examining.[42] *Toward an Intellectual History*, though, focuses primarily on more well-known Black women activists and formal, published writers. Keisha Blain's *Set the World on Fire* examines the nationalist thought of Black working women, showing how the ideas of Black nationalist working women traversed the globe, even if they could not.[43]

Continually Working considers the economic and intellectual activism of a community of Black women in the urban Midwest. In so doing, it builds on and brings together several historical conversations related to Black women's activism, the nature of civil rights, and the unfinished struggle for economic justice in the region and in the nation.

Milwaukee's Bronzeville: An Overview

To understand Black working women's experiences, thoughts, and activism, it is important to lay out a brief overview of the history

TABLE 1. The Black population in Milwaukee between 1910 and 1970

Year	Black population	Percent of total Milwaukee population
1910	980	.2%
1920	2,229	.4%
1930	7,501	1.2%
1940	8,821	1.5%
1950	21,772	3.4%
1960	62, 458	8.42%
1970	105,088	14.65%

Data from the United States Census of the Population

of Black people in Milwaukee. Black women fought for economic justice in a dramatically and continually changing urban context, especially in Milwaukee. Migration transformed the nature of the African American community in Milwaukee. Black people lived in Wisconsin as early as the 1700s, although their population was negligible for much of this time. Even with the advent of the Great Migration, in which many Black Americans moved to northern cities, Milwaukee's African American population remained relatively small and did not compare to the Black population in cities such as Chicago and Detroit.

In 1910, African American Milwaukeeans numbered 980, or 0.2 percent of the city's total population (approximately 373,000).[44] By 1920, the Black population had increased 127.4 percent but still only equaled 0.4 percent of the city's total population.[45] By 1930, the city's Black population had reached 7,501, or 1.2 percent of Milwaukee's total population, which by then was over 578,000.[46] Compared to the high level of migration to cities such as Chicago and Detroit during this same period, Black migration to Milwaukee seems miniscule. For example, in Detroit over the twenty-year period from 1910 to 1930, the Black population grew from 5,741 to 120,066. Black migration to Chicago during this period was just as dramatic: the population increased from 44,103 to 233,903. Milwaukee saw the greatest increase from the 1940s through the 1960s. In 1940, the Black population was 8,821, or 1.5 percent of the total population. In 1950, the

Black population had grown to 21,772, and by 1960 the population had reached 62,458, with the majority of the new migrants arriving between 1956 and 1960. By 1970, the Black population had grown to 14.65 percent of the city's total population.[47] Because of the dramatic increase in the Black population between 1940 and 1970, historian Paul Geib described this period as the Late, Great Migration.[48]

While Black people migrated to Milwaukee for many reasons, one of the biggest attractions was the potential for employment. In the early twentieth century, a Black newspaper in Milwaukee, the *Advocate*, continually placed ads and served as an employment agency for women looking for work in domestic service.[49] Although Black workers most often migrated to the North in search of industrial jobs, domestic service positions in the North paid more than the same jobs in the South, and Southern Black women also came in search of these better paying positions.[50] Black men fared somewhat better than women in that they were able to obtain jobs in factories and plants. However, these jobs were typically the lowest paid, dirtiest, and most physically demanding of the industrial sector. These jobs gave Black male laborers access to steady work, higher wages, and sometimes union involvement. Black men's footing in the industrial labor force was precarious, but not as precarious as the position of Black women. While Black women gained industrial jobs during the First World War, they lost these jobs after the war. After the Second World War, some Black women kept industrial jobs, but by the 1950s and 1960s low-paying service jobs in hospitals, restaurants, and stores had replaced domestic service as a top employment option for Black women. In sum, although some African Americans realized the promise of better jobs, many found that their economic dreams of life in the North were difficult to achieve because of structural racism and discrimination.

As a result of residential segregation, a Black community (eventually called Bronzeville, after Chicago's Bronzeville community) developed in Milwaukee. In the 1930s almost all Black people in Milwaukee lived within a confined fifty-six square block area, from Highland Boulevard to Walnut Street and from Third Street to Twelfth Street. The precipitous growth of the African American population caused this area to expand, and by 1960 Bronzeville had grown by several blocks, though its boundaries and its residents were still constrained.[51] At first Bronzeville's boundaries lie within the city's sixth ward, however redistricting expanded the neighborhood's boundaries into the second ward as well. As Bronzeville's population and boundaries expanded, so too did its social and political offerings for Black residents. With each passing decade, Bronzeville transformed and grew tremendously. The community thrived until the 1960s, when highway expansion forcibly removed long-term residents and businesses from the area.

Although the Black population in Milwaukee was relatively small prior to World War II, Bronzeville residents had already begun to develop a community life that reflected those in other cities, in characteristics if not in scale. Mirroring Grand Boulevard in Chicago's Bronzeville, Walnut Street, sometimes called Chocolate Boulevard, was the central commercial district in Milwaukee's Bronzeville.[52] Up and down Walnut Street, from Third Street to Twelfth Street, Bronzeville residents could find several Black-owned businesses and offices—from cleaners and tailors to restaurants, gas stations, beauty salons, and barber shops, and even the first Black-owned financial institution in the state, Columbia Savings and Loan Association. Bronzeville was also home to several bars and clubs and a theater, which became a primary source of leisure for Bronzeville's residents. In fact, Bronzeville's music scene touted many of the popular artists of the time as they came through Milwaukee on tour.[53]

Another source of leisure for Bronzeville residents—the game of policy—developed as a result of financial need.[54] Policy was an illegal lottery game that was popular until the 1940s. Black residents who participated in policy placed small bets that sometimes yielded big winnings. Although policy was illegal and considered disreputable, for Black Milwaukeeans in difficult financial circumstances, winning a game of policy often enabled them to pay rent, buy household necessities, and travel to and from work. In addition, the game supported and financed several Black-owned businesses in the community.[55] The game of policy, though social in its operation, met a very real economic need.

FIGURE 1. Businesses on Twelfth and Walnut. 1958. Historic Photo Collection, Milwaukee Public Library

In addition to commercial and leisure opportunities, Bronzeville was home to several religious organizations, mainly various Christian denominations. An individual's economic class often dictated the church he or she attended.[56] For example, many middle-class Black worshippers chose to attend Saint Mark African Methodist Episcopal Church, which was known for its reserved and formal worship atmosphere. In contrast, Calvary Baptist Church had a much more colorful worship style; with northern migration, a few Sanctified or Holiness storefront churches opened, and these were even more flamboyant than Calvary. The wide variety of religious denominations meant Black Milwaukeeans had many religious opportunities from which to choose.

Black Milwaukeeans also established several chapters of national self-help institutions. The Milwaukee National Association for the Advancement of Colored People (MNAACP) was established in 1915 and the Milwaukee Urban League (MUL) was established in 1919. Because internal strife hampered the MNAACP, especially during the 1930s and 1940s, the Urban League was more popular in the early years of Bronzeville. In addition to self-help institutions, residents established Black branches of organizations such as the Young Women's Christian Association (YWCA) and the Young Men's Christian Association (YMCA) in Bronzeville. These branches, which offered many social, political, recreational, and leisure opportunities to Bronzeville residents, became the center of community life.

Bronzeville has a long history of Black women's clubs that have linked Milwaukee clubwomen to the state and national club movement. In the early 1900s, Black women established clubs to engage in leisure, social, and charity activities. By the 1930s, the local clubs had affiliated with the National Association of Colored Women's Clubs, and members began participating in state and national conferences. Representatives from the city of Milwaukee and the state of Wisconsin often attended regional and national meetings of the National Association of Colored Women's Clubs. In addition, Wisconsin club members served in elected and appointed positions at the regional and national levels. In a similar vein as Black clubs, local chapters of Black fraternal and sororal organizations also existed in Milwaukee. Bernice Lindsay, a Black community leader and intellectual whose life I explore in Chapter 1, was both a club woman and sorority member. She helped organize the Mary Church Terrell Club in 1933 and was a member of the local graduate chapter of Delta Sigma Theta.

The Black press in Milwaukee had an unstable tenure in Bronzeville.[57] A number of Black newspapers, with runs as short as a few months to as long as twenty-five years, were established during the Bronzeville period; however, at several periods during the era, residents had no Black newspaper and relied on news from nearby sources such as the *Chicago Defender*. The longest-running Black newspaper in Wisconsin, the *Wisconsin Enterprise Blade*, was published in Milwaukee from 1916 through 1941. The paper's twenty-five-year run was commendable, especially given the shaky history of the Black press in Wisconsin prior to its existence. Other Black newspapers began in the 1950s, including the *Milwaukee Defender*, an affiliate of the *Chicago Defender* that lasted less than five years. It would not be until the 1960s that a local Black newspaper was consistently published in the city.

William Albert Vick has suggested that "business and employment took precedence over politics in Black Milwaukee," because while Black Milwaukeeans created an important institutional base during the early to mid-twentieth century, it was not until the late 1950s that Black Milwaukee's political base was solidified in the form of representation on the city's Common Council.[58] This lack of political representation, coupled with Milwaukee's brand of socialist politics, often referred to as "sewer socialism" because of its focus on infrastructural reform, resulted in the passage of policies that negatively affected Black residents.

Milwaukee's status as a socialist city, especially during the heyday of Black Bronzeville, has been written about extensively.[59] From 1910 to 1960, socialist mayors governed the city. Historians have written about race and socialism in Milwaukee, underscoring that while there were Black socialists in the city, they had little influence on local socialist politics overall because white socialists held racist ideas and practices. Notably the national socialist leader, Milwaukee teacher, newspaper publisher, and US congressman Victor Berger, made his views on Black people widely known.[60] Race-based tensions were not peculiar to the Milwaukee context—there was a race problem within socialist circles nationwide.[61] Despite the racial tensions, Milwaukee's socialist political context meant that there came to be a strong connection between labor and politics and constituents pushed politicians to implement policies and allocate city funds to address infrastructural needs and social service programs. Milwaukee's sewer socialism played a role in the devastation of Bronzeville because politicians and other city leaders connected race with urban decay.

By calling the Bronzeville area a "slum," politicians justified the city's decision to build a highway through it that allowed easier access, specifically for white people who had moved into the suburbs, to the city's downtown area. Official reports disseminated by the city's health department repeatedly linked disease and crime to "blighted" and "slum" areas.[62] While these reports did note that neglected, dilapidated housing, as well as absentee landlords, contributed to blight, the reports often blamed Black residents for the condition of their dwellings, claiming that they did not want to maintain their residences. In addition, city leaders, newspaper outlets, and white Milwaukeeans continually connected the terms *blight*, *slum*, *death*, *decay*, and *crime* to Bronzeville, until eventually the city's

Black residents became synonymous with, and were ultimately seen as responsible for, the rapid disintegration of the inner city. Because of this slum rhetoric, in the 1950s Bronzeville was deemed a part of the city's urban renewal redevelopment efforts; by the mid-1960s, highway construction projects had destroyed nearly eight thousand homes and businesses in the Bronzeville community. These projects effectively decimated the center of Black Milwaukee—its flourishing business and commercial district.[63] Bronzeville never recovered and the community's decline, coupled with continually deteriorating economic opportunities, created the conditions that incited African American Milwaukeeans to engage in direct-action protests and demonstrations in the 1960s.[64]

Black women's struggles for economic justice in Milwaukee must be understood within the context of Black life in Bronzeville. Expectations regarding the local government's responsibilities to its residents shaped Black women's economic thought and action. In other words, they expected the city and its leaders to do something about the plight of Black working people in the city. *Continually Working* uncovers Black women's varied responses to this rapidly changing urban landscape. During the twentieth century, despite gains Black women's economic opportunities continued to be dismal, even through the Milwaukee industrial economy's most prosperous periods.

Weaving together Black women's struggles against the Jim Crow job system and the intellectual practices that undergirded this resistance, *Continually Working* is organized into five chronological chapters. This book begins in the 1940s by examining the actions of the Black working women who labored at the Milwaukee Young Women's Christian Association (MYWCA), a predominantly white-led organization that aimed to improve its programs and services for Black urban women. Hired to increase, coordinate, and manage participation among Black women and children in the city, the Black Y workers did much more than was in their job description. They created a community space for Black working women and girls that provided recreational, social, educational, and leadership development opportunities, allowing them to engage with each other about important topics and issues of the day. Black Y workers did not simply see Y members as participants; they declared them "indigenous neighborhood leaders" who could identify and solve the problems Black Milwaukeeans faced. Together they represented the Y on local committees that addressed the needs of Black workers in the city. While Black Y workers engaged and developed leaders among their membership, they also uncovered the contradiction between the organization's commitment to interracial cooperation and its lack of commitment to equal employment in the 1940s: the organization offered integrated programming for Black and white women and girls, but it did not treat its Black and white workers fairly and equally. Black Y women workers came together as a group, raised this critique, and called upon the MYWCA to rectify the inequality, which the organization refused to do. While Black Y women's attempts were unsuccessful, Chapter 1 uncovers the intellectual practices they used to create community among Black working women and girls, as well as combat the Jim Crow MYWCA.[65]

Defying the Jim Crow job system was also on the minds of Black beauticians as they endeavored to control their own labor and define themselves as licensed professionals in the 1940s and 1950s during a regulatory crackdown by the Wisconsin Division of Cosmetology. Aimed at apprehending hairdressers who engaged in the work without being formally recognized and approved by the state, the Division implemented strict laws to prevent the illegal practice of cosmetology. Seeing that the Division's wrath was being meted out on Black beauticians, many of whom had migrated to Milwaukee from the South, beautician Mattie DeWese started the first Black-owned beauty school in the state, Pressley School of Beauty Culture, and began working to get Black women licensed. In operating the school, DeWese and her students both learned and taught state officials several lessons. Black beauticians exposed the fiction that cosmetology policies were race-neutral and, consequently, revealed the bureaucratic racism embedded in the structure that regulated cosmetology in the state. Chapter 2 shows how, through their beauty work and community involvement, Black beauticians refashioned their identity as licensed professionals, defining themselves as "a credit to their city and their state," ultimately thinking of themselves as adding to, not subtracting from, the local economy and Black community.[66]

Black working women who critiqued the Jim Crow job system by filing complaints with the Wisconsin Industrial Commission during the 1950s and 1960s illustrate the power of raising multiple voices, narratives, and experiences in the struggle against employment injustice. They bravely recounted their experiences of employment discrimination, and their stories, explored in Chapter 3, reveal how power operated within the Jim Crow job system. By characterizing all Black workers as men, the Jim Crow job system erased the specific ways employers kept Black women on the bottom, which included limiting the kinds of labor they could engage in and making them vulnerable to sexualized violence in the workplace. During the heyday of civil rights insurgency in Milwaukee, Black working women raised their voices, articulated their resistance to Jim Crow, and expected that the state-administered complaint making process would lead to just work and working conditions.

What does resistance to economic and employment injustice look like in the post–Civil Rights era, specifically after the passage of Title VII of the 1964 Civil Rights Act, which made employment discrimination illegal? What collective intellectual practices did Black women employ to spread the message that the passage of federal laws did not automatically equate to equality, especially in a context where Black workers struggled against a state apparatus, a business sector, and a labor market that disproportionately cast them as unqualified and unemployable? The last two chapters of this book explore the answers to these questions by examining the activism of Black women engaged in the battle for economic justice on two fronts: one in the struggle for welfare rights and the other in the struggle for equal employment accountability. While these two struggles seem dissimilar, they are more connected than one might think. Both chapters reveal how Black women continually critiqued the state and the business sector.

Through a focus on the local welfare rights movement, Chapter 4 explores how Milwaukee activists employed "militant motherhood" in the fight against poverty, standing up for themselves and their children by demanding dignity and justice. While the primary focus of welfare rights activists' critique was the state, specifically the Milwaukee County Welfare Department, welfare activists also pressured profitable big businesses operating in Milwaukee to distribute their wealth by supplementing the county welfare budget where it fell short regarding special assistance funds for welfare recipients. Welfare rights activists registered their discontent through strategically planned protests and demonstrations; they also gathered their personal stories and collectively wrote a book to change the narrative about the welfare system and educate others about the injustice they endured at the hands of the state.

Black women who fought for equal employment accountability pressured businesses, but instead of demanding money, they urged businesses to comply with federal policies regarding equal employment and to voluntarily begin increasing the number of Black and women workers or risk having to answer to the federal government. Chapter 5 uncovers the labor of Black women who passionately advocated for equal employment accountability. Women did the mundane, behind the scenes, administrative work—receiving and reviewing paperwork, analyzing data, drafting reports, conducting trainings and workshops, and writing regular communications—to hold businesses responsible in fully eradicating the Jim Crow job system, an enduring structure which would not be dismantled overnight.

These final chapters provide two distinct but connected accounts of Black women's economic justice activism and the community intellectualism that underpinned it in the post–Civil Rights period. Because there is still work to be done, the book's epilogue explores two twenty-first-century examples of Black women's economic activism and community intellectualism, showing how contemporary organizers connect their work to the legacy of Milwaukee's historic Bronzeville community. The epilogue reiterates the main point of *Continually Working*: the importance of connecting Black women's resistance to economic inequality with their collective intellectual practices as they pursue a just future for themselves and their community.

CHAPTER 1

"More Than a Job"

Black Women's Midcentury Struggles at the Milwaukee Young Women's Christian Association

In June 1950 the entire Black women workforce of the Milwaukee Young Women's Christian Association (MYWCA) resigned. The reasons why Nana Baker, Jeanne Hopkins, and Bernice Lindsay left the predominantly white organization were not a mystery. Prior to their mass resignation, Baker, Hopkins, and Lindsay wrote several reports describing their contributions to the organization, making plain their critiques, and offering solutions that could make the MYWCA a better workplace. As a result of their steady work and community outreach over the years, a dedicated group of Black women and girls attended and planned book club meetings, implemented social and cultural programs and outings, fundraised for organizational and community projects, and represented the MYWCA at the regional and national level. Black Y members could also be found on citywide committees, commissions, and planning groups advocating for housing, jobs, and other social services. While the Black Y workers knew their work mattered, they found themselves hard pressed to convince the MYWCA's leaders—the nearly all-white Board of Directors—to give them adequate funding and a permanent location for their activities. Year after year, despite consistently reporting on the necessity and popularity of their work, they were told they had to do more with less money, space, staff, and support.

Finally, the workers reached a breaking point in the 1949–1950 fiscal year. After refusing to invest in a permanent location in Bronzeville (the north side neighborhood where most Black Milwaukeeans resided) the MYWCA let the lease run out on its Walnut Street Center. This effectively forcibly—and hastily, without proper planning—integrated the MYWCA's programming. The activities ran by and designed for Black women and girls were subsumed into those that occurred at the Downtown YWCA location, a facility supposedly open to all MYWCA members but predominantly frequented by white members. This reduced Black Y participation by 80 percent. Also, moving the Black MYWCA women's offices to the Downtown location exposed the inequality that existed among workers at the organization. Shared workspaces and forced collaboration confirmed what Baker, Hopkins, and Lindsay had suspected: the MYWCA paid them less than white Y workers in the same position. Additionally, where there existed duplication in organization and structure—for example both the Downtown Y location and the Walnut Street Center had a Teenage Department— the Downtown Y's preferences and priorities prevailed.

Baker, Hopkins, and Lindsay endured the first few months of integration, saw its impact on their working conditions, and realized that their ties to Bronzeville had been traumatically severed. They tried to convince the MYWCA to address the workplace problems and the declining Black Y membership—which they knew went hand in hand—by increasing their salaries to make them commensurate to white workers in similar positions and committing to taking into consideration the recommendations of the Black staff and membership in the process of securing a permanent home for the Walnut Street Center. If the Y could commit to these requests, the workers would continue to work at the MYWCA. Citing a budget shortfall, the MYWCA dug its heels in, refused to budge, and told the workers if they could not accept the conditions as they were, then they would accept each woman's resignation.

Caught between a rock and a hard place, Baker, Hopkins, and Lindsay resigned. Their resignations exploded in the Black press when the *Chicago Defender* ran a story with the attention-grabbing headline, "Milwaukee Negro YWCA Staff Quits when 'Lily-White' Program Starts."[1] While the headline highlighted the forced integration, the article also detailed the workers' grievances and featured an interview with Bernice Lindsay, the MYWCA staffer who had the longest tenure at the organization. Offering a critique of the MYWCA's disregard for the ideas of the Black women who labored there, Lindsay told the newspaper, "When a Negro board member brought her thinking and that of the Negro staff which called into question some of these decisions, the all-white personnel committee asked for the resignations of the staff." The MYWCA's actions, as well as the Black Y workers refusals, exposed the operation of the Jim Crow job system at the organization.

This chapter engages the ways Black Y women encountered the Jim Crow job system, as well as their responses to it. While historians have focused on Black professional women who worked at the Y, settlement houses, and other community organizations, there is room for more analysis on Black women's workplace experiences, especially at predominantly white, progressive organizations with race-relations-focused missions.[2] Working at the MYWCA revealed a contradiction between the organization's stated goals and practices. While the MYWCA was purportedly interested in the spiritual, social, and economic well-being of Black working women in Milwaukee, it treated its own workers poorly. Not surprisingly, the organization's inequitable treatment of its Black staff directly affected the quality of its programming in Bronzeville. Baker, Hopkins, and Lindsay could only do so much with so little, and they routinely registered their discontent with their work environment by using internal reporting processes, and when that failed, publicly airing their grievances. Ultimately, they resigned.

Baker, Hopkins, and Lindsay's collective resignation reveals much about how they thought about themselves as workers and what they thought the nature of their action should be: together they registered their grievances, together they demanded fair wages, and together they

quit when the MYWCA ignored their complaints. This collective strat-
egizing and action extended to their efforts with the Black women and
girls who came to the MYWCA. Therefore, this chapter also explores
the everyday, group-centered intellectual practices—community
intellectualism—infused within the activities of the Walnut Street
Center. Some of these practices included reading and discussing contemporary debates and books, organizing and attending lectures and
political rallies, going to conferences, and establishing and leading
organizations that advocated for public housing and vocational education. Black Y workers aimed to identify and support "indigenous
neighborhood leaders"—those Black women and girls from, in, and
committed to their neighborhood, working together to improve conditions therein. The MYWCA's Black woman workforce engaged in this
lofty work despite being weighed down by the Jim Crow job system.

Prior to discussing the work of the Black women employed by the
MYWCA, the chapter lays out the national and local contexts from
which the Walnut Street Center emerged. Then the chapter explores
the life of Bernice Lindsay (née Copeland) who, in the MYWCA context, provides one frame through which the pattern of community
intellectualism can be seen. Lindsay dedicated her life to what she
called "group work," and she consistently shifted the focus away
from herself and onto the community in which she lived and labored.
Practically, because Lindsay worked at the MYWCA as the organization's only full-time Black professional worker for over a decade, it
makes sense to discuss her background to understand not only the
machinations of the Jim Crow job system but also her work ethic.
Lindsay's official title of "executive secretary" did little to explain her
actual job at the MYWCA. While it included administrative duties, it
far exceeded that. In her role Lindsay built relationships with Black
women and girls; exposed them to the MYWCA, its programs and
activities; and then encouraged them to create meaningful activities
and groups of their own, which they did in large numbers. Lindsay
supported and advocated for the groups, attended their programs
when she could, and tried to convince her supervisor, and eventually the Board of Directors, to provide financial support. Eventually,
the MYWCA hired additional Black women staff. Together, through

their labor, they amplified the importance of "indigenous neigh-borhood leaders," prioritized group-centered work, and labored for structural change. Ultimately, their efforts bring community intel-lectualism into full view. Through all of this, these women forced the MYWCA to both recognize and compensate their (over)work and to reckon with its racism.

Creating a Program for Black Working Women: National and Local Developments

The MYWCA began its work in Milwaukee in 1892, focusing on white women workers and their physical, spiritual, and social needs. One of the Y's most important resources was the residence it ran, which provided safe, affordable housing in a communal environment. In addition to providing housing, the Y sponsored social events and activities. As a religious organization, the Y took seriously its Chris-tian commitment and provided access to spiritual opportunities as well, taking care not to become a substitute for church attendance in working women's lives. Focusing on a wide range of participants from young girls to older adults, the Y offered participants opportu-nities to attend camp, go bowling, learn etiquette, and socialize with other girls and women. Women and girls could also join one of the myriad clubs based on their age or background. For example, clubs for teenage girls, married women, and women employed in business and professional fields all existed at the Y. One of the most popu-lar type that emerged in Ys all over the country was the "industrial club" for working women. Though the clubs initially formed to tar-get women who worked in manufacturing industries, they came to be filled with working women from a variety of industries, includ-ing those who worked in personal or domestic service.[3] By the time of the Great Migration, the Milwaukee Y had made a name for itself in the city for its focus on working women.

During the Great Migration, and because of World War I, Milwau-kee experienced a large increase in its Black population. This was

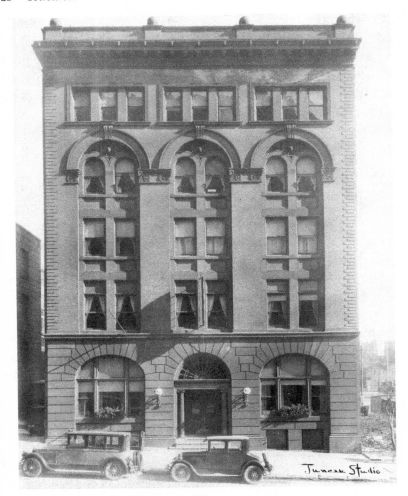

FIGURE 2. "Exterior of old YWCA building." No date. Photograph by Juneau Studio, Wisconsin Historical Society, https://www.wisconsin history.org/Records/Image/IM53705

not unique to Milwaukee, as other Midwestern cities such as Chicago and Detroit also experienced tremendous population growth. While Milwaukee's Black population was much smaller than these two urban metropoles, there was still a discernible increase in new Black residents. In 1910, the Black population in Milwaukee numbered 980. By 1920, the population grew to 2,229, nearly 60 percent of whom were workers between the ages of 20 and 44.[4] Of the 1,329 Black people in this age range, 587 Black women called Milwaukee home. Of course, migration and work went hand in hand, and the census recorded Black women laboring primarily as dressmakers and seamstresses, in tanneries, and in other textile industries—all categorized as "semi-skilled" by the federal government—or in "Domestic and Personal Service" as cleaners, laundresses, waitresses, or servants. Close to 80 percent of Black women in the labor force worked in these two occupational categories. Although very few in number, there were some Black women engaged in professional, clerical, skilled, and small business work. For example, under "Professional," the census counted three music teachers and one religious/charity/welfare worker. Three Black women engaged in "skilled" labor—one working as a tailor and the other two working as forewomen in unspecified manufacturing industries. Not surprising, especially given the housing inequality in Milwaukee, fifteen Black women ran boarding and lodging houses. Finally, the census only recorded four barbers, hairdressers, and manicurists—likely an undercount, especially considering the story of Black beauticians in Milwaukee, which Chapter 2 explores.

The increase in the number of Black workers in the city activated several organizations with goals of helping workers find employment as well as meeting their housing and social needs. Among these were the Milwaukee Urban League (MUL), which was affiliated with the National Urban League (NUL) and organized in Milwaukee in 1919. Like the structure set up by the National Urban League, the Milwaukee affiliate had an interracial board that oversaw the programmatic efforts carried out by a Black staff.[5] The same year MUL was established, it joined with the MYWCA to create and sponsor a programmatic activity for Black working women, La Circle Club. While the MYWCA organized La Circle under the auspices of the industrial club structure described earlier, the organization partnered with the MUL to recruit Black working women to participate.

The La Circle Club for Black working women; Girl Reserves, a club for young Black girls; and the Service Club, with a focus on community service, were the extent of the MYWCA's outreach to

Black people in the city for nearly the next decade. The increase in the Black population, though, led the MYWCA to dedicate more resources and time to Black women workers in Milwaukee. Upon recognizing the growing Black population in the city, the Milwaukee Y allocated funds to human resources and programmatic efforts. They did this by hiring a Black social worker, Bernice Copeland (soon to be Lindsay), whose job duties including overseeing and expanding the Y's programming. The Black Y worker would carry out this work from the central Y association, located in downtown Milwaukee and about one and a half miles from where most of Milwaukee's Black residents lived.

This is where the MYWCA's history slightly diverges from histories of other Black Ys in the country. Most work among Black women in other cities across the nation was organized, from the outset, in segregated branches. In some instances, Black women had to petition the all-white local Ys, and not the national organization, for permission to affiliate. Once affiliated, although Black women ran the programs and led the outreach effort, white women supervised their effort and allocated resources as they saw fit, often resulting in the inequitable distribution of resources. Despite these problems, Black women still saw the benefit of a Y affiliation and fought for them.[6] In the case of the MYWCA, it was proactive in its outreach to Black Milwaukeeans, reaching out first.

The MYWCA's decision to expand its program for Black women was in response to local conditions, but it also coincided with changes at the national level that happened during the 1910s and 1920s. In 1913, the National Y Board of Directors hired its first Black secretary, Eva Bowles. Bowles directed the organization's effort to reach Black women. In 1915, despite the racial prejudice exhibited by many of its Southern affiliates, the organization sponsored an interracial conference in the South. Two developments resulted from this conference, both of which affected the Milwaukee Y. One was a committee of Black and white members tasked with encouraging participation among Black women, and the other was a leadership training program that would prepare Black women to do Y work in their local communities.[7] These two occurrences led to dramatic increases in the number of both Black Y branches and Black Y workers. The most dramatic increase occurred in the number of Black Y workers—from nine in 1915 to eighty-six in 1920.[8]

Black women led the Y in its thinking and action around engaging with Black communities as well as in its work on improving racial relations. Specifically, Eva Bowles pointed out how the Y had failed to increase participation in Black communities, mostly because they had been relying on white workers to do outreach. In 1922, Bowles reported, "this year has proven the futility of an understanding if white people interpret colored people to white people. *Colored people are their own best interpreters.*"[9] Black women could and should speak on behalf of themselves. Bowles recognized the importance of making space for Black women, but she also saw the importance of interracial work because Black women could not do the work of improving race relations alone. Racially progressive white women needed to be involved. To do this work at the Y, Bowles advocated for the creation of interracial committees that she believed could "help bring about happy relationships and also help the growth of racial understanding."[10] These interracial committees operated in several capacities, overseeing outreach to Black communities, "interpreting this work to white leadership," and leading the efforts of improving race relations, both in the Y and in the broader community.[11]

The impact of Black women's leadership and ideas on national Y developments could be seen at the MYWCA. The MYWCA developed its own Interracial Committee, which had a two-fold role. From this committee, the MYWCA committed itself to improving Black and white race relations in the city. This committee also oversaw the "Colored Work Department," which coordinated all their programming and outreach geared toward Black people in the city. To lead these efforts, the MYWCA hired Bernice Copeland, who became the organization's first "colored work executive secretary." While not a part of the dramatic increase in Black women Y workers noted above, Bernice Copeland started her career at the Y in 1924, when she joined the Phillis Wheatley Branch in Indianapolis, Indiana, as a business and industrial secretary. After four years at the Wheatley Branch, the MYWCA hired Copeland to oversee existing clubs such as La Circle Working Women's Club, the Girl Reserves Club, and the Service Club. [12] As the city's Black population increased, so too did her work. Copeland's personal, educational, and professional history had prepared her.

Copeland was born on March 10, 1899, in the small Quaker community of Winchester, Indiana. Her grandfather Dennis Copeland, a self-freed man who had purchased his and his wife's freedom, moved the family to Winchester in 1833, where, according to Copeland, they were fully incorporated and accepted into community life.[13] Though the Copelands were only one of two Black families in Winchester in the 1830s, Indiana counted several free Black communities during this period.[14] The free Black communities of Cabin Creek, less than ten miles away, and Snow Hill, six miles away, benefitted from the support of anti-slavery Quakers. At its peak, Cabin Creek numbered 100 Black families.[15] The people in these communities built their own self-sufficient churches, schools, and businesses. These communities also served as enclaves where escaping bondspeople found provision and cover, especially in an increasingly dangerous environment because of the Fugitive Slave Law enacted in 1850.

Having lived in the area during slavery, the Civil War, and Reconstruction, by the time the first of Copeland's siblings, William, was born in the 1890s, the family's roots in the area ran deep. The Copeland family prized education, with Bernice's father, Benjamin, being the first African American resident to graduate from the town's high school. The next Black person to graduate from Winchester High School was Bernice's older brother William in 1913. Bernice soon followed him, and after graduating, she chose to attend Ohio State University (OSU), probably because it was only around 120 miles away from home. At OSU Copeland became the first African American to earn a journalism degree. While Copeland's journalism major made the news, the story of her minor in social work deserves mentioning, especially since this laid the foundation for her life's work.[16]

While at OSU, a chance meeting with Jane Addams, founder of Chicago's Hull House, had a profound impact on the young Bernice Copeland. The specifics of the meeting are unknown, but perhaps

Copeland was interested in Addams' work with working class and poor people in Chicago. Something may have attracted Copeland to the idea of a settlement house where educated women interacted with community members, and together developed solutions to urban problems, or perhaps Copeland agreed with Addams' sentiment that working people did not desire charity but instead wanted good jobs and the ability to provide for themselves.[17] Whatever the case, after the meeting, Copeland changed her college minor from mathematics to social work.

After graduating from OSU, Copeland returned to Indiana to work in Indianapolis (about ninety miles from her hometown of Winchester) as an industrial secretary at the Phillis Wheatley Branch of the YWCA. The great beauty entrepreneur and philanthropist Madam C. J. Walker had helped establish this Black branch, and Copeland worked with Black Y women who had a vested interest in the lives and empowerment of working women. This initial professional position aided in the development of Copeland's ideas about organizing and community leadership. As industrial secretary, Copeland collaborated with Black working women, organizing activities, events, meetings, and outings. The popular Phillis Wheatley Branch served as a hub and community center offering a wide range of programs and activities that provided social and cultural learning opportunities.[18] Because of the knowledge and skills Copeland gained while working at the Phillis Wheatley Branch, the Milwaukee YWCA hired her to lead its efforts among Black women in 1928.

Copeland both represented the traditional idea that Black professional women could and would represent and speak on behalf of the race and challenged this idea with her own philosophies and beliefs regarding community involvement.[19] She believed that everyone, regardless of educational background or class status, should work together, engaging in what she referred to as "group work." Essentially, group work was Copeland's way of describing community organizing—community members uniting to work on issues of importance. She also cared about empowering "indigenous neighborhood leadership."[20] These neighborhood leaders, she thought, were better able to understand and create solutions to pressing community concerns than city officials who might not even reside in the neighborhood. Although Copeland's personal background, professional experiences, and social class standing might have placed her in a cadre of elite race leaders, her actions and philosophy reveal that she prioritized working collectively to address the needs of her community through strategic thinking and action.

When the MYWCA hired Copeland in 1928, she worked at the downtown Milwaukee headquarters located at 626 North Jackson Street, referred to as the Central building. She was supervised by a white woman, Eva Eubanks, who also served as the chairperson of the Interracial Committee.[21] The Interracial Committee at the MYWCA, a subcommittee of the MYWCA's Board of Directors, could be described as the epicenter of the MWYCA's racially progressive activities. It was through this committee of eight to ten Black and white women that the MYWCA committed itself to improving inter-racial relations and Black community development. Falling under the auspices of the Interracial Committee, the Colored Work Department carried out the MYWCA's imperatives as they related to Black people in the city with Bernice Copeland at the helm.

Working from her philosophy of identifying and encouraging indigenous neighborhood leaders, Bernice Copeland soon petitioned for a location change from the Central building downtown to Bronzeville, which resulted in the Y renting a series of buildings in the neighborhood. Opening a satellite office in Bronzeville increased the participation of Black women and children in its programs, but some Black community members criticized the move because they considered the Bronzeville facilities to be inadequate, especially when compared to Central building facilities. It was true; the Bronzeville facilities were not as well equipped, but Copeland saw the value of being in the community and settled for less than perfect facilities, hoping that the Y would find a permanent home for the Department. She thought increased proximity to the community outweighed the potential benefits of a better-resourced Y building that was inconvenient and costly for community members to get to. Over the course of Copeland's career as executive secretary, the Y never found the

Department a permanent home, and this contributed to the Y's hasty decision to integrate two decades after Copeland began working at the organization. Before getting to that part of the story, it is crucial to explore the nature of Black women's efforts within the Colored Work Department.

Black Y Women's Work in Bronzeville

The Great Depression dampened the work of the Y in the 1930s, but the organization held on and by the 1940s, with the advent of World War II, activity flourished, especially in the Colored Work Department. Due to the Second World War, the Black community in Milwaukee grew once again, putting pressure on an already overcrowded neighborhood. During this time, Bernice Copeland—now Bernice Lindsay, due to marriage—and her colleagues, no more than one or two part- or full-time workers at any given time, grew Black Y membership and participation, turning the location into a neighborhood community center. The Department's location in Bronzeville gave it a first-person view of the neighborhood's growth, as well as the needs of community members. Housing was one of the most pressing needs and the Department invested its resources, time, and energy into the struggle for affordable quality housing. Through their work on neighborhood and citywide clubs, committees, and commissions advocating for public housing, Black working women's practice of community intellectualism comes into view, especially in their vocal critique of inadequate housing and the solutions they developed to address the problem.

Members of the Colored Work Department tackled the problem of housing from several angles. To address the need for immediate, short-term housing, the Department developed a rooms registry. Once a woman arrived in Milwaukee, she could go directly to the Department to learn what rooms were available for rent in the neighborhood. The Department also carried out a house-by-house neighborhood survey where they interviewed residents about their living conditions. The data they gathered highlighted the miserable, unsafe, and run-down conditions of many of the residences in Bronzeville. In some of these dwellings, landlords packed up to ten Black families in homes originally meant for one or two families at most. As a result of Y's survey, the city demolished two of the most infamously dilapidated homes, one of which was referred to as "Noah's Ark" because of the number of families who lived there.

In addition to the rooms registry and the neighborhood survey, Black Y women participated in neighborhood and citywide committees to create affordable housing, such as the Sixth Ward Better Housing Community Club that was established in the 1940s to convince the city to erect public housing in the ward where Bronzeville was located. Member of the Y's La Circle Club and beautician Mattie DeWese, whose beauty school will be examined in the next chapter, actively participated in the Better Housing Community Club, and by the mid-1940s the group elected her as its president. The organization held forums about the benefits of a public housing project in the sixth ward and spoke out against private corporations who disagreed with public housing in the area. Additionally, this organization petitioned city leaders to not only demolish the older, dilapidated buildings that stood in the sixth ward but also to build replacement housing. The Sixth Ward Better Housing Community Club hosted discussions with members in the community, and then broadcasted and advocated for their concerns and needs.

In addition to Black Y members doing what they could to address the housing crisis, Black Y staff members, including Bernice Lindsay and Eva Eubanks, joined citywide committees, such as the Joint Action Committee for Better Housing (JACBH), to advocate for building an affordable housing project in the sixth ward. The JACBH was a coalition of nearly twenty interracial social, political, and public welfare organizations, including the Milwaukee Y. The JACBH wrote letters, circulated petitions, and planned, sponsored, and attended forums that sought to educate the city's residents on the importance of public housing.

Milwaukee was not the only urban area struggling to provide solutions to the problem of inadequate housing for their Black residents. During this time Black urbanites in other northern locales shared

Black Milwaukeeans' experiences. Federally sanctioned redlining and blockbusting confined them to certain neighborhoods.[22] Black folks fared no better after the creation of the United States Housing Authority, whose job it was to administer funds to states or local communities for the construction of public housing. In northern cities across the country, including Milwaukee, the location of public housing projects mirrored local segregation patterns. In Milwaukee, early public housing projects excluded Black people because they were built in white neighborhoods. Therefore, civic leaders tried to influence city leaders to build housing projects in areas where Black people lived, especially since the wards where Black Milwaukeeans lived were among the most impoverished in the city. Black Milwaukeeans saw a housing project as an opportunity for higher quality housing, but not everyone agreed.

Despite disagreements between public and private interests, Milwaukee's Common Council decided to erect public housing in the sixth ward. Finally approved in 1947, construction began on Thursday, January 8, 1948, for the building of the Hillside Terrace Housing Project, the city's first sixth ward housing project. The construction of Hillside did not signify the end of Black Milwaukeeans' housing struggles. A housing project would not address the problems of redlining and blockbusting that circumscribed Black people to the sixth ward in the first place. Neither would it address the economic landscape that kept Black people in low-paying jobs. Nonetheless, the approval of a public housing project was a victory, especially for Black Y women community organizers who saw it as one step in relieving the overcrowded sixth ward environment in which Black workers lived.

Black Y women's diverse responses to inadequate housing illuminates community intellectualism, and their labors with girls through the Teenage Department provides an opportunity to see how ideas of indigenous neighborhood leadership and group work took shape. Nana Reed Baker, the director of the Teenage Department, embodied the idea of "indigenous neighborhood leadership." Baker grew up in Milwaukee, attended North Division High School, and actively participated in the Colored Work Department as a girl, presumably under the leadership of Bernice Copeland Lindsay. After studying at both the Ohio University in Athens, Ohio, and the University of Wisconsin, as well as volunteering at the MYWCA, the organization hired Baker to oversee the Teenage Department.[23] Continuing the cycle of developing indigenous community leaders included offering opportunities for young girls to learn and practice the skills that could employ as leaders in their neighborhood.

The Teenage Department, with its four to six clubs and estimated membership of between 100 and 120 young women and girls, was the most active division of the Colored Work Department. Originally called the Girl Reserves and later Y-Teens, these clubs could be compared to Girl Scouts in that they taught middle and high school-aged girls leadership, organization, planning, communication, and social skills. Over the course of her time as director of the Teenage Department, Baker consistently summarized the work of her department through monthly and annual reports. Her lengthy reports indicated how much was going on in the department, especially when compared to the relatively short length of reports from other areas. In the reports, Baker's overwork and overextension were palpable, especially since she was the only full-time worker employed to manage the activities of the Teenage Department.

The 1945–1946 program year illustrates the types of leadership development opportunities available to neighborhood girls. At the beginning of the year, all the clubs united and organized a membership rally where they visited schools in the community to recruit their peers to become Y members. These rallies allowed girls to practice their presentation and dialogue skills as they talked to their peers to persuade them to join the Y. In addition to these annual recruiting events across the city, Milwaukee girls also planned and hosted regional events with girls from Racine, Wisconsin, and Evanston, Illinois, in attendance. Regional conferences allowed girls to interact with others from nearby areas while also hearing from local and regional speakers on topics related to politics, religion, and race relations.

Planning meetings and conferences allowed girls to exercise one set of leadership skills, while giving back constituted another crucial aspect of indigenous neighborhood leadership, and so community service also featured prominently in the clubs' activities. One of the typical avenues for service was the "adoption" of a community member. Club members communicated with their community member to learn about them, assist in meeting their needs, encourage them, and send care packages, among other things. Clubs usually adopted someone for an entire program year. One year, one of the clubs adopted an entire ward of war veterans at the Soldiers Home Hospital. Another club adopted an elderly woman in the community. The club recognized the elder's birthday and made aprons and tea towels for her. While these actions might seem small, they meant a great deal to community members and taught young people early lessons in responsibility, initiative, and care.

Conferences, community service, and what Baker categorized in her reports as "education" rounded out the most important activities of the department. It is worth noting that education was defined expansively, as were the methods and activities that were considered education. In fact, it might be more appropriate to describe these activities as opportunities to learn. Girls participated in "Let's Get Acquainted" sessions that coincided with their visits to high schools across the city in their recruitment efforts. In these sessions, girls dialogued with each other, and Y members shared with other youngsters about their involvement in the Y. Other learning opportunities the clubs organized included knitting lessons, charm (etiquette) sessions, luncheons where they learned about various topics, health talks, and discussions about relationships between boys and girls. While Reed directed the Teenage Program, a committee of ten adult women helped in supervising the girls' clubs. This committee met once a month, chaperoned events, and served as the nucleus for a parent teacher association at one of the neighborhood schools. Reed described this active group of Black women as one that "work[s] faithfully to accomplish much for the girls and our community."[24]

Although the Colored Work Department stood as a community pillar in Bronzeville, Black women workers, Y members, and volunteers struggled to make the MY's Board of Directors understand its significance and continued growth. Eva Eubanks, the department's supervisor, tried to convince the Board of Directors. One year, Eubanks reported to the Board that the Department's dream was a space big enough to accommodate its programs.[25] Recognizing Nana Reed's work in another year, Eubanks spoke of the need for another person to help. The Y's low wages did not make them competitive enough to entice experienced workers.[26] Eventually though, the Colored Work Department successfully hired a part-time employee, Jeanne Hopkins, who had recently graduated from the University of Wisconsin. Hopkins provided administrative support to a handful of young women's clubs.

Spotlighting and Refusing Racism

Although the Y women accomplished much from their small, underfunded location in Bronzeville, challenges abounded that exposed the racial and economic divides that existed between the work that happened in Bronzeville and at the downtown Y location. Most programming for Black folks occurred in Bronzeville, but there were instances when Black Y clubs and groups used downtown Y rooms and spaces. During these instances, some white volunteers refused services to Black participants or could be overheard making disparaging comments such as the downtown building "was built for white girls" or "Negroes have no business here, anyway. If we make it too pleasant, they'll want to stay and they ought to be sent back where they came from, Africa, anywhere."[27] Clearly, some white Y members felt that Black Y members should only frequent the Bronzeville location and did not welcome them in the downtown building. As a result of this treatment, Black Y members did not feel comfortable attending programs at the Central Building. Additionally, Black Y members' comments about the work of the Colored Work Department revealed that they considered it to be the "back door entrance to the Y."[28] Tired of being spatially, politically, and fiscally marginalized within the organization, in an annual report to the Board of Directors, Bernice Lindsay expressed the need for the Y to shun racism, asserting, "Right and timidity have gone hand in hand too long;

the time has come for them to part company. The partnership must be between right and courage."[29]

After changing the name of the Colored Work Department to the Walnut Street Center, the Center, which offered housing resources to Black working women, faced a housing problem of its own. The building the Walnut Street Center inhabited was slated for demolition. Center staff had less than six months to find a new space; immediately Black Y women set out to find another home. After months of unsuccessful searching, the MYWCA board decided to move the Walnut Street Center downtown to the Central Building, without any input from Black Y staff members. This move, according to Lindsay, was "a real blow." Lindsay described a "disturbing and disheartening" process by which "final policies [were] agreed upon in small committees and boards where there [had] been no Negro representation."[30]

Just a year earlier, the Center had served hundreds of participants in the activities of its groups, clubs, and committees. This tally did not include all the members of the general public who attended forums, cultural events, and other one-time social events or those who visited the Walnut Street Center for meetings or events sponsored by organizations that utilized the Center's meeting spaces. Nor did this number include the 125 people who came seeking and received individualized attention and help.[31] However, after the Walnut Street Center moved into the Central Building, Lindsay noted the immediate impact of the relocation:

> Attendance at club, committee and interest group meetings has reached an all-time low. [Relocation] meant giving up our mass recreation programs or open houses and also the scrapping of our . . . young adult activities program. Our Rooms Registry has practically folded up because the people who came seeking rooms were served "over the counter" and sometimes need[ed] to come back three or four times and Central is too inconvenient for this type of service.[32]

This forced relocation and resulting integration had a devastating impact on the Walnut Street Center. The Center lost its members, the Bronzeville community as a funding source, and the ability to recruit and develop indigenous neighborhood leaders, a hallmark of its programmatic and leadership development philosophy. This quick and forced integration, Lindsay noted, "has worked out much as similar ones in other cities where an unrealistic approach has been made on the problem of integration. Hopes for a grand 'coming of age' year for the department . . . end[ed] in serious dis-integration."[33] What happened to the Walnut Street Center was not unique. Many Black Y branches across the country had experienced the negative impacts of integration into a central city association.[34] The Black Y women staff noted that a forced, fast integration process did not make sense for the organization. Specifically, Jeanne Hopkins wrote, "While the policy of integration is one of slow and gradual process, it is my sincere belief that it is possible but not probable at this time. It is not possible because it is something that cannot be forced upon or superimposed upon any group of peoples. "[35] Hopkins thought Black and white Y members needed much more education and interaction before they were forced together. This compulsory integration was not random; it mirrored patterns in cities across the country where urban renewal systematically destroyed the economic and community development nuclei of Black communities.

While dealing with the loss of their Center, Black Y staffers also endured unequal pay practices, a manifestation of the Jim Crow job system within this nonprofit organization. It was common knowledge that the MYWCA paid white and Black staff members different wages, even if they held the same position. This practice became more difficult to accept as Black and white Y staffers worked side by side. Bernice Lindsay had devoted over twenty years to the MYWCA without a raise and without reaching the uppermost limit of the salary range for her position. Statements made by white Y workers, such as, "It doesn't take much for Negroes to live, so you pay them less than whites even though they are as capable," reflected their belief that it was perfectly fine to discriminate against Black employees.[36] The MYWCA's poor treatment of its workers and its failure to pay them equally affected the quality of programming the Black Y workers could deliver. At the end of one of her annual reports on the activities of the Colored Work Department, Eva Eubanks rightly concluded "this Department of the YWCA is attempting to carry on its program with increasingly inadequate facilities, a too small staff and a too limited budget."[37]

All of this came to a head when, one month after the Walnut Street Center's forced relocation, the Personnel Committee of the MY's Board of Directors sent its full time Black staff members requests to renew their contracts for the 1950–1951 fiscal year. Prior to sending the renewal letters, all the Black Y women workers submitted annual reports for the 1949–1950 fiscal year detailing the impact of compulsory integration on their work. Typically, Eva Eubanks authored the reports of the Walnut Street Center. However, because of the impact of the tumultuous integration of the Walnut Street Center into the downtown Y, it seems the Black Y women workers decided to write and submit their own professional observations directly to the Board of Directors. These reports are one of the few times where Black Y women workers' voices have been preserved in the record. Nana Reed Baker's report focused on the Teenage Department but spoke to broader issues raised in all three of the reports.[38]

Baker, who had worked for the Milwaukee Y for seven years, stated the main point of her report clearly: "Integration seems to be the key word in this summary so far—but though a step forward in plans—our program has suffered all along the way."[39] Baker organized her four-page single-spaced report into several sections that included her thoughts on "Y-Teen Staff and Program Integration," the loss of the adult women volunteers who served on the Y-Teen committee, her "Interpretation of Statistical Changes," and her "Analysis of One Project in Detail." In Baker's detailed report, double its usual length, she lays out her case for how the decision to hastily integrate the Walnut Street Center's programs affected both the Teenage Department and Bronzeville community.

In discussing low participation, Baker reports that the sudden displacement of Walnut Street Center programs to the downtown building led to "a slow disintegration" of the Center's previously well-attended activities. Nothing the staff did, including sending letters in the mail, calling members on the phone, or showing up to members' homes could get them to participate. Sensing that for Y Board members, "actual statistics speak more clearly than words," she cited one of the clubs as an example, noting that prior to the forced move the club had an active membership of thirty participants. After the move, club attendance had ranged from zero to nine members at recent meetings. In addition to low attendance in the clubs, Baker spoke of the loss of the entire group of ten women who served on the Volunteer Committee that provided guidance and support to the clubs. Believing one committee would be sufficient, Y leadership had thought the women of the Walnut Street Center committee could join the one based out of the Central Building,. This resulted in none of the former Walnut Street committee members participating. Baker's report unflinchingly records the devastating impact of the Y's decision to relocate the Walnut Street Center.

It may be obvious to some why participation decreased, but Baker did not take anything for granted. While the downtown Y was less than two miles away from the Bronzeville neighborhood, this distance was huge for women and girls who had to travel after work and school and while balancing their additional personal and professional responsibilities. When Baker queried members from one of the senior youth groups about why their plans to meet at the Central building did not work out, she received several telling responses. First, the girls wanted to be close to home so that they could have a meal before participating. The distance factor was doubly difficult during Wisconsin's long and cold winters. Second, meeting close to home meant they would not have to pay carfare to get to the building. Walking was not an option. Third, many of the girls had responsibilities they needed to attend to before club meetings. Taken together, participation in the Y no longer fit within their schedules, nor was it feasible. Their responses highlighted the importance of proximity and also the physical and financial resources one needed to be able to participate in programs at the Central Building.

In addition to speaking specifically about the impact of the move on the young women of the Teenage Department, Baker spent time reflecting on the decline in volunteer leadership. Specifically, Baker lamented the loss of the entire ten-person committee of adult women noted above. In discussing this point, Baker stated "your leadership is too far removed from the overall picture that those who have jobs cannot make morning meetings and that being women who are vitally interested [in] the problems with the immediate community they frankly possess a desire to assist within the immediate neighborhood." With this Baker raised several points. Baker referring to "your leadership" should be unpacked. This referred to the white Y Board of Directors, typically middle class, who had no knowledge or understanding of the lives of Black working women. Baker also points out that these volunteer leaders wanted to participate but they preferred to do so in their own community and not from the Central Building. Location mattered to them and the distance to the Central Building proved prohibitive, disconnecting them from their neighborhood and home base.

In addition to being frank about the problems facing the Teenage Department, Baker provided ideas for solutions. For example, one practical suggestion related to the involvement of the women on the leadership committee; Baker suggested that instead of morning meetings, evening meetings be considered. Baker's report also included her thoughts on the working environment Black Y women endured. Baker noted lack of communication, failure to include Black Y staffers in decision-making, and putting the onus of integration on the Black Y staffers. Baker recommended the responsibility of integration not be put on only the Black Y staffers, "but that all departments move forward step by step at the same time with an over-all picture clearly visible."[40] With this recommendation Baker was asking for transparency and a clear plan for moving forward with integration. Simply closing the Walnut Street Center and requiring all its programs be combined with what was going on at the Central Building was going horribly wrong, for community members and for Black Y staff members. Baker also recommended open communication and honest discussion among all Y staffers in an effort to gain clarity about the teenage program.[41] Baker hoped Y leadership would heed her practical recommendations.

Baker ended her report with a summary statement worth quoting from in length:

Looking at the picture of the community—from which "Y" Center has been temporarily but completely removed makes one concentrate and observe that therein lies a challenge: Within my province a great challenge to the service of the Teenage Department of the Y.W.C.A. Having grown up within this very community under the guidance and influence of family, the community Y.W.C.A., the community Church, and the community School—makes this challenge all the more vivid to me. . . . In all sincerity, it is my hope that the challenge be so accepted and with humbleness be administered—so that these youth, so encouraged, might grow as people, grow in friendships, and grow in the knowledge and love of God—and in turn be so recognized and included as citizens of the total community.

From her position from within the Black community, Baker could see the full picture of the impact of forced integration. Removing the Walnut Street Center from the Bronzeville neighborhood resulted in formidable challenges. It was up to the Y to accept these challenges and work toward remedies. The future of Bronzeville's youth, specifically young Black girls, depended on it.

Baker's report, as well as the reports written by Jeanne Hopkins and Bernice Lindsay, were presented in the Board of Directors meeting, presumably by Eva Eubanks as Black Y staffers did not usually attend Board of Directors meetings, but there is no indication that the MY followed up directly with its Black staffers regarding their concerns or solutions. Instead, the MY Board accepted and filed the reports then continued with its annual personnel process which included issuing contract renewals to each of the women. To the Board's Personnel Committee, the initiation of the contract renewal process served as a direct message about the quality of their work. The June 1950 Personnel Committee documents the process:

Contracts were sent to Mrs. Lindsay and Mrs. Baker, which would automatically mean that their work had been satisfactory and that the Y would be glad to have them remain on the staff. However, no salary increase was indicated in the contracts for next year. The Personnel Committee tried seriously to evaluate the work done by each of these staff members. . . . In discussing the work of each of the individuals, not on the basis of race, expressed appreciation of service and work done by each; but felt that they had not tried quite hard enough to fit into the picture. They haven't taken the initiative in doing the kinds of things expected of executives in their jobs. [42]

All in all, the Personnel Committee "felt that the [the Black Y staffers] failed to do a superior job of interpreting the Y to their own people."[43] What is telling about the Personnel Committee's assessment of Lindsay and Baker's work is that there is no recognition of the impact of the loss of the Walnut Street Center. Additionally, the Personnel Committee blamed the women for not fitting into the predominantly white work environment of the Central Building. In essence, the MYWCA both ignored and took no responsibility for the racist and hostile work environment it fostered and expected its Black women workers to endure. Given all of this, upon receiving the contract renewal, Nana Reed Baker sent a letter of resignation to the Personnel Committee. She cited the organization's failure to increase her salary as the reason for her leaving the position.[44]

A letter Bernice Lindsay received from Margaret Hill, the acting chairperson of the Personnel Committee, informed Lindsay that although she had been working under "extreme difficulty" and with a salary that was not commensurate with her experience nor the highest for the position, she would not receive a raise due to association-wide budget reductions. Hill enclosed a job agreement and asked Lindsay to sign it and return it by June 1 to retain her position.[45] Lindsay responded to the Personnel Committee but did not sign the enclosed agreement. In her response, Lindsay remarked, "[my] work with the Association has been more than a job, it has been a challenge and satisfaction to give whatever ability I have to the building of human relations."[46] In addition, Lindsay noted that she was aware that the salaries of employees at the Walnut Street Center had historically been lower than salaries of workers in other departments; however, she added because "I feel a certain responsibility as the first Negro secretary and want to prove that inclusiveness in the YWCA is an asset, I tried to be objective and minimize this

FIGURE 3. Bernice Lindsay. April 23, 1967. © *Milwaukee Journal Sentinel* - USA Today Network

difference."[47] Lindsay believed that her education and professional development activities warranted an increase in salary. She had consistently kept herself relevant by attending conferences and taking graduate courses, which she typically funded herself, even with her low salary. Lindsay wrote that she should be receiving the maximum salary and closed her letter by explaining that she accepted the fact that "although we have accepted the theory of integration, we know that the promotion of Negro members to certain jobs is not likely." Lindsay "paid a high price for being the pioneer Negro staff member"; on June 9, 1950, the personnel committee once again offered her the employment terms outlined in the May 1950 letter and added: "if you do not feel you wish to remain on staff under these circumstances, we shall accept your resignation with regret."[48] The absence of Lindsay's signed contract indicated her resignation.

In August 1950 the *Chicago Defender* ran an article with the headline "Milwaukee Negro YWCA Staff Quits When 'Lily-White' Program Starts."[49] Racial discord had always existed within the MYWCA but relocating the Walnut Street Center brought the conflicts into stark relief, and as a result Black Y staff members refused to accept the unfair and unequal treatment they had been receiving. The move to the Central Building could have given the MY Board the opportunity to move toward fair and equal pay and work conditions. Instead, the MYWCA's refusal to elevate the status of its Black workers and its decision to make Black staff work alongside white workers who were paid more for the same jobs pushed Lindsay, Baker, and Hopkins to resign. The physical inhabitation of the Central building by Black women did little to change the MYWCA's racist social and fiscal practices, and by 1950 the MYWCA had lost its foothold in the Black community, and Black working women had lost a leadership and organizing space, as well as a workplace.

Given the MYWCA's early racial agenda, which prioritized Black working women, its actions in 1950 might seem uncharacteristic. The creation of the Colored Work Department and the hiring of Bernice Lindsay occurred when middle class white women's reform efforts centered on improving the urban environment, which provided a small opening for the possibility of interracial and interclass cooperation. By mid-century, however, the Y began to bend to the racial mores of the time and the Board of Directors included members who were not just racially conservative, but explicitly and outwardly racist. The MYWCA's progressive lead in the area of race relations evaporated as the 1950s progressed. Black women, however, did not abandon the Y altogether and continued to work within its confining structures, trying to push it forward toward racial justice. Chapter 5 picks up the story of the Milwaukee Y in the 1970s as it finally committed itself to rooting out racism in its social and fiscal practices.

The next chapter of the book, however, continues the process of uncovering Black women's intellectual and economic activism by focusing on Pressley School of Beauty Culture and its owner Mattie Pressley DeWese, who was involved in the struggle for quality housing in Milwaukee's sixth ward. Serving as president of the Sixth Ward Better Housing Community Club was one way DeWese worked to improve the plight of Black Milwaukeeans. Establishing and running Pressley School of Beauty Culture was another. Presley provided an opportunity for Black working women to get the official training they needed to successfully pass the state of Wisconsin's cosmetology licensing examination. Exploring Pressley continues to reveal community intellectualism, as well as the conflicts that arose between DeWese, Pressley students, and the State, making plain not only how racism and economic injustice operated through bureaucracy, but also Black women's responses to it.

CHAPTER 2

"A Credit to Our City as well as Our State"

Black Beauticians' Professionalization, Progress, and Organization in Milwaukee, 1940s and 1950s

On September 17, 1947, beautician Mary Evelyn Williams wrote to the Cosmetology Division of the Wisconsin State Board of Health on behalf of herself and fellow beautician, Willie M. Mitchell, to request an exemption from the state law that required proof of a tenth grade education to be licensed in the state.[1] In William's hand-written letter she wrote of their commitment to cosmetology and their desire to become licensed. She also mentioned the financial investment they had already made to enroll in Pressley School of Beauty Culture, the only Black beauty school in the state. Although she and Mitchell had practiced cosmetology illegally, without a license, in their kitchen, they had come to the place that "whatever we do we want it to be a credit to our city as well as our state."[2] The Cosmetology Division responded to Williams' request with a form letter restating the requirement and urging both women to take a proficiency exam to obtain proof of a tenth grade education. There is no evidence of either Williams or Mitchell's further action. Short though it is, Williams and Mitchell's story reveals much about Black beauticians' struggles to become licensed professionals—specifically how the state obstructed their desires and the lengths women went to advocate for themselves and resist the crushing nature of the Jim Crow job system.

The story also brings into focus Pressley School, which functioned as an economic and educational gateway for Black working women during a time when most, out of necessity and lack of opportunity, engaged in menial service work. Although World War II did mean some Black women entered manufacturing industries and thus had access to higher paying wartime jobs, after the war they lost these gains, and by the close of the decade according to the 1950 census, 52 percent of Black women in the labor force worked in the domestic service industry.[3]

Despite lacking proof of their education, Pressley owner Mattie DeWese accepted Williams and Mitchell as students and almost certainly encouraged them to write their letter. If the Cosmetology Division had waived the requirement, the decision would have affected an entire group of women in Milwaukee by removing a barrier to economic mobility. While this was not the result of this case, DeWese and her students pressed the division on other matters that affected their standing as professional beauticians, some of which are discussed in this chapter.

The first part of this chapter tells the story of Pressley School of Beauty Culture, which Mattie DeWese opened in 1944 as a response to increased regulation and criminalization of unlicensed beauticians in the state. With Pressley, DeWese provided an opportunity for Black beauticians to get the training they needed to successfully pass the state's licensing examination. DeWese and her students routinely interacted with and challenged the Cosmetology Division's stringent policies and procedures, which often negatively affected Black women like Williams and Mitchell. Records kept and preserved by the Cosmetology Division include correspondence from DeWese, Pressley students, and state officials; notes filed by state inspectors; and statistical reports. These documents expose the bureaucratic racism that permeated the division's structures and practices and include responses and critiques from the community of Pressley women.

Although Pressley School students joined DeWese in resisting state policies and procedures that got in the way of their professional goals, these same students also challenged DeWese's ideas about professionalism and her adherence to the politics of respectability, which, although common for the time, occasionally conflicted with their ability to make a living. They challenged DeWese by refusing to abide by her rules and regulations, absenting themselves, and continuing to do hair in their kitchens despite the risks this posed to their reputations (and DeWese's by association) if caught by state authorities. These conflicts, steeped as they were in class divisions and financial need and amplified by friction that had developed between old settlers and new migrants, as many Black beauticians were, manifested in Pressley while also erupting in churches, organizational spaces, Black media outlets, and public transportation.[4] Short-lived, Pressley closed in 1949 because of DeWese's deteriorating health. By the 1950s cosmetology had become a program of study at public vocational schools in Milwaukee, resulting in more opportunities for Black women to pursue beauty training. This expansion in cosmetology training opportunities coincided with Black beauticians' increasing local, regional, and national organizing efforts.

Therefore, the second part of the chapter explores Black Milwaukee beauticians' participation and leadership in the national Black beauticians' sorority, Alpha Chi Pi Omega (ACPO), founded by Marjorie Stewart Joyner in 1945. Committed to licensure and professional development, public service, and business ownership, involvement in ACPO bolstered Black beauticians collective economic, social, and community status, and resulted in recognition and honor in their communities. In 1951, Milwaukee beauticians chartered a local chapter of the sorority and asserted their identity as professional businesswomen and community leaders. Because sources are more abundant for the national organization than for the local Milwaukee chapter, I explore ACPO's national history and agenda, and a selection of its activities, highlighting where Milwaukee beauticians come into view and using these moments to shed light on the organization's function on the local level.

While historians have written about beauticians' activism and contributions, few have explored the intersection of their economic justice activism and community intellectualism. In exploring this intersection, this chapter uncovers the specific ways Black beauticians advocated for themselves and struggled to control their own labor, especially in an increasingly regulated industry. Together, beauticians critiqued the state and sometimes each other, engaged in community work, and joined national organizations to solidify and amplify their status as professionals. They then used this status to more importantly advocate for and create change in their communities, profession, and society, which they continued doing during the 1960s and beyond.

The Impetus for Pressley School of Beauty Culture

Mattie DeWese opened Pressley School of Beauty Culture because of tightening federal and state regulations that gave rise to new or stricter requirements for beauty culturists, as beauticians initially called themselves. As early as 1919 Wisconsin passed cosmetology laws but had not been stringently enforcing them. [5] However, the 1938 Food, Drug and Cosmetic Act enacted by the Food and Drug Administration (FDA) provided guidelines for beauty products and caused many states to develop or enforce cosmetology regulations.[6] By 1939, the majority of states had created cosmetology laws and boards to regulate them.[7] In Wisconsin's case, the FDA's act prompted the state to become stricter in enforcing its regulations because many women practiced cosmetology without ever having stepped foot in a classroom, and customers began to file complaints to the Department of Health.[8] Several cosmetology schools emerged to handle the influx of beauticians who needed to enroll in a cosmetology course, take the state licensing examination, and earn the required 1,500 hours of apprenticeship. Mirroring the patterns of white-owned salons, none of the existing beauty schools in

FIGURE 4. A sign for a Poro beauty salon in Milwaukee, a national chain started by Annie Turnbo Malone in Saint Louis, Missouri. It reads, "PORO HAIRDRESSING / MARCEL WAVING / FINGER WAVING / MANICURING." January 10, 1930. Historic Photo Collection, Milwaukee Public Library

Wisconsin accepted Black students, which led to a growing number of unlicensed Black beauticians.

With a goal of decreasing the number of unlicensed beauticians, the Cosmetology Division dispatched field inspectors to Milwaukee, where the majority of unlicensed Black beauticians resided, to disseminate information about licensing requirements and to offer them the opportunity to take the state's licensing examination.[9] If beauticians could prove they had practiced prior to 1938, they would only be required to take the state examination.[10] They only needed a licensed beautician to vouch for them. All other beauticians would have to enroll in a cosmetology course and provide proof of

1,500 hours of apprenticeship under a licensed beautician. Despite its outreach efforts, the state struggled to decrease the number of unlicensed Black beauticians.[11] Eventually, the Cosmetology Division enlisted Black beauticians who had taken the state's licensing examination to help in the effort.

Mattie DeWese, originally from Georgia, was one of these women. Before migrating to Milwaukee and opening her own beauty salon, DeWese had lived in Chicago, where she completed her beauty training at an integrated beauty school, Moeller Beauty Culture College.[12] DeWese moved to Milwaukee in the 1930s and realized that although cosmetology regulations were becoming stricter, there was no systematic way for Black beauticians to learn the required skills and accumulate the hours the Cosmetology Division mandated. This realization promoted DeWese to open Pressley School of Beauty Culture in 1944, with her first class commencing on July 1.[13]

Historian Julia Kirk Blackwelder describes the period from the 1930s to the 1960s as the "golden age of black beauty education."[14] This golden age of education directly followed the "golden age of black business," from 1900 to 1930, when many Black women became successful beauty products manufacturers and distributors.[15] These women excelled in the area of beauty culture, prompting interest in and providing economic opportunities to working women who had previously had limited economic opportunities. During the golden age of Black business, women like Annie Turnbo Malone, Madam C. J. Walker, and Sara Spencer Washington developed their own products and hired sales associates who promoted those products and taught their hairstyling methods. With so many products flooding the market, Black beauticians realized the importance of training programs and began to open their own schools because cosmetology education was segregated in some cities.

Black beauty school owners saw themselves as educators, businesspeople, and race leaders.[16] As successful beauty entrepreneurs had proved, the business of Black beauty culture could be lucrative. Women engaged in this field were among the race's first twentieth century social entrepreneurs and philanthropists, donating large proceeds from their profits and resources to building and supporting

Black community organizations to uplift the race.[17] Black beauty educators saw themselves in this same vein. By opening these schools, they "trained eager matriculates to provide hair care for black patrons and groomed their students to lead model lives as citizens and as tradespeople independent of white employers."[18] Therefore, Black beauty education had a political and economic component that spoke to racial uplift and progress, for both the individual beautician who completed the course and for the community that would benefit from her services and community involvement. DeWese's beauty school served this same purpose in Milwaukee.

The Struggle to Become Licensed in Milwaukee

While DeWese had a great vision for helping Black women become licensed beauticians, state regulations made this task difficult to accomplish. Although the cosmetology code developed by the State Department of Health made no mention of race, the impact of state licensing and sanitary regulations on Black beauticians could often be detrimental. Black women who enrolled in Pressley School of Beauty Culture began the program with high hopes—after nine months of study and 1,500 hours of practice, they would become licensed beauticians and be free to work in a shop or continue their studies to obtain a manager's license, which would allow them to open their own shop. Wisconsin Cosmetology regulations at times created insurmountable barriers though. For example, cosmetology regulations mirrored Jim Crow job system requirements of needing proof of birth and high school education. Specifically, future licensed beauticians needed documents certifying that they were seventeen years old and that they had the equivalent of a tenth-grade education. Often Pressley School enrollees had recently migrated from the South and lacked proof of either their age or educational attainment. A birth certificate or baptismal record could serve as proof of one's age. Only official transcripts or a diploma could serve as proof of one's educational attainment. These requirements obstructed Black women's ability to become licensed beauticians.

Stories of Pressley students who encountered difficulties with the state's proof of age requirement are common in Pressley School's records. In one instance, for example, Norma Hadley submitted a document that she hoped would meet the requirements of proving her age. Since she did not have her birth certificate in her possession before the start of school on September 1, 1947, she submitted a verification letter from the high school she had attended. The Cosmetology Division rejected the document. saying it had been altered. In a letter to DeWese, the Division wrote, "If she had really been born in 1932 and we took her in, she would only be 15 and we would be wrong."[19] Hadley's mother submitted an additional letter of verification, but because the letter arrived to the Cosmetology Division after the start of the semester, Hadley lost credit for the hours she had already completed. Mattie DeWese repeatedly asked the Cosmetology Division, by letter, in person, and via phone to reinstate Hadley's hours, especially since she met the age requirement by the time school started and because she commuted from Kenosha—forty miles away—to attend Pressley. The Division refused.

A year later, in 1948, Pressley School instructor and daughter of Mattie DeWese, Flora Simms, wrote to Cosmetology supervisor Marion Groth on behalf of a student. This time the student, Lillie Mae Brown, had migrated from Mississippi. Brown had written to her church to request a copy of her baptismal records, but unfortunately the church did not keep official records. She submitted a letter of verification to the Cosmetology Division that she hoped would serve as an acceptable substitute as she waited for a copy of her birth record from the county in Mississippi where she was born. There was no response to Simms's written inquiry in the Cosmetology Division records.[20]

In addition to facing difficulties verifying their age, many of Pressley's students found it nearly impossible to meet Wisconsin's educational prerequisites because they had been born and raised in the South. Opportunities for secondary education for African Americans in the South, especially during the 1930s, when many of these women would have been enrolled in school, were limited at best.[21] Additionally, the state of Wisconsin required more education than other states and was among the few states that required a high school diploma.[22] Most did not; for example, Texas only required beauticians to have proof of a seventh-grade education to qualify for a beautician's license. Therefore, many Black women experienced the same obstacles as Mary Evelyn Williams and Willie Mitchell as described in the opening vignette. Despite this, Williams and Mitchell enrolled in Pressley School anyway. After paying the enrollment fee and going to class, they received word from the Cosmetology Division that unless they provided proof of a tenth-grade education, their enrollment at Pressley would not count. In response to this, they wrote to the Cosmetology Division.[23] In the letter they detailed their past experiences, their vision for themselves, and their request to the Division:

> We are both one of the many people who have bootleged [*sic*] or work in our kitchens without a license.
>
> But now we have come to the place that what-ever [*sic*] we do, we want to do it right. What-ever we do we want it to be a credit to our city as well as our state. . . .
>
> We both like the work very much and would like to be granted the privilege to continue our studies.
>
> We know that we haven't proof that we have a 10th grade education, but we are begging you to please let us by. Please give us the "Go Signal." We'll be happy and so grateful to you.
>
> If there be any extra charges we will be glad to pay. . . .

Williams and Mitchell already considered themselves beauticians and wanted the opportunity to formalize their education at Pressley, which would prepare them for the state examination. Becoming licensed beauticians would remove the stigmatizing label of bootlegger and make their work credible in the eyes of their community, the city, and the state. Becoming licensed, therefore, was an individual achievement that had far-reaching social and economic implications. A beautician's inability to become licensed in the state of Wisconsin meant she would not be officially recognized and she could not practice legitimately. As a result, women like Mary Williams and Willie Mitchell would have to resort to practicing cosmetology illegally in their kitchens.

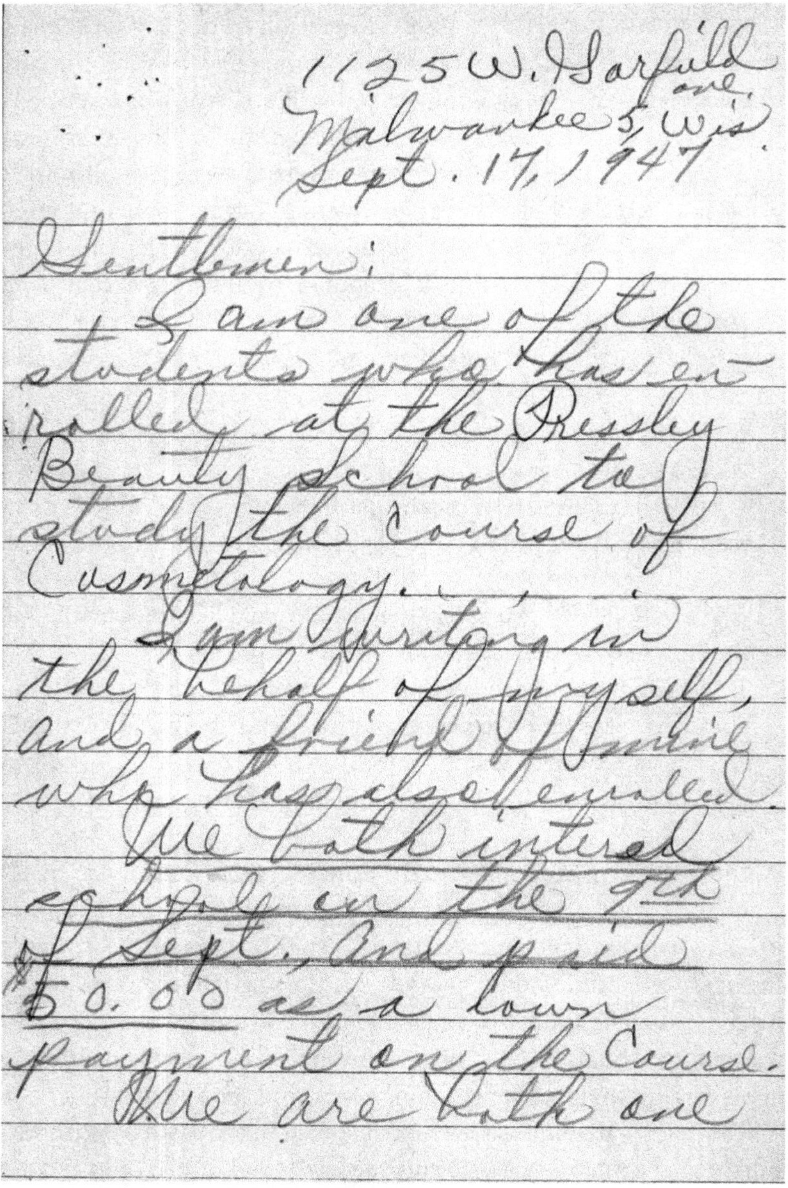
1125 W. Garfield ave.
Milwaukee 5, Wis.
Sept. 17, 1947

Gentlemen;
I am one of the students who has enrolled at the Pressley Beauty School to study the Course of Cosmetology.
I am writing in the behalf of myself, and a friend of mine who has also enrolled.
We both intered school on the 9th of Sept. And paid $50.00 as a down payment on the Course.
We are both one

FIGURE 5. The first page of the handwritten letter written by Mary Evelyn Williams and Willie M. Mitchell. Pressley Beauty School Records, Wisconsin Historical Society of the many people who have bootleged or, work in our kitchens without a license.

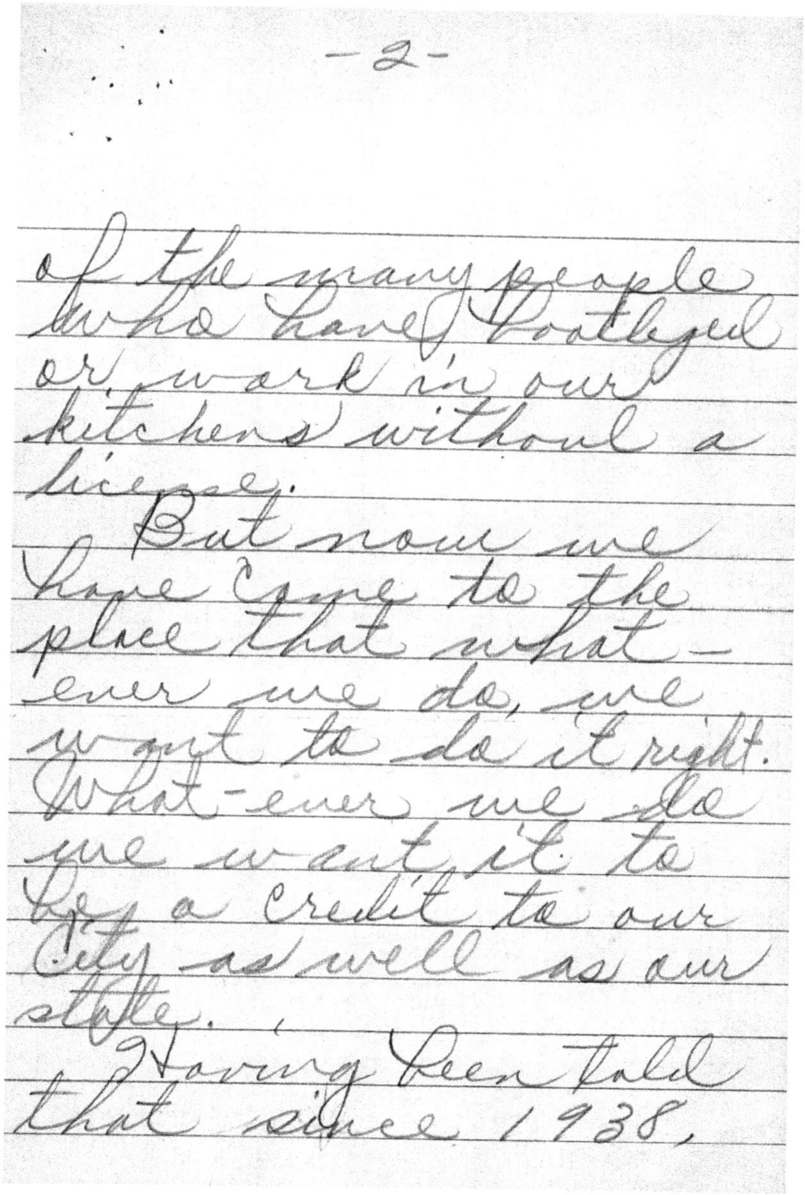

But now we have come to the place that what-ever we do, we want to do it right. What-ever we do we want, it to be a credit to our City as well as our state. Having been told that since 1938,

FIGURE 6. The second page of the handwritten letter written by Mary Evelyn Williams and Willie M. Mitchell. Pressley Beauty School Records, Wisconsin Historical Society

The repercussions for not being able to secure a license could be severe, especially if a beautician continued doing hair illegally. Since the state required licensure, beauticians could neither be hired nor operate their own shop without the credential. Practicing hair illegally was a criminal offense, and beauticians who violated state law could be punished by jail time and/or a fine.[24] The Division of Cosmetology routinely sent state beauty inspectors to the homes of women suspected of practicing cosmetology illegally. When they visited women's homes, a sheriff came along and arrested women on the spot.[25] Therefore, an inability to secure a license could be humiliating and detrimental to a beautician on financial, legal, and social levels. Black women like Williams and Mitchell struggled to get licensed in Milwaukee, but they enrolled in Pressley and advocated for themselves by directly communicating with the state in the hope that they could be a "credit" to their local communities.

DeWese supported her students and engaged in what scholars of Black women's history refer to as "broker politics."[26] With broker politics, Black women activists made their presence and their community's needs known so that "they would be factored into policy decisions and empowered to participate in decision-making processes."[27] In the cosmetology sector, this translated to Black beauticians working through state bureaucracies to influence how state boards of health and cosmetology divisions implemented policies and procedures. Mattie DeWese corresponded and negotiated with the Cosmetology Division, educating them on the effects of state policy on her students and insisting they revise or relax certain policies so that both her students and the school could succeed. These negotiations sometimes resulted in changes that benefitted the school; they also reveal the depths of the state's bureaucratic racism, which was made manifest through officials who enforced the state's cosmetology regulations.

Pressley School and the Challenge of State Regulation

To remain a registered cosmetology school, the Cosmetology Division required periodic inspections from state officials, most often white women, to ensure that schools upheld sanitary and health codes and followed regulations. After each visit, state inspectors submitted a report that detailed their observations and recommendations. While these reports included basic information about the school, such as number of students or the topic of instruction for that day's visit, the reports also reveal the racial attitudes some inspectors held as well as the attempts DeWese and her student made to navigate these attitudes. An early report submitted by state inspector Leah Nelson exposed her prejudices toward Black people. In this report she wrote, "Many of those who are licensed admitted to me that they did not tell these girls because they felt that they were being especially favored by being notified. There seems to be a peculiar pride and jealousy among the colored people."[28] In this statement, Leah Nelson accused licensed Black beauticians of withholding information related to licensing opportunities from those who were unlicensed. While these beauticians' may have withheld information from each other, Nelson stereotyped and generalized about an entire group of people. In another report, Nelson noted that the push to license Black beauticians resulted in a five-year headache causing her to "wake up at night seeing *dark* clouds hovering around" her.[29]

After Leah Nelson left the Cosmetology Division, Hazel Kratsch replaced her and began visiting Pressley. Kratsch also described her relationships with Pressley School and Mattie DeWese. Early on she noted, "I have tried to make these colored folks like me and if I succeed they will be easier to work with as time goes on."[30] After visiting the school regularly, it seems her relationship with Pressley School and its students did improve. She wrote, "I am really getting a thrill out of the cooperation that these colored folks are giving me. I try very hard to make them like and respect me." She continued, "They are trying very hard in their slow way to keep things in order, as they never know when I am going to drop in. A little praise goes a long way with them."[31] A week later Kratsch noted "it was a real pleasure to work with these people."[32] Months later, Kratsch wrote, "I am very glad that I have won these colored folks over. I find them very cooperative and willing to listen and follow out some suggestions that I have given them. I do find, though, that they need constance [*sic*] checking to keep them in line."³³ Both Leah Nelson and Hazel Kratsch's reports included their personal feelings and emotions, revealing their racist and paternalist views about Black women. The state validated these women's views, not only by receiving, recording, and preserving these reports, but also by acting on their recommendations.

Kratsch attributed her improved relationship with Pressley to her own behavior, failing to consider that DeWese and her students understood the power state inspectors had and that it would be strategic to be on good terms with the state—not because they wanted to be Kratsch's friend, but because they knew Kratsch held the keys that could unlock their successful licensing. If DeWese had shown any antagonism towards Kratsch or the state, surely Pressley students would have been negatively affected. For example, it was the role of the state inspectors to make sure beauty schools taught proper techniques so that students would be prepared for the state examinations. Also, state inspectors provided resources, information, and updates from the State Board of Health as it related to new cosmetology regulations and licensing requirements. Therefore, fractured relationships with state inspectors could result in out-of-date information, missed deadlines, and the inability to keep students abreast of changes in cosmetology techniques.

Managing relationships with state inspectors could be challenging, and so was adhering to some of the Cosmetology Division's regulations. However, DeWese employed broker politics to convince the Cosmetology Division to give the school an exception regarding a difficult to achieve regulation. The state mandated all beauty schools have a licensed physician on the instructor's roster to teach beauty classes related to the biological aspects of the skin and the scalp. During the time Pressley was open, fulfillment of this requirement was difficult at best. No white physicians would teach at the school and there were only a few Black physicians in the city who could potentially teach at the school. Unfortunately, these physicians had full caseloads and were unable to add instruction to their list of professional responsibilities. As a result of these two realities, Mattie DeWese continuously petitioned the State Board of Health for an exemption to this rule.[34] She asked for permission to enlist the services of a Black nurse instead of a Black physician. The State Board of Health originally denied DeWese's request, citing the state requirement and that the Board would have to vote on an exception. In the meantime, they encouraged DeWese to continue searching for a physician. DeWese tried and eventually was able to find a physician, but the school was at the mercy of this physician's schedule, which could change at any time and leave them in the lurch. After being stood up several times by this physician, DeWese approached the State Board of Health once again. After nearly a year of corresponding about this issue, the Board finally agreed to allow a nurse to teach the required course.[35] In this case, DeWese's action resulted in a policy exception that benefited the school and her students.

Another example from Pressley's records illustrates DeWese's blatant disregard of state policy when it did not suit her personal and community agenda. In September of 1949, the Cosmetology Division reprimanded Mattie DeWese. The previous chapter discussed DeWese's leadership as the president of the Sixth Ward Better Housing Club, making her attuned to the housing difficulties those in her community faced. She had been letting a family sleep in the unused rooms of her beauty school during the summer term while school was not in session. Earlier that year, DeWese shared her plans to do this with an inspector and had been encouraged not to do so, especially since state laws mandated that beauty salons and schools be separate from residential dwellings. Specifically, the regulation stipulated that for health and sanitation reasons, neither beauty schools nor beauty parlors could be used as or located in a residential dwelling unless the parlor and or school was totally separate from the residential dwelling. DeWese explained that letting the family reside in the school would be temporary until they located a permanent residence. However, when it came time to open the school in the fall, the family had not yet found a place to live and were still occupying rooms of the school. Since the school only had one bathroom, the state inspector scolded DeWese and told her she could not open her school until the family vacated the premises. Eventually, the family moved out and Pressley School of Beauty Culture opened for business.

Professionalization and the Politics of Respectability

Although DeWese disagreed with the Cosmetology Division on several issues, she unwaveringly upheld the division's code of professionalism, which dovetailed with her adherence to the politics of respectability. Historians have written about how efforts to professionalize industries coincided with some Black women's use of the politics of respectability as a strategy for racial uplift. Focusing on behavior, morality, Christian principles, and temperance, the moral codes embedded in professions such as nursing, teaching, and in some cases, cosmetology, meshed with the behavioral standards required for the politics of respectability.[36] For example, in addition to standards of cleanliness and sanitation, the Division required that beauticians always look "neat and professional."[37] Beauty school students' professional attire included school-specific insignia, which all students were required to wear when at school. Insignias were important because they identified the students as beauty professionals in training. Pressley School students had a habit of not wearing their insignias, and one day state inspector Hazel Kratsch, with DeWese's approval, lectured them about this, resulting in a commitment from the students to wear them.[38]

Another incident that occurred at Pressley brought up similar issues regarding professionalization, practicing cosmetology illegally, and the politics of respectability, but also illustrates the tension that sometimes developed between DeWese and her students, especially as they refused to adhere to the state's restrictions and instead opted to act in their own economic best interest. On the weekend of Easter in 1948, none of DeWese's students showed up for class on Friday or Saturday. This upset DeWese because she had lined up several customers and had counted on her students to assist. DeWese assumed her students skipped classes to do the hair of their own friends and family, especially since they could potentially make more money outside of the school environment. Additionally, the students had less than three months before they took their licensing examination and perhaps they reasoned that doing their friends' and family members' hair provided them with more experience, bolstering their client base so that when they finished school they would already have a following. Whatever the rationale, they consciously defied DeWese's instructions and refused to report to school on the holiday weekend.

As a result of their unexcused absences and to "keep them in line," DeWese invited state inspector Hazel Kratsch to talk to the students about absenteeism and the repercussions of practicing without a license.[39] Kratsch told the students about the time she brought law enforcement with her to arrest a beautician who had violated state law. Initially, the students did not believe the repercussions could be so severe and thought the story a joke. Eventually, after a long conversation, students understood the potential consequences of violating state cosmetology regulations.

While DeWese saw this as a moment to teach students about absenteeism and the dangers of violating beauty regulations, this incident reveals much about DeWese and her adherence to professionalism and the politics of respectability. DeWese "was very much upset" over her students' failure to show up because it increased her workload and also made her look bad.[40] Looking bad in front of customers was secondary to DeWese's fear of the repercussions that came with getting caught doing hair without a license. Getting arrested and going to jail—and the community's knowledge of it—would not only taint the student, but also the school and DeWese. This fear, as well as the loss of customers and money during the holiday weekend, could have contributed to DeWese's decision to join forces with the state to teach her students a lesson. This was a potentially dangerous liaison, because now the state was aware of students who had been practicing illegally, and since DeWese provided the state with the contact information of all of Pressley students as required by state regulation, a state inspector could randomly show up at a student's place of residence to check if they were practicing illegally. Fortunately, there is no record of this ever happening.

DeWese and her students lived in an ever-changing urban context, where the number of Black migrants increased, especially after World War II. The influx of new Black migrants to the city exposed the fault lines among Black Milwaukeeans especially as the segregated city and physically constrained Bronzeville neighborhood struggled to integrate new residents into a structure that was already inadequate and unequal. Fear of new Black migrants getting involved in criminal activity and making conditions worse for everyone prevailed, and one response to this was for long-term residents to call out and lecture Black migrants about their behavior, in public and private forums. Therefore, contextualizing DeWese response to her students' behavior within a broader context is important.

DeWese continued her own professional development by pursuing educational opportunities to increase and improve her understanding of the procedures and science behind beauty and cosmetology. By June of 1949, DeWese had finished a course on cosmetic chemistry. Additionally, she enrolled in a cosmetology course for African American instructors in Washington, DC, later that summer. After this year of professional development, unfortunately, Mattie DeWese did not open Pressley during the 1950 academic year. Personal correspondence with state inspectors revealed her husband's health issues, as well as declining enrollment among students.[41] Although this same correspondence never indicated any of Mattie DeWese's ailments, a 1956 *Baltimore Afro American* obituary announced her death after a lengthy battle with illness.[42]

Despite the difficulties DeWese and her students endured striving to become licensed, after completing Pressley's cosmetology course, students did go on to pass the state's licensing examination. Pressley School of Beauty Culture was only open for a few short years, but it provided opportunities for Black women to pursue employment opportunities that allowed for more flexibility and autonomy within the Jim Crow job system. During the 1950s, after Pressley closed, cosmetology education shifted from being predominantly run by private schools to become an area of study at local vocational schools, which Black women took advantage of. Even though there are no complete lists of Pressley School graduates available, in 1973, decades after Pressley closed, the *Milwaukee Courier*, a Black newspaper, featured the school in a profile of Milwaukee's historic Black Bronzeville community. Included in this feature was an image of a graduating class of Pressley School students along with Mattie DeWese and her daughter, Flora Simms. According to the picture's caption, "Many of Milwaukee's favorite and most popular beauticians graduated from this school."[43]

Professionalization through Organization: Local to National Considerations

While the first part of this chapter focused on the women of Pressley School, there is evidence that community activism among Milwaukee beauticians flourished in Milwaukee in the 1940s. For example, news of beauticians' community involvement and organizing reached the *Chicago Defender*. DeWese's daughter, Flora Simms, participated in community organizations and joined the ranks of other well-known local leaders such as Columbia Building and Loan–co-founder Wilbur Halyard, whose co-founder and wife, Ardie Halyard, is discussed in Chapter 3. Simms and Halyard joined Milwaukee Urban League president William V. Kelly as members of the Children's Service Association. The Children's Service Association was established to provide social services for neglected Black children in the city.[44] In addition to community-oriented activities, another *Chicago Defender* article reported the activities of the Milwaukee Hairdressers Association, which had a business meeting and holiday party in early January of 1941.[45]

These short articles point to two things. One, beauticians involved themselves in community issues and DeWese was not alone in her community development endeavors. Two, although very little archival material exists, the second of these two articles illustrates, not surprisingly, that beauticians had been organizing themselves even before DeWese's school. Therefore, when an opportunity for Milwaukee beauticians to join a national beauticians' organization presented itself, they jumped at the chance. At least three members of the early Milwaukee Hairdressers Association, Freddie Banks, Sally Marshall, and Augusta Perkins, became members of the newly established national beautician's fraternal organization, Alpha Chi Pi Omega Sorority and Fraternity (ACPO), or the Greek Letter Beauticians as they referred to themselves. While there is no definitive record identifying Mattie DeWese or her daughter Flora Simms as members of ACPO, they would have known of the organization and DeWese might have attended the same beauty college in Chicago as the organization's founder, Marjorie Joyner. Even if DeWese and Joyner did not know each personally, Marjorie Joyner's leadership in the beauty education field meant DeWese might have known of her, with the two potentially crossing paths at some point.

Successful Black beautician and organizer Marjorie Stewart Joyner established ACPO in conjunction with the United Beauty School Owners and Teachers Association (UBSOTA) in 1946, following decades of experience as a professional beautician and educator. Joyner attended Chicago's A. B. Moler Beauty School and graduated in 1916. She got her start when her mother-in-law suggested and paid for her to take a course on the Madam C. J. Walker Method taught by Walker herself. Joyner took additional classes and impressed the beauty mogul with her own skills—hair weaving techniques she had learned and perfected from her time at the Moler School. Joyner traveled with Walker, and eventually by herself, teaching Walker's hair techniques as well as her own. After Walker died, the company named Joyner National Supervisor of Walker Schools, which had locations in Dallas, Tulsa, Chicago, Indianapolis, New York, and Baltimore. While her home base remained in Chicago, Joyner supervised these schools and traveled extensively. Traveling on behalf of the Walker Company to train Black beauticians and sales agents, Joyner took advantage of Black church networks to spread the Walker technique. For example, the Baptist church's annual conventions and access to community space provided Joyner with an opportunity to recruit new students and offer professional development opportunities for existing beauticians using the Walker Method.[46]

Not only was Marjorie Joyner a leading educator with the Madam C. J. Walker Manufacturing Company, but she also made a name for herself on the state level regarding beauty education. In the mid-1920s, Illinois became one of the early states to develop cosmetology codes that regulated beauty parlors and schools. Because of Marjorie Joyner's experience and success as a beauty educator with the Walker schools, she was one of only three women who helped write the state's beauty regulations. In 1926 she became the first Black woman licensed beautician in the state of Illinois.[47] Joyner's achievements as a beauty educator continued in the 1930s despite the devastating effects of the Great Depression. In fact, due to low enrollments in the early 1930s, Joyner designed a Walker method mail-in beauty correspondence course that interested people could complete to open a shop in their homes. Of course, this course was mostly sold outside of Illinois in states that did not yet have a cosmetology licensing code. Providing employment opportunities through beauty culture during a time when most Black women worked in domestic service was one of the ways Joyner made an impact on Black women in both her local community and across the nation.

Joyner's commitment to her local community and her organizing efforts—both characteristics of Black beauticians and beauty school owners—extended beyond the beauty field and into her hometown of Chicago. For example, she helped to found Cosmopolitan Community Church in Chicago in 1934. Additionally, Joyner oversaw the *Chicago Defender*'s charity bureau, which, among its many activities, sponsored an annual parade and scholarship for Black youth. Her oversight of the Defender's charity bureau as well as her involvement with the Cosmopolitan Community Church led to her recognition as a community leader. This recognition brought national attention and during World War II, President Franklin Roosevelt's administration tapped her to direct a center for Black servicemen in the city.

All her professional and community work primed her to create a professional beauty organization of her own, which she did when she established ACPO and UBSOTA. The creation of ACPO/UBSOTA was a direct result of her commitment to the field of cosmetology and her dedication to Black community development. Although

Joyner was also a member of the African American National Beauty Culturists League (NBCL), which had been founded in 1919, and served as its president, in 1930 the NBCL shifted its priority from the national to the local level.[48] ACPO/UBSOTA aimed to refocus Black beauty school owners and professionals' attention on national cosmetology policies and practices. Joyner's success and determination attracted the attention of nationally known educator Mary McLeod Bethune, who supported the establishment of the ACPO/UBSOTA. As a result of Bethune and Joyner's relationship, beauticians formally supported Bethune's Bethune Cookman College in Daytona Beach, Florida, through considerable financial donations.

The development of the Greek Letter Beauticians mirrored a national trend regarding Black Greek letter organizations (BGLOs). Originally established as collegiate societies as early as 1906, BGLOs developed to provide Black students on predominantly white college campuses an opportunity to join affinity groups with other like-minded, same-gender Black students. Therefore, the early goals of BGLOs tended to be mostly social in nature, although the oldest sororities, Alpha Kappa Alpha, founded in 1908, and Delta Sigma Theta, founded in 1913, affiliated with and supported Black clubwomen through the National Association of Colored Women. However, by the post–World War II period and the advent of civil rights campaigns, the mission of BGLOs shifted to political activities and community engagement, such that by the 1950s they had developed agendas that made Black community development a priority. In Milwaukee, Alpha Kappa Alpha and Delta Sigma Theta sponsored social, cultural, and political events. Additionally, some of the Black community's most prominent leaders held membership in these historic groups. For example, Bernice Lindsay, from Chapter 1, joined Delta Sigma Theta as an undergraduate student at Ohio State University. Upon arriving in Milwaukee, she joined the graduate chapter—an act that distinguishes Black from white Greek letter organizations. In BGLOs, members remain active after graduating from college, join a local chapter, and continue their community service projects. Black beauticians modeled their sorority after Black Greek letter organizations that had developed during the early part of the twentieth century.

Milwaukee Beauticians Join the Greek Letter Beauticians

Milwaukee beauticians joined ACPO/UBSOTA by chartering a chapter of the organization in Milwaukee in 1951. By joining the sorority, Milwaukee beauticians committed themselves to its economic, political, social, and educational ideals, thrusts, and programs. The Constitution and Bylaws of ACPO/UBSOTA stated that both the fraternal organization and the association were organized for two main reasons: "to promote the business abilities of those who join" and "to lift the educational standards of the beauticians."[49] Any person enrolled in a beauty or barber school could join, as well any person already licensed who had been practicing at least two years. A 1952 booklet of the fraternal organization's international conference featured a fourteen-point list explaining the organization's goals for itself.[50] First on the list was its desire "to let the general public know that we are accredited business people." Members of the organization owned beauty parlors, barbershops, and cosmetology schools that were lucrative and contributed much to the economy of many communities across the country. In addition to defining themselves as businesspeople, members of the organization were committed to civic involvement and philanthropy. ACPO/UBSOTA also encouraged a Black business and economic agenda, directing members of the organization to buy directly from Black-owned businesses or white-owned businesses that employed Black workers. The organization defined beauticians as businesspeople and professionals and insisted that beauticians attend the organization's national conventions because continually advancing one's knowledge of the field was the mark of a true professional.

In addition to providing Black beauticians a formal organizing space, the organization also advocated on behalf of Black beauticians at the national level, especially since national officers like Joyner had influence and clout in the beauty industry. National officers used their connections to lift up the interest of beauty students, operators, and schools. Specifically, national officers took it as their duty to remain apprised of any updates from the federal Department of Agriculture, especially as they related to regulations and laws regarding cosmetics or skin and hair products. They did this in addition to staying informed about any other economic developments, national or international, that would have an impact on the work and welfare of beauticians.

Milwaukee beauticians joined ACPO/UBSOTA and started the Alpha Iota Mu Chapter in 1951. A year later, Milwaukee chapter president Lillian Cosgrove and chapter member Mary Spottswood participated in ACPO/UBSOTA's first international trip to Port-au-Prince, Haiti, the first week of March 1952. According to a *Chicago Defender* article, the trip signified a crucial step in "building international understanding," a new undertaking for the group.[51] Historian Tiffany Gill writes about the importance of this international trip in the development of the Black beauty association as a professional organization.[52]

During the trip, beauticians received full cooperation from Haiti's top officials. Specifically, President Paul Magloire saw the potential of the trip in building connections, understanding, and relationships between the United States and Haiti. In addition to meeting with the president and First Lady of Haiti, beauticians met with other Haitian leaders including Cleante Desgraves, president of the Women's League for Social Action in Haiti. Beauticians also met with Jean F. Brierre, member of Haiti's Council of Government and M. Marc, Haiti's director of National Education. US officials including Acting Ambassador Robert Folsom, press relations officer Homer Gain, and director of the Haitian American Institute James Cassidy also met with the group of beauticians while they visited.

Beauticians planned and held activities at the Haitian American Institute that included joint seminars, mass meetings, and special presentations. US beauticians and Haitian women participated in a one-day seminar as well as a mass meeting where *Chicago Defender* journalist Vernice Spraggs spoke about the segregation and discrimination endured by Black people, their commitment to democracy, and the ongoing struggle for attaining full human rights.[53] Haiti's secretary of commerce Jules Domond also addressed beauticians to explain the procedures for doing business in Haiti, especially the regulations regarding manufacturing and selling cosmetics. While ACPO/UBSOTA's original plans included providing four scholarships to Haitian girls for beauty training in the United States, by the end of the trip, this commitment had increased to twenty-one scholarships as additional beauty school owners pledged their own commitment to the development of this international exchange. After several days of social, educational, and political networking, the beauticians returned to the United States by way of Daytona Beach, stopping at Bethune Cookman College and visiting with school founder and ACPO/UBSOTA supporter, Mary McLeod Bethune. During the international trip, Black beauticians connected their business activities with education and training, sharing what they learned with others, highlighting community intellectualism, as we saw with Mattie DeWese earlier in the chapter.

Not only did Milwaukee beauticians participate in national conventions and international excursions with ACPO/UBSOTA, but they also quickly gained prominent leadership roles within the organization. Within a year of starting the Milwaukee chapter, ACPO/UBSOTA leadership appointed Milwaukee chapter president Lillian Cosgrove as a state director. Additionally, in the 1960s, Wilhelmina Hardy served as the secretary of the Great Lakes Region of ACPO/UBSOTA. Even those without formal leadership roles represented Milwaukee at important sorority events. For example, seven members of the Milwaukee chapter attended a Chicago chapter banquet in 1953. The banquet resembled a cotillion in that the chapter introduced new ACPO/UBSOTA members to notable Black civic, professional, and educational leaders, including publisher of the *Chicago Defender* John Sengstacke, as well as executive secretary of the Chicago Urban League Sidney Williams. At the banquet, beauticians spoke about their community work and support of Black institutions such as the Washington Park Young Men's Christian Association (YMCA) and Provident Hospital.

Six years after being organized in Milwaukee, through the leadership and involvement of its members on the national, state, and regional levels, the Alpha Iota Mu chapter of ACPO was already recognized as a preeminent organization. A March 28, 1957, *Milwaukee Defender* article announced a cultural event the group would sponsor the following week. Although the headline of the article announced that the beauticians would bring an internally known music group to the city, Payne Calypso Group, the article also recognized the local chapter for its community efforts. "Each year," according to the article, "the sorority has contributed to some worthwhile organization." [54] These organizations included the local YMCA and of course, Bethune Cookman College in Florida. Finally, the article described the women as "licensed graduate beauticians" and as "one of Milwaukee's leading groups of women." A week after the Calypso event the *Milwaukee Defender* reported the success of the event and saluted the hard work of beauticians in Milwaukee, noting that because of the "time and effort that our many Licensed Beauticians have spent in glorifying our women . . . it is no wonder that the beauty shop has taken on a greater importance not only to the women, but to the entire community." [55] Milwaukee beauticians continued their community activism and leadership in ACPO.

In 1962 ACPO held its Great Lakes regional meeting in Milwaukee. Planned and sponsored by the Milwaukee chapter, the theme for the 1962 conference was "Forging Ahead." Like all ACPO conferences and conventions, one of the purposes of the gathering was educational advancement in the field. Regional meetings were condensed versions of national conventions and usually included hair demonstrations as well educational sessions related to business administration, English, economics, teaching methods, and physiology, as the most recent national convention had featured earlier that spring. In addition to lectures and demonstrations, the beauticians invited Dr. Louis Maxey, a plastic surgeon, to deliver a morning lecture. Social activities included a luncheon and fashion show, to which prominent female leaders were invited such as the first and only Black female member of the Milwaukee Council, Vel Phillips, and Ernestine O'Bee, owner of O'Bee Funeral Home and officer on the national board of the United Church Women of America.

Milwaukee beauticians continued their involvement and leadership in ACPO/UBSOTA throughout the 1960s. By then, in the midst of the national Black freedom struggle, ACPO/UBSOTA began promoting a five-point program that guided the organization's work on national and local levels and cemented the organization's priorities as they revolved around beautician's economic development and political involvement.[56] In connecting professional development and training of students interested in the profession, one aspect of the five-point program established regional scholarships. ACPO/UBSOTA would partner with the Office of Economic Opportunity, the National Urban League, and the Phi Delta Kappa teacher's sorority to establish the scholarships. The second point related to volunteerism and civic activism, and it committed members to volunteer at vocational schools, hospitals, and rehabilitation centers. Beautifying local communities connected the third and fourth points. In 1965, the federal government created the Head Start program, which was an eight-week summer program meant to prepare disadvantaged young people for starting kindergarten. Beauticians would support their local Head Start programs by participating in the ACPO/UBSOTA seed packet program, where beauticians would distribute packets of flower seeds to Head Start centers to encourage an interest in science and planting among young children. Along the same lines as the seed project, a fourth point included participation of local beauty shops in "Beautify America." With this project, beauticians planned to pass out literature to their clients about sprucing up and improving their neighborhoods by cleaning up, painting, and planting flowers.

The final point in the Greek Letter beauticians' five-point program spelled out their stance on and commitment to voting. The ACPO/UBSOTA national convention met in June 1965, after the Voting Rights bill passed in the US Senate and while the US House debated the legislation. Acknowledging the importance of the moment, the beauticians asserted, "Members of the beauty trade profession have always believed in the importance of citizenship responsibility at the ballot box."[57] For them this responsibility translated into a year-round voter education program that encouraged their customers to register to vote and actually cast their ballots. ACPO/UBSOTA laid out concrete action steps for this important component of its five-point program:

Beauticians will be on the alert to move into action immediately once the Voter Registration Bill in Congress becomes law. They will distribute literature through the shops urging their customers to register and vote. Every shop and school will be supplied with posters to display the sign of good citizenship, "be a registered voter." In addition, beauticians will be urged to join with local registration committees to help in whatever way they can to speed up the drive. Of all the programs in the "Great Society," none is more important than getting people to register and vote.[58]

Although records for the local chapter are extremely scarce, national records of the ACPO/UBSOTA show that Milwaukee beauticians stayed active with ACPO/UBSOTA, led at the regional and state level, and brought the mission and vision of the organization to the city.

Conclusion

Unrecognized by the state of Wisconsin prior to the 1930s, Black beauticians had come a long way by the 1960s. Decades after it closed, Pressley School and its impact was still remembered by Black Milwaukeeans. Pressley should also be remembered for what it reveals about community intellectualism. While DeWese opened Pressley to provide a service to Black beauticians, both she and her community of students exposed the bureaucratic racism inherent within the state cosmetology division while also proposing solutions to maneuver around policies and procedures that held them back, sometimes refusing these regulations altogether. In the case of DeWese's students, their refusals surfaced intra-racial class tensions that existed between Black Milwaukeeans. Differences in class and economic positioning factored into Black working women's financial decisions. For some Pressley students, it was worth the risk to do hair without a license, because the income enabled them to pay rent or buy groceries. They weighed their options, which sometimes meant their actions and ideas differed from DeWese's. Community intellectualism was a dynamic process, and Pressley women's actions reveal this.

After Pressley closed, Black beauticians in Milwaukee affiliated with a new national organization, participating on the state and regional levels by creating a community that focused on civic activism and continued professional development, similar to what we saw in the example of Mattie DeWese. Milwaukee beauticians took their service and craft seriously and developed a reputation for their work. The Black professionally trained beauticians who joined ACPO/UBSOTA immediately became leaders on the state, regional, and national level, even traveling internationally with the organization. At a time when most Black working women toiled in low-paying service positions, beauty work provided a measure of economic autonomy, giving women an opportunity to give back to their community and thus fulfill their desire to be a "credit" to their city, state, and nation.

In the next chapter, the focus shifts away from Milwaukee's Black beauticians and onto Black working women laboring in manufacturing, clerical, and other service industries in the city. Several aspects of these women's work experiences connect with those of Black beauticians including their refusal to be mistreated by and within the Jim Crow job system, their engagement with and critique of the state, and their insistence on articulating their experiences of racial and gender discrimination. The main difference was the context; instead of the beauty school, beauty shop, or kitchen, the Black working women in the next chapter worked in factories, hospitals, and offices and shared their experiences in MNAACP or MUL offices, or with the Wisconsin Industrial Commission, the state apparatus responsible for remedying employment discrimination. Their actions coincided with Milwaukee's direct action civil rights movement, which peaked in the 1960s.

CHAPTER 3

Working toward a Remedy

Exposing the Experiences of Black Women during the Civil Rights Era

In March of 1963 twenty-three-year-old Hazel Williamson moved to Milwaukee from Indianapolis, Indiana, in search of a better job. Having worked as a punch press operator for the past five years in Indianapolis, she was told by relatives that finding a better-paying job in Milwaukee was possible, so she made the move. Recognized as a "superior worker" by her previous supervisor, Williamson left Indianapolis confident in her work experience and skills.[1] Upon arriving in Milwaukee, Williamson noticed job advertisements for manufacturing positions at Globe Union, Incorporated, which produced electronic components, automotive spark plugs, and batteries and employed nearly three thousand workers in its plant and administrative offices. Williamson went to Globe Union and filled out an application to work in the manufacturing plant.

By April, Williamson had not heard back from Globe Union regarding her initial application, but she did see an advertisement that the company was now hiring for punch press operators with at least one year's work experience. Seeing as this was the work she had been doing in Indianapolis, Williamson went back to Globe Union to complete another application. Although Williamson specifically asked for an application for the punch operator position, the receptionist gave her an application for a job in the manufacturing plant, in error.

As with most jobs in the city, proof of one's age needed to be provided, usually in the form of an official birth certificate. Unfortunately, Williamson did not have her birth certificate on hand, so the receptionist placed her application in a pile with other incomplete applications. Williamson's birth certificate was in Indiana, so she contacted her mother, who sent it immediately. During the time that Williamson waited for her birth certificate to arrive, she contacted Globe Union to verify that the position was still open. The birth certificate arrived within a week, and Williamson brought it to Globe Union as soon as she received it. While there, Williamson once again confirmed with the receptionist that the punch press operator position was still open. After confirming it was, the receptionist updated Williamson's application and put it aside.

Williamson waited to hear back from Globe Union about the punch press operator position but heard nothing. While Williamson waited, unbeknownst to her, a white woman with nine months experience applied for the job. Globe Union verified the woman's age, contacted her references, and hired her. Desperately in need of a job because she had been out of work, Williamson returned to Globe Union to fill out another application, her second time applying for a factory position. Globe Union never contacted Williamson for any position even though it continually advertised that it had open positions and that it was an "equal opportunity employer."

Believing that Globe Union did not consider her for any of the open positions because of her race, Williamson went to the Milwaukee Urban League to enlist their help. With the Milwaukee Urban League, Hazel Williamson filed a complaint with the Wisconsin Industrial Commission accusing Globe Union of race-based employment discrimination. Within three months of filing the complaint, the Industrial Commission heard Williamson's case but found that Globe Union had not discriminated against Williamson because the company provided evidence that it did hire other Black workers. Although the Commission ruled in Globe Union's favor, it did reprimand the company and order it to reform its hiring procedures, including the multiple application form system and its disorganized filing system, which had resulted in Williamson's applications being misfiled and ultimately misplaced. Because it took so long for the Industrial Commission to investigate and make its determination, Williamson ended up leaving Milwaukee and going back to Indianapolis. She was out of work for the several months it took the Commission to complete its investigation, which involved meeting with the Milwaukee Urban League, corresponding with Globe Union, and interviewing Williamson and representatives from the company several times.

Williamson's story reveals how the Jim Crow job system operated, implicating private companies and, as Chapter 2 explored, the state as well. Although the Industrial Commission determined that Globe Union should revise its procedures, doing so would not change Williamson's experience, account for the time and money she lost, or get her a job—which is what she ultimately wanted. Neither Williamson nor countless other Black women before her received justice, and like the previous chapter illustrated, the state played a major part in keeping the Jim Crow job system functioning.

The decisions of Black working women, like Williamson, to submit complaints to the Industrial Commission during the 1950s and 1960s illustrate aspects of community intellectualism. Specifically, their actions make clear the power of raising critiques, testifying multiple narratives, and publicly refusing employment injustice. Telling their stories reveals the diverse ways they responded to the Jim Crow job system that mistreated them and demanded their subordination. Some moved on when they refused to settle for jobs that never materialized. Others crafted their own work experiences, managing their laboring lives within an exploitative system. We see examples of Black working women's varied responses by studying the complaints they filed.

Records of these complaints come from several sources. In the 1950s, some Black workers filed complaints with the Milwaukee chapters of the National Association for the Advancement of Colored People (MNAACP) and the Urban League (MUL), which at times acted as intermediaries between Milwaukee-area companies and Black workers. If the MNAACP or MUL failed to reach a resolution with local companies, these organizations took complaints to the Wisconsin Industrial Commission, the state-level apparatus that heard cases of alleged employment discrimination through its Fair Employment Practices Division.[2] Increasingly though, especially because of the civil rights and Black power movements, Black working women filed their own complaints directly with the Commission, which by the mid-1960s had created an Equal Rights Division.

The overall structure of this chapter takes the form of four chronologically ordered sections. The first section discusses Black working women's industrial labor situation by zooming in on the work experiences of well-known activist Sylvia Bell White, who like many Black working women, moved to Milwaukee during the Second Great Migration and tried to get work in Milwaukee's manufacturing industries. This section of the chapter analyzes national and local census data to put Sylvia Bell White's experiences within a broader context. The second section delves into complaints filed by Black working women in the 1950s that illuminate the range of employment discrimination they experienced as well as their strategy of working through the NAACP and the Urban League to make their voices heard. A third section narrates the heyday of civil rights insurgency in Milwaukee in the 1960s, an era that serves as the backdrop for the final section of the chapter, which analyzes complaints filed with the Industrial Commission directly by Black working women in the late 1960s and early 1970s.

In all, examining this sample of Black working women's complaints exposes their experiences of employment discrimination and reveals how power operated within the Jim Crow job system: by characterizing all Black workers as men, the system erased the specific ways employers kept Black women on the bottom, limiting the kinds of labor they could engage in and making them vulnerable to sexualized violence in the workplace. Black working women envisioned that participating in the complaint-making process would lead to more just work and working conditions. This chapter positions Black working women and their complaint-making activities at the center of 1960s struggles for Black freedom in Milwaukee.

Black Working Women and Milwaukee's Industrial Labor Situation

Although Milwaukee was home to many successful urban industrial workers, Black women aspiring to postwar careers in the city's manufacturing firms often experienced a different reality. Take, for example, the story of well-known activist Sylvia Bell White. Born Sylvia Bell in Milwaukee, she and her parents relocated to their home state of Louisiana where Bell grew up. She moved back to Milwaukee from Springfield, Louisiana, in 1947. Seventeen years old at the time, Bell left her small Louisiana town because she believed she would have more opportunities in the urban Midwest. When Bell returned to Milwaukee as a teenager, she had two goals: enroll in school and find a job. These two goals, intimately connected, proved to be near impossible. Bell quickly felt the inadequacy of her Louisianan schooling; it had not prepared her to seamlessly continue her educational journey in Milwaukee. After taking placement exams in Milwaukee, Bell learned that she only had a sixth-grade education. Undeterred, she enrolled in school part time and earned her eighth-grade diploma over the course of several years.[3] Because Bell ultimately wanted to become a nurse, she continued taking classes part-time at Milwaukee Vocational and Adult School. Her lack of a high school diploma proved limiting. At one point she took and passed the city's civil service exam. However, because she did not have her high school diploma, she was not hired for one of the open positions.[4]

Bell continually encountered the resoluteness of the Jim Crow job system. Although she was aware that many higher-paying manufacturing companies had open positions, they would not hire her. In an oral history interview, she recalls trying to get a job at a large bakery near where she lived.[5] Every morning she observed what seemed to her to be scores of people entering the facility. She just knew there were open positions, yet every time she went to ask about working there, they told her that there were no jobs available. She took that to mean that there were no jobs available to *people like her*, especially since she never saw Black workers entering or leaving the facility.

Soon Bell began working in the typical low-paying, labor-intensive jobs available to Black women in the city: nurse's aide and domestic service worker. Bell found work as a nurse's aide at Milwaukee County Hospital, which primarily served people with mental illness, but only after the hospital removed the required exam, opening the doors for Black women who wanted to work at the facility but had trouble passing the exam. The hospital relaxed its requirements after realizing that there was a nursing shortage and that white women thought these positions undesirable. Eventually, Bell left the job because of the emotional toll the work took on its workers. One of the physicians in the hospital with whom she worked closely committed suicide.[6] After leaving the job, Bell began working in the domestic-service industry, cleaning the homes of well-to-do Jewish women in prosperous Milwaukee neighborhoods such as Whitefish Bay and Fox Point. While domestic work came with its difficulties, Bell noted that the women she worked for offered flexibility and accommodations. For example, when she could not find childcare for her young son, her employer allowed him to come with her to the job.[7] These conditions, however, did not diminish the fact this work was lowly paid and came with no benefits, no retirement fund, and no opportunities for advancement. Despite the difficulties Sylvia Bell faced advancing her education and obtaining quality work, her younger brothers, Daniel and Walter, followed her to Milwaukee for similar reasons.

In the 1950s and 1960s, constantly encountering the painful realities of the Jim Crow job system, Bell worked in many jobs but never found a career that provided retirement benefits, what she defined as a good job. Later in her life, she reflected,

> I have went everywhere to try to get a job. I ended up working in nursing homes. Oh, I was continually workin'. . . . I've always worked. And, that

FIGURE 7. Twenty-year-old Annie Tabor works in a Milwaukee supercharger plant. October 1942. Official Office of War Information photo by Ann Rosener. Library of Congress Prints and Photographs Division, https://lccn.loc.gov/2017694610

wasn't easy, tryin' to work for some of these people. They will kick you in the behind or say something, just to make you get off the job. Then, if you jump up'n leave, it ain't nothin' they loss. It's your loss. Oh God! What a life! I tried. I tried and tried and tried. But I never got one of those good jobs where you get retirement . . . I coulda had it. There was no reason why I shouldn't have had a good job.[8]

The discrimination Sylvia Bell and other Black women like her faced in Milwaukee resonated with longstanding national patterns where Black female workers had the hardest time getting jobs.[9] Many Black women left farms and domestic service to successfully find manufacturing work, but they were still underrepresented in factories. This was especially true in Milwaukee.

Examining employment-related national census data from 1860 to 1960, sociologist Enobong Hannah Branch found that although the numbers of Black women employed as operatives in manufacturing industries steadily increased, their percentages when compared to white men, white women, and Black men have historically been the lowest. Men received high enough industrial wages to escape poverty, but working women, especially Black women who were relegated to the lowest-paying positions, did not receive these same high wages.[10]

Milwaukee was among the most industrialized cities in the urban Midwest, and although Black women there did better than Black women nationally when it came to manufacturing jobs, the number of Black women employed in Milwaukee's factories was still far less than Black men, which followed the national trend.[11] In 1940, 66 percent of Black men in the Milwaukee labor force worked as skilled, semi-skilled, or unskilled workers in industrial settings, but only 21 percent of Black women. Most Black women workers (64 percent) were domestic workers or service workers like beauticians, barbers, charwomen, janitors, cooks, waitresses, or elevator operators. As a result of World War II, by 1950 the number of Black women employed as industrial operatives increased to 30 percent, but still 52 percent worked in domestic or other service work, while 79 percent of men in the labor force worked in manufacturing positions. By the 1960s, Black women had lost many of the gains they had made in the manufacturing industries while holding relatively steady in service industries at 48 percent. Black men lost positions in the manufacturing industry as well, although 70 percent remained employed as skilled, semi-skilled, or unskilled workers.[12]

While in 1950 and 1960 Black women in Milwaukee outpaced white women as industrial operatives, this was because white women in the city took on an increasing number of higher-paying and less physically demanding clerical jobs, which Black women struggled to obtain (see figure 10).[13] State historian William Thompson wrote of the period, "But in all the Milwaukee metropolitan area, only eighty-eight of the 4,444 typists, forty-six of the 9,721 secretaries, twenty-four of the 3,146 stenographers, thirty-eight of the 1,996 telephone operators, sixteen of the 4,970 bookkeepers, 129 of the 4,268 professional nurses and sixty-six of the 13,283 retail clerks were black women."[14]

TABLE 2. Female occupation by sex and race for Wisconsin and Milwaukee, 1950 and 1960

Occupation	1950			1960		
	Total Female, Wisconsin (N=359,429)	Black Female, Milwaukee (N=2,708)	White Female, Milwaukee (N=110,875)	Total Female, Wisconsin (N=457,307)	Black Female, Milwaukee (N=7,263)	White Female, Milwaukee (N=161,463)
Craftsmen	1.60%	1.20%	3%	1.30%	0.80%	1.40%
Operatives	17.30%	30%	20.20%	14.70%	23.70%	16.30%
Professional	12.20%	2.50%	11.40%	12.60%	6.10%	11.10%
Clerical	25.30%	5.10%	33.80%	28.40%	7.40%	34.20%
Private Household Workers	5.20%	23.30%	3.42%	5.20%	16.30%	3.80%
Service Workers	13%	28.50%	12.60%	16%	32%	14.50%

Although Black women made minor gains in post–World War II Milwaukee, these statistics back up Bell's experiences and substantiate the point that Black working women never really gained a foothold in Milwaukee's manufacturing labor force, specifically in well paid positions. Many Black working women in Milwaukee remained locked out of the manufacturing and clerical labor forces and were circumscribed to low-paying service occupations, even within companies claiming to be "equal opportunity employers."

Increased migration to Milwaukee during the 1950s and 1960s laid bare Black women's inability to get quality work in Milwaukee, but also resulted in Black political representation in the city's Common Council for the first time. Like Hazel Williamson and Sylvia Bell, Black people came to Milwaukee in droves, with the last few years of the 1950s seeing a dramatic increase in the population. Specifically, from 1950 to 1960, the Black population increased from 21,772 to 62,458. This increase in population, which led to redrawn district lines, created a new aldermanic position representing the census tract where most Black people lived in the city. In 1956, Vel Phillips became the first woman and African American elected to the Common Council. As the only Black person and woman, she faced an uphill battle in convincing the eighteen white male aldermen she served with to create city policies that addressed the inequality that persisted in areas that affected Black migrants the most such as housing and employment. Despite this, Phillips continually pushed for civil rights through her position on the city council.[15]

Filing Complaints through Black Civil Rights Organizations in the 1950s

Increased Black migration to Milwaukee opened the doors for Black political representation on the local level and ramped up Black Milwaukeeans' efforts to hold the state accountable for addressing racial discrimination in employment. Black Milwaukeeans had taken advantage of the federal Fair Employment Practices Committee (FEPC), which had Midwestern offices in nearby Chicago and operated between 1941 and 1946.[16] After pressure from A. Philip Randolph and the threat of a march on Washington as a protest against discrimination in defense-related employment, President Franklin Roosevelt issued Executive Order 8802, which forbade racial discrimination in companies that had contracts with the federal government.[17] With the executive order, President Roosevelt also created the Fair Employment Practices Committee to receive and hear complaints of employment-based discrimination. If the FEPC decided that racial discrimination had occurred, it also determined a remedy. The federal committee opened regional offices around the country, and while it had some success in opening up opportunities for Black men, Black women had a hard time getting hearings before the commission. By the end of World War II, the FEPC transitioned into a fact-finding committee without any real enforcement power.

After the end of World War II, the state legislature passed Wisconsin's first fair employment law in 1945, banning discrimination in employment based on race, color, national origin, or ancestry. As a result of this new labor law, the state created a Fair Employment

Practices Division (FEPD), which would be administered by the Wisconsin Industrial Commission (WIC). With the FEPD, the state legislature "authorized the Industrial Commission to receive and investigate complaints charging discrimination or discriminatory practices and give publicity to its findings with respect thereto."[18] If the WIC found "probable cause" to believe discrimination had occurred, "it was authorized to immediately endeavor to eliminate the practice by conference, conciliation, and persuasion."[19] The WIC held hearings, determined and publicized findings, and also recommended action.

Unfortunately, though, nearly a decade after the creation of the FEPD, most companies "wriggled out of discrimination charges," thus leaving the Black community "apathetic" to the FEPD and the WIC.[20] This apathy emerged because in a vast majority of the cases submitted by Black workers, the WIC found that it was "not probable" that racial discrimination had occurred. Additionally, in instances where the Industrial Commission determined that racial discrimination had occurred, the commission had no power to enforce its recommendations.

In 1952, Isaac Coggs became the first Black politician elected to the Wisconsin State Assembly and he targeted the Jim Crow job system during his tenure as state assemblyman. Coggs saw how ineffective the Industrial Commission had been in enforcing fair employment law. A 1957 state supreme court case that upheld a craft union's right to restrict membership based on race solidified the need to pass what he considered a fair employment practices law "with teeth."[21] Coggs introduced a bill that would give power to the state to sue businesses engaged in employment discrimination.[22] The bill passed in the Wisconsin State Assembly, but by this time few Black workers believed businesses would be held accountable for their part in maintaining the Jim Crow job system.[23] Even so, Black working women used this channel to register their complaints.

Throughout the 1950s, some Black working women registered their complaints with the Milwaukee Urban League or NAACP chapters whose officials then decided which cases they would back. By the 1960s, however, some Black women would eschew these middle class brokers and instead register complaints on their own behalf. Black working women in Milwaukee, like many around the nation, insisted that state institutions hear their stories. The next few examples highlight the experiences of Black working women who, throughout the 1950s, partnered with the MNAACP or MUL to file their complaints.

Cases Brought to the MNAACP in the 1950s

In 1951 the MNAACP elected its first Black woman branch president, Ardie Halyard, and solidified the branch as one where working people, specifically Black women, could seek help in resolving instances of employment discrimination they experienced. Halyard was well known in the city for having founded, along with her husband Wilbur, the first Black-owned financial institution in the city, Columbia Savings and Loan Association. While the couple strove to get Columbia off the ground in the 1920s and 1930s, Halyard labored full time for Goodwill Industries, working her way from being a donations sorter to the personnel director and eventually director of rehabilitation.[24] Like many Black working women, though she had the educational background and the skills to teach, the jobs immediately available to her were neither in her field nor highly paid. However, by the time of her election to the MNAACP presidency, she had decades of work experience and connections in the city and state. During her MNAACP presidency, from 1951 to 1953, she continued the organization's objectives regarding addressing employment discrimination. The year before she assumed her duties as branch president, the branch published its annual program calendar and list of activities, which laid out the branch's mandate "to explore the housing and employment needs in our locality, to determine the extent of inadequacy or discrimination, if and where it exists and work toward a remedy."[25] During Halyard's tenure as president, one way she carried out this mandate was assisting the Black working women who came to the MNAACP to report their encounters with the Jim Crow job system. Ardie Halyard saved evidence of several requests, and the stories narrated here illustrate the types of cases she championed during her time as MNAACP president.

DR. LELABELLE FREEMAN AND THE MILWAUKEE DEPARTMENT OF HEALTH

In 1952 Dr. Lelabelle Freeman, from Chicago, Illinois, wrote the MNAACP to enlist the help of the organization in what she believed to be a case of employment hiring discrimination on the part of the Milwaukee Department of Health. Upon receipt of the letter, Ardie Halyard sprang into action using her direct connection to Milwaukee mayor Frank Zeidler to advocate for Dr. Freeman. Ardie Halyard requested a meeting with Mayor Zeidler, and on May 8, 1952, she recounted Dr. Freeman's story. Halyard explained that Dr. Freeman had been in contact with Dr. Virginia Downs, an administrator at the Milwaukee Department of Health, regarding a position with the department. After communicating for several months via mail, Dr. Freeman set up an appointment to see Dr. Downs regarding a position in the department. Prior to the appointment, Dr. Downs realized that Dr. Freeman was a Black woman. She then wrote to Dr. Freeman stating there were no longer any open positions with the department. Dr. Downs also sent a copy of that letter as well as the following memo to the Milwaukee commissioner of Health, Dr. E. R. Krumbeigel:

> Re: Lelabelle Christine Freeman, M.D.
>
> This person was recommended to us, race unknown, before commitments. The application reveals that she is a graduate of Howard University and is a colored physician. The case should be handled with tact.[26]

Although copies of the letter and memo were placed on the commissioner's desk, Dr. Krumbeigel claimed to have never seen them because Dr. Downs eventually removed the documents from his desk. During her scheduled meeting with Dr. Downs, Dr. Freeman noticed the memo, after which she reported her experience to the MNAACP.

While meeting with Ardie Halyard, and upon learning of the memo, the mayor realized the severity of the case and called Dr. Krumbeigel to his office to discuss the incident. Because the letter and memo had been removed from his desk, Dr. Krumbeigel told the mayor he was unaware of the situation and suggested that Dr. Downs be invited to the meeting. The mayor then requested that Dr. Krumbeigel investigate the matter and submit a report to him.

Dr. Krumbeigel did submit a report, which the mayor then sent to Ardie Halyard. In the report, Dr. Krumbeigel defended Dr. Downs by asserting that Dr. Downs' prior experience working with and supervising Black physicians made discrimination on her part unlikely. In addition, Krumbeigel referenced the employment of another Black physician in the department. Although the physician had been recently terminated, Krumbeigel explained that his termination was due to job performance and not because of his race. This example was meant to illustrate the fact that because the department employed Black physicians, it was improbable that Dr. Freeman had experienced any discrimination. Finally, Dr. Krumbeigel asserted that there was simply no evidence of mistreatment. He concluded the report by describing Dr. Downs' efforts to go above and beyond to help Dr. Freeman, including making her aware of other available positions in the area. According to Dr. Krumbeigel, no other white applicant received such assistance, insinuating that Dr. Freeman had received special treatment.[27]

Upon receipt of the report, Halyard drafted a Milwaukee NAACP resolution to prompt Mayor Zeidler to act. The resolution accused the mayor of making no statement and taking no action regarding the incident. The document insisted both that Dr. Freeman be given the position in the Milwaukee Health Department and that the mayor commit to forbidding employment discrimination as well as disciplining city workers who engaged in the practice.[28] In addition to the resolution, Halyard also wrote a letter criticizing Dr. Krumbeigel's report. She noted several inconsistencies in the report, but she was most disturbed by Dr. Krumbeigel's refusal to acknowledge that an unfortunate incident had happened at all.[29] Halyard pointed out the larger implications of these behaviors by recognizing them as not isolated but as a "pattern used again and again in situations where Negroes are securing jobs." Black workers are supposedly given "special" attention, one "goes out of his way to be helpful to them, but as [in] this case, such pretentious magnanimity is followed by a courteous denial of the position in question. They are invariably just 'handled with tact.'"[30] Black workers did not ask for special attention, but to be considered and hired for the jobs for which they were qualified. Halyard stated adamantly, Black workers "do not ask for, nor do they wish favors. They want nothing special. They only want justice." Although Dr. Freeman eventually accepted a position in Washington, DC, Ardie Halyard used this unfortunate experience to remind Mayor Zeidler of his commitment to "democratic ideals," ideals that included ending employment discrimination. Although Mayor Zeidler acknowledged Halyard's letter, he took no further action regarding the Milwaukee Health Department, Dr. Krumbeigel, or Dr. Downs. Dr. Freeman's experiences trying to get a job at the Milwaukee Department of Health make clear that Black working women of various educational and professional backgrounds collided with the concrete wall of the Jim Crow job system.

Dr. Freeman's and Ardie Halyard's responses are important to consider. After meeting with Dr. Downs and noticing a note she was never supposed to see, Dr. Freeman suspected she was being treated unfairly. Her first response was to go to Ardie Halyard at the MNAACP. Halyard used her influence with the mayor to get an audience with him. Halyard also engaged the formal procedure of resolution-making. Resolutions served several purposes. In many instances they provided a historical record of a problem, the organization's solution, and any resulting action. Unlike regular committee meeting minutes, which may or may not have been always publicly available, resolutions were typically made public during an official meeting of the organization. Resolutions were formal measures and had to be voted on by the organizational body in order to be acted upon. Therefore, as political acts, resolutions had power, and Halyard used one to make a statement detesting the employment discrimination experienced by Dr. Freeman and demanding the mayor act. But resolutions are also intellectual acts, and with this resolution Halyard made a declaration that mirrored the demands she wrote in her correspondence with the mayor—Black workers do not want special treatment, but equality and justice. Although the mayor did not respond the way Halyard would have liked, this failure to act did not discourage Ardie Halyard or stop Black women workers from coming to the MNAACP to register their experiences of employment discrimination. Because of Ardie Halyard's diligence, word got around that the MNAACP was a place people could come to seek help.

ROSETTA THOMPSON, DAISY THOMPSON, AND JANETTA DICKINSON AND MISERICORDIA HOSPITAL

In the spring of 1954, several hospital workers came to the Milwaukee NAACP to get aid regarding incidents that happened the previous year. At least eight Black women workers came to the organization, which prompted it to act on their behalf. In the NAACP records, the formal statements of Rosetta Thompson, Daisy Thompson, and Janetta Dickinson are preserved.[31] These three women either worked at or tried to obtain employment at Misericordia Hospital, a Catholic hospital in the city.

The basis of Rosetta Thompson's complaint centered on the personnel manager's refusal to give her raises as promised when she was hired. After inquiring several times about the promised raises, the personnel manager, a Mr. Casper, told her, "You are not going to get a raise, you are not going to get a vacation, in fact you are fired."[32] Having received no prior complaints of her work, Thompson left the hospital stunned, and in her words, "not knowing the reason for his action."[33]

Daisy Thompson also worked at Misericordia and interacted with the same personnel manager. In her formal statement, Thompson noted that she worked at Misericordia from February until April 1953 after which Casper fired her. Like Rosetta Thompson, Daisy had received no complaints of her work. When she approached Casper to inquire about the reason for her termination, he said the night supervisor complained about her work. Daisy Thompson told him that the night supervisor had never shared this with her, nor had she ever not willingly complied with the requests of her supervisor. Daisy Thompson inquired if she should speak with the supervisor about these complaints. Casper told Daisy Thompson no, but she did anyway and discovered that the night supervisor had filed no complaints about her work. Still, Casper upheld the termination. In addition to firing Daisy Thompson without cause, Casper also refused to pay her for the last two weeks of her employment at the hospital, claiming that there was no state law requiring him to do so.[34]

A final complaint received in the NAACP office regarding Casper came from Janetta Dickinson. Dickinson attempted to apply for a position at Misericordia because she had been told they needed workers. Casper interviewed Dickinson and during the interview he questioned Dickinson's need for work. According to Dickinson's statement, Casper "asked if my husband did not earn enough to support me and stated that I only wanted to work to buy a car so my husband can run up and down Walnut Street." Dickinson tried to explain to Casper that this was not the case. After the interview she never heard from Misericordia Hospital. Janetta Dickinson stated that she knew the reason she hadn't heard from Casper. Dickinson and other Black women workers figured out Casper had been firing Black women and replacing them with white women workers. In addition to these complaints, the NAACP compiled instances of racial discrimination experienced by Black working women at other Catholic hospitals across the city. At these hospitals Jim Crow operated fully: hospitals maintained separate restroom facilities for African American workers, Black workers could purchase food but could not eat in the dining facilities, and they were being fired when ill even though they had doctor's orders not to work.

Casper created a hostile working environment for Black working women that demanded their subordination and punished them when they questioned white supervisory authority. But lest this example be interpreted as the case of one errant supervisor, the MNAACP records indicate that Black women workers experienced this type of treatment at other Catholic hospitals across the city. Black women workers at these hospitals exposed that their employment was based on the whims of white supervisors and that they could be hired or fired, not based on their own actions or work records but because of the unfounded, illogical, downright harmful, and explicit racism of white managers. Again, Black women workers came to the

MNAACP because of its practice of resisting the Jim Crow job system. Their complaints prompted the MNAACP to draw up a memo entitled "Problem: Re Hospitals," listing these complaints. It is not clear what action the NAACP took, although it is clear the memo was circulated among the MNAACP leadership. By this time Ardie Halyard had moved on from the position of branch president and was now president of the Wisconsin State Council of Branches. This new position meant that she no longer directly received Black working women's complaints, but her efforts in this area over her term as branch president helped keep jobs justice a priority for the local organization.

Complaints Brought to the Milwaukee Urban League in the 1950s

Because of the efforts of Ardie Halyard, the MNAACP became known as an advocate for Black women workers struggling against the Jim Crow job system. The MUL's track record in regards to Black working women needed some rehabilitation, especially after William Kelley, the MUL's executive secretary, actively discouraged Black women from filing complaints during the World War II period.[35] During the war, President Roosevelt's Fair Employment Practices Committee, whose regional offices were in Chicago, was known for dismissing Black working women's complaints, citing that they did not have enough documentation of the employment discrimination they experienced.[36] In *Black Milwaukee: The Making of an Urban Proletariat 1915–1945*, historian Joe Trotter writes that some Black working women got fed up and wrote directly to Eleanor Roosevelt, thinking they had a better chance getting justice with her than with the FEPC.[37] When the FEPC dissolved after World War II, some Black working women filed complaints with the Wisconsin Industrial Commission through the MUL. They probably approached the MUL for several reasons, among them being that the organization was still the most well-known organization in the city dedicated to Black workers. The organization's access to legal aid and resources most likely factored into their decisions as well. The next examples are cases that Black women filed at the MUL; one had a hearing before the WIC while the other appeared in the MUL records but included no formal resolution. Both offer different yet instructive perspectives on Black working women's experiences with the Jim Crow job system.

FRENCHIE BELL AND COLONIAL TANNING COMPANY

In 1952, supported by the MUL, the Wisconsin Industrial Commission heard the case of Frenchie Bell, who had filed a complaint against the Colonial Tanning Company, which she believed had fired her because of her race.[38] While at Colonial Tanning Company, Bell worked in the leather trimming department. Workers trimmed leather in two different phases. During the first phase of the work, workers trimmed large pieces that hung on a line that moved at a regulated speed. During the second phase, workers cut individual, smaller pieces of leather at a table at their own pace and were paid by the piece. Men mostly worked the line because of the size of the pieces and the speed at which the work needed to be done. Women usually did piecework. According to Bell, the foreman, George Nance, placed her on the line without proper training. Consequently, she had trouble with the work. Nance accused Bell of slowing down the line and discarding a large amount of usable leather during the trimming process. Nance submitted a complaint to Colonial's Advisory Committee, which arbitrated such grievances. The Advisory Committee heard Bell's case and considered firing her, but because this was Bell's only official reprimand, the Committee warned her instead and decreased her rate of pay. After this first hearing, Bell continued to face difficulties with George Nance. He again accused her of being careless in her trimming. Even though Bell told Nance she preferred piecework, he placed her back on the line and then complained that she requested assistance from her male coworkers, hung fewer pieces, and decreased the department's productivity.

Nance submitted another complaint and the Advisory Committee held another hearing. This time, Nance brought in fifteen pounds of scrap leather that he claimed Bell had carelessly discarded. Bell denied this charge and insisted that there was only one box in the shop used to discard scraps. She accused the foreman of framing her; Bell claimed she "watched George Nance when he picked up all that leather. He picked it from the floor, from around and from that box." Bell continually asserted that she did her job as best she could with the minimal training she had received from Nance. Despite this testimony, Colonial Tanning Company fired her. During the WIC hearing, the examiner asked Bell why she thought Colonial had terminated her and she stated, "I think because purely Mr. Nance's dislike for me." Bell recounted an exchange with Nance where he stated that "if [you] didn't like [the job], you can get the hell out of here." Bell testified that Nance kept asking her why she remained at Colonial Tanning Company and during one episode he told her, "You're not doing this right . . . you people don't know how to work." Bell understood "you people" as referring to Black workers. Despite Bell's testimony, the WIC decided that probable cause for racial discrimination had not been proven.

Frenchie Bell's case against the Colonial Tanning Company is representative of the kinds of treatment Black working women endured in Milwaukee's manufacturing industries. The transcripts of the Wisconsin Industrial Commission hearing provide an accounting of Bell's tenure with the company, and a deeper analysis of Bell's experiences reveal that throughout her time at Colonial she tried to resist Nance's racist and sexist actions. Nance's initial complaint of Bell centered on her inability to keep with the pace of the line. We might read this not as incompetence on Bell's part, as Nance alleged, but as a conscious decision to resist impractical and unfair labor conditions. Bell tried to perform quality work, but the speed of the line made this impossible, especially since she had not been trained properly. Rather than perform the work quickly and with errors, Bell slowed down and asked for help from her fellow coworkers. Bell's efforts to recast her work as careful and skillful were misread as inefficient and wasteful.

Additionally, Bell's request to do piece work with the other women illustrated her desire to have autonomy over her work conditions and assert her womanhood. In requesting to work with the other women, Bell challenged pejorative stereotypes that masculinized Black women workers and demeaned their womanhood. Requesting to do piece work also might have freed Bell from being on the line with mostly men and possibly subjected to verbal harassment, both racist and sexual in nature. Bell's complaint was not only about work conditions and it certainly was not only about racial discrimination. Before she submitted her complaint, she tried to resist Nance's discriminatory behavior. Bell's complaint centered on dignity, respect, and autonomy, which Black working women rarely received in Milwaukee's manufacturing industries.

Although Bell did not win her job back at Colonial, her case is still important to consider. In addition to revealing how notions of gender and race worked together to oppress Black working women in the industrial labor force, it also exposes how the white-male-dominated manufacturing industry maintained economic order by suppressing and ejecting Black working women. It is telling that a Black female coworker Frenchie Bell called upon to testify on her behalf, Ella Mae Thomas, also employed in Nance's department, was fired after she testified. When Black working women joined together to resist the racist and sexist conditions of the industrial workplace, white bosses responded with a devastating blow and a message that reverberated across the city: Black working women who resist the Jim Crow job system are not welcome.

EDRIS WASHINGTON AND THE LAW OFFICES OF BASS AND GOLDSTEIN

Despite a state-level Fair Employment Practices law on the books, employers blatantly discriminated against, intimidated, or harassed Black workers because they knew they would not face any repercussions. Edris Washington's story is a prime example.[39] In 1958, Washington filed a complaint with the MUL regarding her experiences at the law offices of Bass and Goldstein. Eighteen-year-old Edris Washington heard of a clerical job at the firm and sought employment. After a successful interview, the firm hired Washington and instructed her to report to work. When she arrived at work, she reported to Goldstein, her new supervisor. In her official complaint, Washington noted that Goldstein was getting dressed in the office. She went into another room until he finished and afterwards, he called her into his office where he, once again, explained to her what the duties of the job would be, information she had received in her initial interview. In addition to recounting information she had already been told, Washington wrote that he spoke to her in detail about the sexual assault cases on which he had worked. This conversation made Washington uncomfortable, so she excused herself, leaving his office to practice her skills on the firm's stenographic equipment. While she was working in the other room, Goldstein asked her to retrieve a paper towel from the ladies' room and when she entered his office, she realized he did not have any clothes on. In her complaint Washington noted that she ignored his state of undress and immediately left the room. When he was dressed, Goldstein called Washington back into his office to discuss the job duties again. During the meeting, Goldstein noticed Washington was quiet. The meeting soon ended with Goldstein telling Washington to think more about the job and that he would call her to follow-up. After this, Washington left the office and never returned.

This horrifying experience of sexual intimidation and harassment speaks to the intersectional experiences of Black working women in the labor force. Edris Washington registered her complaint at the MUL where it was filed as a racial complaint. While there was no way to indicate sexual harassment, Washington was correct to read Goldstein's tactics as employment intimidation. Washington's decision not only to tell her story but to also have it certified by a notary public highlights that not all Black women were bound by a culture of dissemblance that would have them remain silent in the face of sexual mistreatment.[40] Unfortunately, the record is not clear regarding the Urban League's response to this case. This case is significant, nonetheless, because it provides another layer to the employment-related injustice Black women endured in Milwaukee's labor force. Black women's employment complaints abound in the record, and taken together they tell a story of exclusion and marginalization but also resistance.

Because many Black workers like Edris Washington routinely went to the MUL to lodge their complaints, in 1963 the Wisconsin Industrial Commission partnered with the Milwaukee Urban League to bolster its efforts against employment discrimination in the city.[41]

Local Congress of Racial Equality (CORE) activists did not believe much would come from the partnership because of the state's record so far.[42] Despite the commission's existence, neither local businesses nor companies had been held fully accountable for discriminating against or harassing Black workers and this, according to CORE activists, led African Americans to distrust the state's work on behalf of fair employment. In 1965, Wisconsin expanded its Fair Employment Practices Division (FEPD) and became the Equal Opportunities Division. By 1967, the state consolidated the work of the Governor's Commission on Human Rights and the Equal Opportunities Division into the Equal Rights Division, which became responsible for administering state law as it related to discrimination wherever it occurred and in whatever form.

Despite Wisconsin's lengthy history in attempting to address employment discrimination, Black workers rightly believed that the state law "had no teeth," especially since little changed for them in the state. In fact, Virginia Huebner, the director of the Fair Employment Practices Division told the *Milwaukee Defender*, "While resistance to the principles of fair employment practices in Wisconsin may be decreasing, nevertheless, the actual practice of discrimination in employment because of race, creed, color, national origin or ancestry has not, in the same degree, lessened."[43] Democratic congressman Henry S. Reuss, a member of the Governor's Commission on Human Rights, said as much on a public radio broadcast. "The present law," Reuss asserted, "actually permits discrimination in employment against Negroes. The court can do no more than interpret the law. It is the Republican dominated legislature which is to blame for having an unenforceable [fair employment] act on the books."[44] In 1967, over a decade after its existence, the Fair Employment Practices Act had no power.

Heightened Civil Rights Activism in Milwaukee

Those who resisted the Jim Crow job system faced powerful institutional opposition, and their resistance dovetailed with heightened civil rights activism in the city. In the case of Sylvia Bell White, whose story was mentioned earlier, she and her family were thrust in the spotlight after her younger brother's fatal encounter with two Milwaukee police officers.[45] Daniel Bell had migrated to Milwaukee for the same reason as Sylvia and other family members: economic opportunity. And like his sister, he faced structural barriers to better employment because of the inadequacy of the education he had received in Louisiana. This had a lethal impact on him because he was never able to pass the written portion of the Wisconsin driver's license test and so he drove without a license.[46]

Tragically, a Milwaukee police officer murdered Daniel Bell on February 2, 1958. That evening, Bell drove with a broken taillight, for which two officers, Thomas Grady and Louis Krause, attempted to pull him over. Afraid that he would be arrested and put in jail for driving without a license, Bell pulled his car over, got out, and fled from the officers. The officers chased him and Grady shot Daniel Bell in the back of his neck, point blank. Knowing that he had no legal justification for using deadly force, Grady planted a knife on Bell and fabricated a story about him yelling, "I'm a hold-up man," which would indicate he had a prior criminal record, providing a justification for using excessive force.[47] Heartbroken and understandably distraught after hearing that their brother had been killed, Sylvia and her other siblings went down to the police station for more information and to identify his body. After demanding to know what happened, officers accused the family of making a scene, brushed them off, and demanded they leave the police station or face charges of their own. When the two officers were put on trial, both were acquitted.

Daniel Bell's murder and the failure to hold the police officers accountable brought Black Milwaukeeans together, if only briefly, with a common goal of getting justice for the Bell family. After an initial mass meeting that brought 450 people together, several groups had ideas about what should be done next. Many of these ideas reflected divisions in the community, especially relating to conflict between newer migrants and older residents.[48] Echoing a "culture of poverty" mentality wherein Black people's behavior was blamed for structural racism and discrimination, the Reverend T. T. Lovelace and the members of his Mount Zion Baptist Church agreed to start the Institute of Social Adjustment to "improve the general behavior of the Negro community."[49] Some thought the response should be more holistic and address the needs of Black Milwaukeeans in areas including but not limited to education, recreation, and employment. Headed by longstanding residents and community leaders Lucinda and Grant Gordon, the Lapham-Garfield Neighborhood Council held its first public gathering the same month as Daniel Bell's killing. Auto worker and activist Calvin Sherard also started a new organization, the Citizen's Committee to Protest the Murder of Daniel Bell, which partnered with Reverend R. L. Lathan of the New Hope Baptist Church to propose a prayer protest, and was endorsed by state assemblyman Isaac Coggs. The prayer protest never happened, but activists did invite Birmingham, Alabama, civil rights activist Reverend Fred Shuttlesworth to speak at a mass meeting. After Reverend Shuttlesworth's sermon, he led the attendees, including Sylvia Bell White, on a brief march down Walnut Street. That demonstration was the only direct action and there was very little follow-up afterwards. Although Bell White marched, she did not participate in any further civil rights action in the city. She remembered, "I couldn't even think about goin' cause I was too busy workin' for a nickel and a dime. With a child, tryin' to pay the house note and everything. If I'da went . . . , they'da shut off my lights, shut off my gas. They woulda. I had to work. So I couldn't get into that . . ."[50]

Although Sylvia Bell White could not actively participate, throughout the 1960s radical Black and liberal white Milwaukeeans engaged in what historian Patrick Jones describes as civil rights insurgency.[51] Engaging in civil rights activism and employing their own brand of Black power rhetoric, activists led by the Milwaukee NAACP Youth Council and its advisor, white Catholic priest Father James Groppi, demonstrated for fair housing and fought for the desegregation of private social clubs that excluded African Americans. In 1967, Black city dwellers rebelled against police brutality and the repressive urban conditions they experienced on a daily basis, in what the press labeled a "riot," one of many that summer and part of what historian Peter Levy refers to as "the great uprising."[52] The environment

FIGURE 8. During the summer of 1967, activists participated in a series of demonstrations and protests, including the woman in this photograph. July 6, 1967. Photographer: Sherman A. Gessert Jr., © *Milwaukee Journal Sentinel -* USA Today Network

was volatile but Black people nationwide and in Milwaukee were fed up with inequality. Black working women joined the movement and put their bodies on the line, in the street and at work.

The 1960s also saw a renewed effort and focus on employment activism, this time by Black workers who endeavored to make the city's labor movement take responsibility for the continuing employment discrimination that people of color of faced. For example, Calvin Sherard, the auto worker who started the grassroots organization protesting Daniel Bell's murder, also established the Crusaders Civic and Social League in 1960, which the same year affiliated with the national Negro American Labor Council (NALC) that had been started by A. Philip Randolph in 1959. Randolph established the NALC as a result of conflict between him and AFL-CIO leadership over its slow process and reluctance to deal with racism in the labor movement. Randolph brought together Black union leaders from across the United States to create the NALC, which had a goal "to ensure Afro-Americans a more influential role in the shaping of policies and programs of the American trade union movement on all levels."[53] Randolph did not create the NALC to be a labor union or to clash with the AFL-CIO, but he did encourage all Black labor union members to affiliate with the NALC.

Impressed by Randolph, Calvin Sherard's Crusaders worked on employment discrimination, and particularly they "argued that all businesses located in the inner core ought to hire from the Black community."[54] Bolstered by the 1960s sit-in movement sweeping the country, the Crusaders picketed several local businesses.[55] Their sit-ins, picketing, and negotiations resulted in some of these businesses agreeing to and subsequently hiring more Black workers in their establishments. By the end of 1960, after affiliating with NALC and becoming the Milwaukee Negro American Labor Council (MNALC), the organization built on its early success and started a "Grocery Store Campaign" with the goal of pressuring grocery stores to hire more Black workers. The Grocery Store Campaign used picketing as a strategy and received varying degrees of support from Black Milwaukeeans. Many crossed picket lines, which discouraged members of the MNALC.[56] By 1965, the MNALC joined other Milwaukee activists in the escalating fight for school integration—which became one of the publicized focuses of the civil rights movement in Milwaukee.[57] Because of the MNALC's shift in focus and Calvin Sherard's subsequent departure from Milwaukee, job-related activism did not attract media attention. This, however, did not mean Black activists discontinued their action. Black women relentlessly pursued employment-related economic justice throughout the 1960s and the early 1970s, and they used the newly passed Title VII of the 1964 Civil Rights Act to ramp up their critique of both racial and gender injustice in the workplace and in unions.

Complaints during the Civil Rights and Black Power Era

In the late 1960s and thereafter, more Black working women filed their complaints directly with the WIC, bypassing the MNAACP, the MUL, and their Black middle-class intermediaries. The complaint analyzed in this section illuminates how white managers' impoverished understandings of gender contributed to Black working women's treatment within the Jim Crow job system. The state complaint-making process made it difficult to correctly categorize these acts of discrimination, though, forcing Black women workers to describe their treatment as race-based discrimination when it was clear that discrimination based on gender occurred as well.

Anna Mae Finney, Bobbie Chappel, and Kromer Cap Company

On September 7, 1967, Anna Mae Finney and Bobbie Chappel submitted a complaint directly to the WIC against their former employer, Kromer Cap Company. They accused Kromer of firing them because of their race. Their case revolved around statements made by their union steward, Grace Russo. According to Finney and Chappel, they got into an argument with Russo after she repeated several times during a union meeting, "Why don't you people [Negroes] stay up on the north side on 10th Street where you belong?" After the meeting Finney and Chappel confronted Russo, asking her to repeat and clarify her statement. Russo refused, ran away, and reported that she had been hit by the two Black women.[58] As a result of the quarrel, Kromer Cap Company terminated all three women. Finney and Chappel filed a complaint with the WIC because they believed their termination was race-based and without due cause. Although Finney and Chappel met with Kromer Cap Company president Richard

Grossman to get their jobs reinstated, he refused to reverse the decision.

The WIC investigated and spoke with Grossman to hear his side of the story. Grossman confirmed that Russo did, in fact, make the statements Finney and Chappel described.[59] Grossman also stated that five workers witnessed the assault on Russo. After the meeting, Grossman wrote a letter to the WIC and explained his decision to terminate all three women. According to Grossman, the altercation disrupted and upset other workers, causing them to fear for their safety. Grossman explained that all three women had been terminated because of employment misconduct. He insisted that race did not factor into his firing the women. Instead, he said, their "unladylike behavior" caused their termination.[60]

On October 4, 1967, the WIC decided that because Kromer fired all three women, race had not played a role in their termination.[61] But race absolutely played a major role in the incident. Wrapped up in the complaint against Kromer Cap Company was a demand to hold Russo responsible for the racial comments she made repeatedly and the impact this had on the work environment. Finney and Chappel asserted to Grossman that this was not the first time Russo had made comments like this. Because they had not filed a complaint for these prior instances, we do not know how they responded in those cases—we can only assume that they did what most Black workers did: they bore it.

By refusing to acknowledge the complaint, firing all three women, and accusing them of unladylike behavior, Grossman downplayed the role that racial slurs played in the incident and recused himself from having to deal with the real issue at hand: the racist working environment of his company. While one racist worker lost her job, his refusal to acknowledge the larger racial implications of Finney and Chappel's complaint did nothing to change the racially charged environment at Kromer Cap Company.

Grossman's reactions also reveal the gender politics at play. The Wisconsin Industrial Commission ruled that racial discrimination had not occurred while simultaneously upholding Grossman's sexist behavior. Because the three women, two of them African American, failed, in his eyes, to act like respectable women, they were fired. Loud, confrontational women who disrupted and challenged the status quo, as Finney and Chappel did, were not welcome at Kromer. Finney and Chappell's racial identity and Grossman's understandings of what constituted respectable womanhood contributed to his decision to classify their behavior in the manner that he did, behavior that resulted in their termination.

It is also important to contextualize Russo's inflammatory accusations of physical assault within the immediate context of the urban rebellion that had taken place in Milwaukee that summer. Tensions remained high; Finney's and Chappel's response to Russo's racist and inflammatory language illustrates this. From the records of the WIC, there was a history of verbal harassment at Kromer Cap Company. Knowing there were few structures that could help them, Finney and Chappell tried to resolve the issue on their own by first approaching the union steward directly, and only then the WIC. But the WIC continued to reinforce the same lesson as before: Black working women who resisted were not welcome in Milwaukee's manufacturing industries.

Finally, that this incident occurred in the context of a union meeting and with a union steward matters too. While Black women had more access to unions by this time, racism and prejudiced beliefs permeated these organizations, making their experiences in unions extremely fraught.[62] Despite this, some Black women workers, like Finney and Chappel, got involved because they knew the benefits of union membership, some of which included the power of collective bargaining and job security. As it turns out, unions, which supposedly protected workers, continued to be a site of racial and social hostility and inequality.

Conclusion

Although Title VII of the Civil Rights Act of 1964 outlawed employment discrimination, Black women workers still experienced Jim Crow conditions as companies and organizations struggled to implement the law and change the culture of their workplaces. Filing complaints was one way Black women workers exposed the inequality of the Jim Crow job system. Black women's complaints also expose how generalizing the experiences of Black workers resulted in Black women's experiences being ignored and erased.

Black women's complaint-making actions, specifically their determined efforts to tell their painful stories of discrimination and its emotional, personal, and financial impact, demonstrate their commitment to racial and gender justice in Milwaukee. While their actions rarely made it to the headlines, or even in most local histories, awareness of their struggles and resistance provides a fuller picture of Black Milwaukeeans' experiences in an urban landscape teeming not only with racism but with sexism as well. In many ways, Milwaukee's local civil rights movement was like others in that the activists thrust into the spotlight were typically male, with a commitment to direct action and militant masculinity.[63] While Black women in Milwaukee had always participated in the movement, many of them did so in ways largely unrecognized by the public or media, like filing complaints. While Black working women's complaints were ultimately unsuccessful in dismantling the Jim Crow job system, they reveal what Black working women were up against and uncover the power of raising multiple voices and narratives to testify against employment injustice. This strategy of raising multiple voices and narratives to expose economic injustice persisted as Black women activists shifted from civil rights to welfare rights—the topic of the next chapter.

CHAPTER 4

"What the Mothers Have to Say"

Welfare Rights Activism in 1970s Milwaukee

On Sunday, September 21, 1969, seventy-six welfare rights activists left St. Boniface Catholic Church to begin a ninety-mile trek from Milwaukee to Madison to protest budget cuts that would decrease the state's Aid to Families and Dependent Children budget by 20 percent. Organized by the Nat Turner Welfare Mothers group, the Mothers March to Madison planned to arrive just in time for a special legislative session scheduled by the governor, Warren Knowles. Over the course of their weeklong march, mother activists and their supporters, including well-known local civil rights leader Father James Groppi, braved the elements as well as hostility from rural Wisconsinites whose towns they passed through in route to the capitol city.

By the time of their arrival to the state's seat of power the following Sunday, their numbers had swelled to five hundred, and at a Sunday afternoon rally held on the campus of University of Wisconsin–Madison, less than one mile away from the capitol building, the welfare rights activists poured out their emotions at the proposed cuts. Gertrude Strean, Clementina Castro, and Cassie Downer were among the mother activists who spoke at the rally. Strean and Castro stressed that the budget cuts would negatively impact children, with Castro tearfully telling rally goers that her kids were her priority and that she had come a long way for them. Downer reflected on the promises of the American dream and told the crowd, "They say this is the land of opportunity and I would like to see it in my lifetime, while I'm living."[1]

The next day, Monday, September 29, 1969, around one thousand protestors marched from the University of Wisconsin–Madison to the state capitol where they arrived just prior to Governor Knowles' scheduled address to the legislature. Flooding the capital building, they entered the chamber where politicians gathered and demanded to be heard. Taking over the chamber for eleven hours, they chanted, sang, made speeches, and got into heated arguments with legislators. Within hours, Dane County sheriffs, police officers, and eventually the National Guard arrived, forcing protestors out of the building and onto the capitol grounds. Although they had been forced out, protestors declared that they would remain in Madison until politicians restored the budget cuts.[2] Protestors did remain in Madison over the next several days with some, including Father James Groppi, ending up in jail. Groppi's arrest deflected media attention away from the reason for the march and sit-ins—the budget cuts, which unfortunately, were never reversed. Disgusted by the treatment they endured, mother activists turned their anger into activism, joined together and created a new organization: the Milwaukee County Welfare Rights Organization (MCWRO), which was a collective of previously existing neighborhood-based groups.

After the Mothers March to Madison, the newly formed MCWRO organized mother activists, planned demonstrations to agitate for more funding, established daycares, and eventually wrote a book where they shared their stories and experiences with poverty with the goal of educating their community and the nation about the potential of eradicating poverty, not through handouts, but through the restoration of dignity and power.

With the MCWRO and the mother activists who started it at the center of the story, this chapter explores the history of the welfare rights movement in Milwaukee. In 1970s Milwaukee, poor mothers agitated for and expanded the definition of economic justice. For mother activists, economic justice centered on the needs of the unwanted, the neglected, and those who society most often ignored: poor people.

Defining economic justice with poor people at the center went hand in hand with their methods for pursuing economic justice, which included direct action protests as well as education and storytelling. Their activism coalesced into a book they published in 1972, *Welfare Mothers Speak Out*, a collection of essays, transcribed speeches, and social science research featuring the experiences of mother activists.[3] Originally a fundraising effort for both the National Welfare Rights Organization (NWRO) and the local Milwaukee chapter, the book shined a national spotlight on Milwaukee mothers, showing how their experiences transcended the local, putting into words the feelings and experiences of mother recipients from around the country. Unfortunately, the proceeds from the publication of *Welfare Mothers Speak Out* did little to stave off the continuing financial instability both the NWRO and the MCWRO experienced and by the mid-1970s both organizations ceased to exist. Though the welfare rights movement was short lived, it had an important impact; Milwaukee activists continued their activism in other venues, organizations, and contexts.

Organized into several sections, this chapter chronicles the history of the Milwaukee organization, teasing out their economic activism and community intellectualism. The first section details early welfare rights activism in the city, which culminated in the emergence of the MCWRO in 1969. The next section lays out "militant motherhood," the strategy welfare rights activists deployed as they confronted and challenged economic injustice. Like the Milwaukee NAACP Youth Council Commandos who defended civil rights activists as they marched into hostile environments, militant mothers, who were on the front lines of the War on Poverty, defended their children, as well as their right to motherhood. Their defense of themselves and their families was not rooted in social, moral, or behavioral reform, but in structural reform. They fought to overhaul the economic system and, if successful, transform the lives of their children, themselves, and in the process, all poor people. The next two sections show activists putting militant motherhood into practice, in their Winter Clothing Campaign and in the development of two daycare centers. Focusing on the material and educational needs of children, these campaigns also highlight how mothers used every opportunity at their disposal to disrupt structures that kept them impoverished and powerless. The chapter concludes by discussing *Welfare Mothers Speak Out* and the demise of the MCWRO and the NWRO due to financial instability.

Early Welfare Rights Activism in the City and the Emergence of the Milwaukee County Welfare Rights Organization

The year 1968 was pivotal for welfare rights organizing in Milwaukee. Several welfare rights groups sprouted up in the city. State records provide incorporation dates for the United Welfare Recipients, incorporated on June 11, 1968; the Northside Welfare Recipients, incorporated on October 4, 1968; and the Nat Turner Welfare Mothers, incorporated on November 11, 1968.[4] Union Benefica Hispana also existed in 1968 although members did not incorporate the organization until 1970.[5] Of these groups, only the establishment of the Nat Turner Welfare Mothers group received any media attention. A Black newspaper, the *Greater Milwaukee Star*, reported on the formation of the organization, noting its leadership and its clear rationale for forming: "getting the basic needs [of] welfare mothers and children" met.[6] Thirty-two mothers joined the organization, and its officers included president Mattie Gulley, vice president Alice Gransberry, secretary Bessie Bresby, treasurer Lonnie Johnson, and program chairman Etta Turnell.

Pretty soon after the formation of these neighborhood-based groups, their actions began to attract the attention of local Black journalists who began to consistently report their activities. Black journalists' efforts to chronicle welfare rights activism was crucial and they often took pains to interview mother activists, recounting narratives of their actions word for word. This reporting was often at odds with mainstream, white media outlets that demonized Black mothers and those who received public assistance. Therefore, the role Black journalists played in collaborating with mothers to provide an alternative narrative while also preserving the actions and words of these mothers cannot be understated.

In December 1968, the *Soul City Times* reported on the activities of the Northside Welfare Recipients group, which had organized over one hundred mothers in a demonstration at the County Welfare Department's office to demand an additional $25 per family member. Mothers wanted the supplement so that they could buy Christmas toys for their children.[7] What began as a peaceful demonstration devolved into conflict, resulting in the arrest of fourteen activists, including Mary Loggins. Journalist Gregory Stanford interviewed Loggins who shared her reasons for participating. She noted that while she had children of her own, she did not join the demonstrations for them because they were old enough to understand that finances might not permit Christmas presents. Instead, Loggins participated to support mothers with younger children and because she saw firsthand that societal stigmatization of poverty and public assistance had a grave impact on children. Her greater purpose was "to see . . . black children stand tall and proud."[8]

Two weeks later the police arrested Mary Loggins again.[9] A day before her arrest, she had returned to the County Welfare Department's office with another group of mother activists to vocalize their displeasure that their aid checks had been delayed and to request that the Department issue duplicate checks. This time activists from the Northside Welfare Recipients and the Nat Turner Welfare Mothers groups joined forces. Members, including Mary Loggins, spoke to multiple white, male welfare department workers who explained the lengthy process of getting a duplicate check, a process that included speaking with a caseworker. Highly upset and aggravated by the delay and bureaucratic response that both inconvenienced them and threatened their ability to provide for their children, the mothers demanded their checks immediately. After going back and forth, the welfare workers told the mothers to return to the office the next day.

The following day, Loggins and five other mother activists went back to the office as instructed. No checks were ready to be picked up. Demanding to know why, Loggins got into a heated exchange with a white female caseworker that became physical. According to Loggins, the caseworker waved her finger in Loggins' face "as if to reprimand her" and Loggins slapped it away. After this, the caseworker had the sheriff called on Loggins, and he promptly arrested her. After her release, she told her story, once again, to Gregory Stanford, whose paper, the *Soul City Times*, continued to report on welfare rights organizing in the city, even when other newspapers did not.

While welfare mothers continued their organizing efforts and put fire under the feet of the county welfare department, the next year they took their battle to the state level through the Mothers March to Madison, the rally and eleven-hour sit-in described in the introduction to this chapter. The impact of this sit-in was tremendous, with different groups remembering and characterizing the events of that day differently.[10] Politicians and the media referred to the demonstrators as "storm troopers" for taking over the chambers.[11] According to Milwaukee mother activist Mildred Calvert, during the protest she "learned how bad the system is, how we are really hated, and how people could make you feel degraded and how humiliating it really is to be a welfare recipient to a person who really doesn't understand."[12] She and the other activists occupied the chambers of those who had been elected to represent the interest of the people of Wisconsin, including theirs. Instead of hearing their concerns, legislators refused to listen and instead demeaned and threatened them.[13] Filled with emotions and overwhelmed by the gravity of the situation, Calvert cried as she protested. The takeover of the capitol ended with the arrest of several activists, including well-known Milwaukee civil rights activist Father James Groppi. Unfortunately, while the media made a big deal out of Groppi's arrest, neither the demonstration itself nor Groppi's participation swayed politicians. The state legislature never approved Governor Knowles' proposed Urban Aid Package, nor did it restore the cuts to Aid to Families with Dependent Children (AFDC).

Undeterred, activists went back to Milwaukee more resolute than ever. Upon their return to Milwaukee, several of the welfare mothers' groups united to create the Milwaukee County Welfare Rights Organization (MCWRO) in 1969. Existing organizations that joined the MCWRO included the Northside Welfare Recipients and Union

Benefica Hispana.[14] Even though the Nat Turner Welfare Mothers group had played such a pivotal role in organizing the Mothers March to Madison the month prior, the group did not join the MCWRO. Inconclusive evidence points to a dispute between leaders of the group and an NWRO staff member, but neither records of this nor accounts of the group's continued action exists.[15]

Defining Militant Motherhood, Civil Rights and Black Power Connections, and Disrupting Welfare Myths

After the Mothers March on Madison, Mildred Calvert and other mothers returned "determined to fight," deploying "militant motherhood" in their struggle for welfare rights.[16] In contrast to the militant masculinity of the Milwaukee civil rights and Black Power movements, which minimized women's leadership and involvement, militant motherhood opened spaces for women to defend and protect their children, assert their anger about injustice, demand their rights, and imagine a new society where everyone had access to economic security, if not mobility. Multiracial in nature, militant motherhood brought activists from different racial and ethnic backgrounds together in a coalition.

The subtitle of the MCWRO's book *Welfare Mothers Speak Out* is instructive regarding militant motherhood: *We Ain't Gonna Shuffle Anymore*. This subtitle was a refrain from a popular movement song activists sang during demonstrations. Civil rights activists remixed the song, a traditional Black spiritual, into a freedom song.[17] Welfare rights activists revised it for their use, too:

We're gonna lay down our shufflin' shoes
Down by the welfare door,
Down by the welfare door,
Down by the welfare door,
We're gonna lay down our shufflin' shoes,
Down by the welfare door,
'Cause we ain't gonna shuffle anymore.[18]

The song, remixed from the African American spiritual "Down by the Riverside," speaks of one "laying down their sword and shield" by the riverside after battle. In the song there is a yearning for peace, peace that comes after fighting for and winning justice. In saying they were laying their shufflin' shoes at the doors of the welfare department, activists made a statement about the future. Being able to lay down their shuffling shoes meant they would no longer be taken advantage of or fighting for basic rights. Using this refrain as the book's subtitle illuminates that mother activists knew they were engaged in a battle and they would not be dragging their feet. Fighting a battle not yet won, welfare rights activists deployed militant motherhood as a strategy.

Militant mothers furiously called out injustice despite the risks. They were not afraid to speak their unvarnished truth and invite others to join them in the movement. These militant mothers defended their rights to the resources they needed to take care of their children. Take for example welfare recipient and rights leader Betty Niedzwiecki who declared herself "at war with the War on Poverty."[19] According to Niedzwiecki, she continually had to fight the bureaucracy of the Milwaukee County Welfare Department to get resources for her family and other welfare recipients.[20] She also had to deal with the stigma of being on welfare as well as society's mistrust of poor people. In the case of the Milwaukee Welfare Department, this mistrust translated into the policing of poor people, especially those affiliated with the MCWRO, at welfare agencies. There was always a police presence at the Welfare Department, especially during the days when people came to pick up food stamps. The Welfare Department justified the police presence as preventative in nature.[21] Instead of policing caseworkers who routinely refused to follow procedure when it came to disbursing funds for welfare recipients to buy appliances, furniture, or even pay for medical procedures, police officers and sheriffs targeted welfare rights activists. According to Niedzwiecki, she "would be there yelling at a caseworker because he won't give a woman $100 for a washing machine—he'll only give her $75." She continued: "the laws says she can get $100, but who are the cops after? Me, not the caseworker."[22] As a welfare rights activist, using militant motherhood as a strategy, Niedzwiecki fought against more than poverty—she fought against societal misperceptions about poor people in general and poor mothers specifically as well as a broken welfare system that rarely had the alleviation of poverty as its priority.

Connections between Civil Rights, Black Power, and Welfare Rights

Niedzwiecki's upfront and confrontational style of agitating for the rights of welfare recipients at the Welfare Department was reminiscent of tactics employed by civil rights activists during the mid-to-late 1960s, which was made visible by the activism of the Milwaukee NAACP Youth Council, and as mentioned previously, Father James Groppi. Father Groppi combined nonviolent, direct action strategies with Black Power ideology. Having participated in the Southern civil rights campaigns in Selma, Alabama, Father Groppi had been exposed to nonviolence and brought this strategy back to Milwaukee. Upon his return, the increasingly radical NAACP Youth Council asked Groppi to be their advisor. In the 1950s, Ardie Halyard played a crucial role in organizing the Youth Council although, by the 1960s, its more direct style was much different than her earlier approach of using broker politics to push for change.[23] Once Father Groppi accepted the Youth Council's invitation, together they stood at the forefront of civil rights struggle in Milwaukee.

Not long after the Youth Council selected Groppi to be its advisor, in 1966 the group began its first civil rights campaign—protesting the segregated Eagles Club. The Eagles Club was an all-male social club frequented by the city's top political, business, and economic leaders. The club was also exclusively white. In its laid-back atmosphere the city's leading businessmen and politicians made significant financial deals and political decisions. Therefore, Black men's inability to access this space meant that they could not participate in negotiating these deals and decisions and, by the time they were formalized publicly, it was too late. The Eagles Club stood as an important physical, political, economic, and racial reminder that the powerbrokers in the city of Milwaukee were white men—Black men were excluded. The Youth Council organized a protest to integrate the Eagles Club. For several weeks, they set up a picket line outside of the Eagles Club and urged prominent white members, such as the mayor of Milwaukee, Henry Maier, to terminate their membership. After picketing at the Club did little to change its racial policies, the Youth Council decided to protest outside the homes of other prominent public officials, such as circuit judge Robert Cannon, county judge Christ Seraphim, and judge Robert Hansen, to urge these men to terminate their memberships. Unfortunately, their protests yielded very little results as these Eagles Club members cited that it was their prerogative to join any private club they wanted, regardless of its racially restrictive membership policies.

During the Youth Council's Eagles Club campaigns, rowdy white counterdemonstrators gathered in opposition, especially while protestors picketed outside circuit court judge Robert Cannon's home. These crowds shouted insults and threw objects at the demonstrators. As a result, Governor Warren Knowles called out the National Guard to preserve order and to protect the activists' right to protest.[24] In response to white counterdemonstrators' violent opposition, the Youth Council created the Commandos, whose main purpose was to preserve the strategy of nonviolence by protecting civil rights activists and Father Groppi from angry counterdemonstrators. Soon after its inception, the Commandos assumed the primary responsibility of making key decisions regarding the plans and tactics for the Eagles campaign and eventually all of the Youth Council's direct action campaigns. The Commandos provided a space for young Black men in Milwaukee to grapple with and construct their own definitions of masculinity. Many of the Commandos grew up poor or working class in Milwaukee's Black community, and for some this became their first chance to prove themselves as men and leaders in their community.

As the vanguard of Milwaukee's movement leadership, the Commandos, according to historian Patrick Jones, "project[ed] a masculine verbosity and toughness of style," leaving little space for women to be publicly recognized as leaders in Milwaukee's civil rights movement.[25] This aggressive and protective masculinity contributed to the Commandos' development of their understanding of Black Power. For Commandos, adhering to Black Power meant protecting the community, building Black institutions, racial pride,

FIGURE 9. During the summer of 1967, activists participated in a series of demonstrations and protests. This photograph, with no identifying information included, was taken two days before activists commenced marching for two hundred consecutive days for fair housing. August 26, 1967. © *Milwaukee Journal Sentinel* - USA Today Network

self-determination and "not-violence."[26] Because of this, civil rights leadership in Milwaukee tended to be portrayed as predominantly male, although several women participated formally and informally in the movement's direct action campaigns.[27]

Although Father Groppi's and the Commandos' masculinist leadership style often obscured women's contributions and leadership during the height of the movement, women were drawn to their militant Black Power ideology. Many people, including welfare rights activist

Mildred Calvert and her children, were encouraged by Groppi's charisma, high energy and decisive stance against white supremacy.[28] In fact, Calvert's children's decision to join a civil rights march prompted her to join as well. She recounted, "but when the kids decided that they were going—the march came right by our house—I had to go with them. So, I went and followed Father Groppi."[29] Calvert's involvement with the civil rights movement led to her participation in welfare rights organizing in Milwaukee, which to her felt like a huge risk, especially since it was known that welfare department officials retaliated against recipients who got involved with the movement. Calvert's fear was also justified, especially given the historic ways Black women have had to defend Black motherhood as well as the way society vilified mothers who took advantage of public assistance.

Disrupting Myths about Black Motherhood and Welfare Assistance

Deviant Black motherhood and matriarchy contributed to urban poverty and high rates of welfare, according to Daniel Patrick Moynihan in his controversial report *The Negro Family: The Case for National Action*.[30] In this report, Moynihan argued that the destruction of the Black family during slavery and Jim Crow contributed to a matriarchal family model that essentially emasculated Black fathers. Because Black fathers could not provide for their families, this increased the poverty rate of Black families. In this report, Moynihan laid blame on and demonized Black women, instead of seriously considering the societal and structural causes of urban poverty. The Moynihan report also reinforced stigmas and stereotypes about welfare, making welfare synonymous with race and single parent families, specifically families led by Black mothers. Three years after the publication of the Moynihan report, welfare rights organizing commenced in Milwaukee.

Welfare rights activists in Milwaukee continually challenged the ideas perpetuated by the Moynihan report, while also contending with general myths about welfare. In Milwaukee and other northern cities, a common myth that prevailed asserted that most welfare recipients were Black migrants who moved north simply to take advantage of welfare. This damaging myth did two things: it correlated welfare and public aid with African Americans and minimized the societal and structural causes of poverty, which included employment discrimination, deindustrialization, and the resulting lack of quality of employment. While many journeyed north in search of economic opportunities, they did so with quality employment in mind, not welfare. This myth prevailed even though in 1970, 55 percent of welfare recipients were white while 39 percent were Black and 6 percent were Native Americans and other people of color.[31] Milwaukee welfare mother Rosie Hudson challenged this myth when she asserted, "Too many people are saying welfare's a black problem, when it's really a green problem. Why don't we have decent food, clothing, or shelter? It's simple. We don't have enough money."[32] To Hudson the focus on race shifted the focus away from economics and her comment reveals the idea that for too long welfare had not answered the primary problem it was supposedly designed to alleviate: poverty.

Another myth Milwaukee mothers challenged was the one that asserted welfare mothers continually had children to abuse the system. In 1970, the average mother on welfare had 2.7 children, which was comparable to the national average of 2.4.[33] The myth that "all welfare mothers do is have illegitimate children" was blown apart by this data and by mothers themselves.[34] Again, another Milwaukee mother, Anne Henderson, confronted this myth when she asserted:

> If you think I'm gonna have a baby—and watch that child grow up with no food or clothing; and then watch him go to school where teachers don't teach him anything; and worry that he's gonna become a pimp or start shooting dope; and finally, when he's raised, see him go into the army and get really shot up in there—if you think I'm gonna go through all that pain and suffering for an extra $50, or $100, or even $500 a month, why you must be crazy.[35]

Henderson argued that it was absurd to think mothers would purposely have children, aware of the financial struggle that would ensue, just to get a few more bucks from the government.

One of the most damaging myths accused welfare recipients of mismanaging their monthly grants:

You'll give those lazy, shiftless, good for nothings an inch and they'll take a mile. You have to make it tougher on them. They're getting away with murder now. You have to catch all those cheaters and put them to work or put them in jail. Get them off the welfare rolls. I'm tired of those niggers coming to our state to get on welfare. I'm tired of paying their bills just so they can sit around home having babies, watching their color televisions and driving Cadillacs.[36]

This angry diatribe, printed anonymously in *Welfare Mothers Speak Out*, represented the views of many regarding recipients of public aid. Again, Milwaukee mothers often told a different story that was diametrically opposed to how they were portrayed.

While Milwaukee's mainstream newspapers often misrepresented the truth in regard to poor people and justice, a rare campaign in the *Milwaukee Journal* shed light on the human faces of public assistance, highlighting the story of Gertrude Strean, a welfare rights leader who lived in Fond du Lac, Wisconsin. Strean's experience on welfare, similar to many others, offered a counter to the angry diatribe printed in *Welfare Mothers Speak Out*. Originally from North Dakota, Strean tried exactly what many dissenters suggested she do—get a job—and yet the wages from her full-time job did not provide her with enough income to care for herself and her six children adequately. Strean, armed with typing and shorthand skills, still only received a monthly salary of $360, ironically from doing office work at an anti-poverty agency. Of the $360, Strean lost $100 to taxes because welfare mothers could not claim themselves or their children as exemptions. Not enough to support six children and an adult, Strean applied for welfare benefits. Once Strean's oldest child was able to work, he did so in order to help support the family. Unfortunately, because of welfare restrictions, he could only keep $20 of his $252 earnings, the rest went to the welfare department. By the time he was a junior in high school, he was able to save most of his earnings for his college education. However, after being diagnosed with rheumatoid arthritis, he quit school, and as a result, all the savings he had accumulated toward his college degree went to the welfare department. Rather than help recipients better themselves economically, the restrictions, rules, and bureaucracy of the AFDC program trapped recipients in a cycle of poverty.

Strean also enrolled in college at the suggestion of a caseworker. Strean exhausted herself going to work full time, caring for her six children, doing all the housework, and going to school.[37] After two and half years of going to school part-time, Strean only had twelve credits. She realized it would take twenty years to earn her degree at the pace she was going. Under the new budget, Strean's AFDC check had been reduced from $343 to $258 and after she paid rent and utilities, only $81 remained for household supplies, transportation and any other expenses that might come up. Strean applied for a full-time job that would provide enough so that she didn't have to be on welfare, and she also had a contingency plan: "If the job doesn't come through, I'll just go to the factory and forget school."[38] Gertrude Strean participated in the September Mothers March to Madison to bring attention to her plight and to challenge the prevailing myths about welfare recipients spending government money on expensive televisions and fancy cars. Clearly, Strean hardly had time to sleep, let alone watch television. In terms of a car, Strean could barely afford to provide the basic necessities for her family. By telling her story to the *Milwaukee Journal*, Strean exposed the myth of lazy, shiftless, greedy welfare mothers as a fabrication.

Strean shared her story to challenge misconceptions about welfare recipients in the media, and Frankie Patterson combatted the stereotype of recipients as cheaters during a welfare rights demonstration. At the event a woman who opposed welfare told Patterson, "Welfare recipients have no right to complain."[39] This woman, a widow and mother of four children, had to get a job as a waitress because social security did not cover all of her family's expenses. Answering her, Patterson declared, "If people can get a just wage and still raise their children decently, they should work. The problem is that no mother can get a just wage." She asked the woman, "How much do you make on your job?" The woman told Patterson that she made $1.10 an hour. Patterson asked her, "Do you think that's a just wage?" The woman exclaimed, "No!" Patterson continued, "Well, if you want to submit yourself to an injustice, that's your privilege, but you shouldn't condemn us because we refuse." Continuing the conversation, the woman told Patterson that her wage, tips, and social security provided enough for her to provide for her family. She also accused welfare recipients of cheating the system. Patterson challenged the woman by asking, "Do you pay taxes on the tips you get?" The woman responded, "Of course not! If I did that, I wouldn't be able to survive." Patterson exposed this woman's faulty logic and invited her join the movement when she replied, "Well then, you're cheating, because the law says you have to pay taxes on those tips. You're forced to cheat and that's an injustice. No one should be forced to cheat in order to survive. So why don't you join the rest of us cheaters and fight for a country where no one has to cheat in order to live?"[40] In this exchange, Patterson exposed the unfairness of a society that forced people to have to resort to illegal means to provide for themselves and their families. Patterson could have brought out the data that buttressed the fact that cases of fraud were extremely rare, both nationwide and in Milwaukee, or the fact that the vast majority of people who qualify for welfare were not even aware that they qualified. Instead she criticized the system that did not work for the vast majority of people and offered her opponent an invitation to join in the movement to remake the system so that everyone could have what they needed in life. Milwaukee activists continually spoke truth to power, using the strategy of militant motherhood in their campaigns.

"Welfare Mothers Reject Used Garb": The MCWRO's Winter Clothing Campaign

The confrontational strategy of militant motherhood could be seen in the MCWRO's Winter Clothing Campaign. On Monday, January 26, 1970, welfare mothers from Milwaukee made the national and local news once again for their activism. Five hundred welfare rights activists converged on downtown Milwaukee's Boston Store, removing clothes from racks and knocking down counters.[41] This spontaneous demonstration occurred three hours after and in response to the Milwaukee County Welfare Board's failure to pass a resolution to create a $100,000 contingency fund from which grants would be dispersed to welfare recipients so that they could buy winter clothing for their children. County Board supervisors supportive of welfare rights, Gerard B. Skibinski, James G. Lippert, and Calvin C. Moody, had introduced the resolution to create the contingency fund at a special meeting earlier that day.

Welfare rights activists demonstrated at the Boston Store as a way to apply pressure to city officials. MCWRO chairperson Cassie Downer said specifically, "the welfare protestors, by going to the Welfare Department and the County Board, had tried 'to play the ball game' the way society says it should be played. 'But . . . we found that poor people cannot even be heard, so we're going to play the game their way.'" She continued, "This man yesterday (a county supervisor) said he had to wear used clothing when he was little. What he was saying was that because he had to suffer my children have to suffer. He was saying that because he was unhappy we should be unhappy. So we're unhappy and we're going to do it their way. We're going to make society unhappy." Downer also noted that the Boston Store damage was the result of activists' frustration and anger. Calling attention to a deadly double standard, Downer said she "place[d] greater value on human life than property. . . . People take their frustration out on property, and the police take theirs out on people." NWRO staff member Bruce Thomas added to Downer's commentary by saying, "If they're willing to spend more money on repression than on the basic needs of people, which is what they have been doing, that's their decision."[42] The MCWRO committed to its protest with the goal of pressing the county to forgo the clothing drive and instead provide the money for the contingency fund.

Two days after the demonstration at the Boston Store, welfare mothers gathered at the Milwaukee County Welfare Board to convince the board to disperse money to welfare mothers so that they could purchase winter clothing for their children. Some county officials and supportive community leaders spoke out, too. For example, Arthur Silverman, the deputy county welfare director, shared how the recent decreases in welfare grants hurt families. In a time of rising costs, he thought it harmful that welfare assistance in the form of grants had dropped.[43] The League of Women Voters also supported the resolution, and Frances Ponder, the chairperson of the League's Welfare Study Committee, came to the County Welfare Board meeting to show her support.

Instead of allocating the funds, which would have amounted to about $50 per child, the County Welfare Board instead decided to launch a used clothing drive.[44] Revealing the economic and social rationale for the opposition to the used clothing drive, Bruce Thomas responded "We will no longer take the garbage out of white folks' cellars and attics for our kids. . . . These mothers want the dignity to go down and shop for themselves. They demand that." Welfare mothers did not desire used clothes and hand-me-downs. They wanted the freedom to shop where they wanted and purchase what they thought was best for their children, not what was given to them as charity. One unidentified mother spoke out on her children's experiences being teased when she said, "We are sick and tired of the kids being criticized by other children because they are walking the streets like tramps." In tears, another unnamed mother posed a question on the minds of many mothers: "When they have no clothes to go to school with, what am I to do?"[45] Although these two mothers' names are not included in the records of the event, MCWRO chairperson Cassie Downer's comment resonated with theirs when she stated, "The natural parents feel they are entitled to the same treatment that foster parents are. . . . When a child is in a foster home, he has a better chance of getting decent clothing than he has in the home of his own parents, and that's not right."[46] Another welfare rights activist, Helen Hopkins, spoke to the practicality of being able to purchase clothing from stores, when she suggested "used clothing should be provided only as a supplement since it was not always available in the sizes needed."[47] It was not just about winter clothing, it was about freedom to determine the way one would participate in the consumer market. Welfare mothers, through their rejection of used clothing, made a statement that said despite their dependence on the state, they still desired to live with dignity and be recognized as consumers and citizens.

In spite of hearing from welfare rights activists and receiving petitions from Cassie Downer on behalf of five thousand welfare recipients, the chairman of the Welfare County Board, William F. O'Donnell, supported the used clothing drive as a solution to the lack of winter clothes because he did not believe the contingency fund would go far enough. He asserted, "The $100,000 isn't going to accomplish anything. . . . You know it and I know it." He thought the used clothing drive was more feasible and pledged the county would provide clean, used clothing. Rejecting this, Bruce Thomas directed, "Just keep it out of our neighborhoods."[48]

After meeting with the County Welfare Board on Wednesday, January 28, 1970, and realizing that the board did not intend to pass the resolution for the $100,000 contingency fund, the MCWRO planned another march to Milwaukee's downtown shopping area on Saturday, January 31, 1970. The idea was that if activists disrupted business, thereby decreasing their profits, businesses would be inclined to support providing direct funds to poor people.[49] Activists targeted consumers too, asking them to refrain from shopping on that day in support of the needs of welfare mothers and until their needs were met.[50] On that Saturday, about 450 activists marched downtown to pressure business owners to support their cause. Business owners responded, not by closing their businesses, but by locking protestors out of their stores. Mothers and their supporters continued protesting, but by February, the Milwaukee County Board had officially rejected the $100,000 resolution.

Welfare rights activists once again demanded a clothing fund the following year, but with new tactics. On January 3, 1971, the steering committee of the MCWRO met to discuss strategy for a protest the next day.[51] The unplanned, impromptu 1970 protest resulted in the arrests of several of the demonstrators, as well as property damage. Mothers protested out of anger, and the demonstration was unorganized. With Cassie Downer leading the charge, activists developed a strategy that clearly laid out the goals, directions, and purpose of the protest. The purpose of the demonstration was to pressure members of the Milwaukee Association of Commerce, a network of downtown businessmen, to meet with the MCWRO to discuss creating an emergency clothing fund. Minutes from the MCWRO steering committee meeting laid out the plan. The organization targeted the Boston Store once again, but once all the demonstrators arrived, they would stay together, unlike the last demonstration where everyone scattered. If store employees prevented them from entering the store, they planned to start a picket line and pass out flyers. Because they knew the demonstration could be tense, the organization encouraged participants to not intentionally provoke the police by mocking them or engaging in name-calling. Those who did so would be asked to leave. Activists estimated that approximately 150 protestors would join the demonstration, with representatives from several of the MCWRO area affiliates.

As a result of the strategically planned demonstration, activists successfully convinced the Association of Commerce to meet with them. At this meeting, the association agreed to partner with the MCWRO to help raise funds for clothing.[52] By the end of January the Milwaukee County Welfare board joined in the partnership to officially sponsor the fundraiser, which county board executive, John Doyne, announced. Doyne encouraged businesses, organizations, churches, and individuals to contribute. Funds raised would be collected by the county treasurer's office and dispersed to the Welfare Department, which would then issue vouchers for children's clothing. Doyne acknowledged that the clothing drive the county had sponsored the previous year had actually cost $60,000 and did little to relieve the clothing needs of children. The clothing that had been donated via the clothing drive was unusable and inadequate because, while people donated many items, mothers could not find the specific types of winter clothing they needed. Most of what was donated was for adults and not children, as activists had predicted. Doyne acknowledged the failure of the used clothing drive and emphasized money, not clothing, was the priority. In addition to the Milwaukee Association of Commerce and the MCWRO, organizations such as the United Community Services and Greater Milwaukee Conference of Religion and Urban Affairs endorsed the fundraiser. The Milwaukee Association of Commerce immediately donated $50,000 to the fund and nearly $25,000 more had been raised by March.[53] Also in March, county supervisor Michael

Barron submitted a revised proposal to appropriate $100,000 for clothing, but this resolution failed once again.

Symbolic on multiple levels, the MCWRO's winter clothing campaign signified welfare mothers' rejection of social and economic oppression that affected them and their children as welfare recipients. Welfare mothers not only desired the economic freedom to participate as consumers, theirs also was a fight for dignity and inclusion in the economic system as equals, even though they received assistance from the state. Clothing their children properly was their responsibility as mothers. Accepting used clothing robbed them of their rights to take responsibility for their children and painted them as "deviant mothers," lacking maternal virtue. Welfare mothers refused to be depicted this way and rejected any "hand-me-downs" that might characterize them in this way.

The Winter Clothing Campaign was the MCWRO's first protest action following the Mothers March, and the campaign solidified the organization's place in the city as the leading welfare rights organization. By 1971, the MCWRO was the largest welfare rights organization in the state. Over half of the state's one-thousand-plus members belonged to the MCWRO, with the other half spread out over nine other counties in Wisconsin.[54] Both the Milwaukee organization and the state organization were multiracial. The state's membership was 50 percent Black, 25 percent white, 20 percent Native American, and 15 percent Latin American.[55] Together these women claimed their right to welfare and tried to shield their children from the ravages of poverty.

"Mother Power": The MWCRO and UW Milwaukee School of Education Day Care Training Program

After a successful Winter Clothing Campaign, the MCWRO shifted its focus to education, specifically for preschoolers. On February 16, 1971, the MWRCO submitted a grant application to the Community Relations–Social Development Commission of Milwaukee County to open a Day Care Training Center.[56] These centers would provide developmentally appropriate educational support for children and include parents as staff members and volunteers, training them to run centers of their own. According to the MCWRO, in 1971 over six thousand poor children in the city under the age of five could benefit from going to an educational day care center. In addition to benefiting these children, members of the MCWRO believed day care centers could also impact mothers, since MCWRO's goal was to train mothers to run the centers themselves. The MCWRO's decision to pursue day care training came at a time when many agencies, both private and public, were focused on day care. Day care centers were not simply babysitting services; the impetus for them came as a result of the federal Head Start program, which was developed in 1965 to give low-income children an educational jumpstart before they began kindergarten.[57] Originally conceived of as a summer program, educators realized that some children needed more than a few weeks in the summer to prepare them for kindergarten.[58]

As a response to the growing need to prepare children before they began kindergarten, community members from organizations across Milwaukee joined forces to develop education programs for the city's poor children. For example, community members established the Community Board for Community Education Centers for Young Children.[59] MCWRO chairman Cassie Downer and members of the MCWRO sat on this board. Additionally, the Urban League received and reviewed a business plan from a Milwaukee mother, Nellie Thomas, to open her own daycare.[60] The University of Wisconsin School of Education opened its own Day Care Training Center on its east side Milwaukee campus. Therefore, the MCWRO's proposal to start a training center for mothers to learn how to operate day care centers met a real need and was in line with a citywide focus on the needs of young children and their mothers.

The MCWRO partnered with the University of Wisconsin Milwaukee School of Education Day Care Training Center to bring a Day Care Training Center to a more convenient area where mothers lived. Since many residents who lived in the poorest areas of Milwaukee could not afford to travel to the UW Milwaukee campus on the east side of the city, the MCWRO proposed that the center be located closer to where they lived.[61] The MCWRO anticipated serving forty families a week with a $75,000 operating budget that included salaries for the mothers employed by the center.[62]

The MCWRO submitted a detailed proposal that described the two-fold goals of their center. Their primary goal was a comprehensive program that provided meals, as well as educational and physical activities for the children who participated.[63] The MCWRO desired their training center and the resulting day care centers to be on the cutting edge, employing innovative methods that encouraged exploration, discovery, and freedom in preschool children.[64] In addition to tending to the needs of young children, the center also planned to train mothers on how to direct a day care center of their own and in their own communities, the second goal.

In 1971, with the support of the UW Milwaukee School of Education, the MCWRO started the Bread and Justice Day Care Training Center and opened two day care centers: Jolly Juneau and La Causa.[65] Opened in March of 1971, Jolly Juneau Day Care Center was located on the north side. Within a couple months of opening, Jolly Juneau had an average of about thirty children between the ages of two and five participating in its program. Volunteers and MCWRO staff ran the center on weekdays.[66] La Causa was opened in September 1971 by a group of Latina welfare rights activists including Clementina Castro, who contributed to *Welfare Mothers Speak Out*. Castro had also participated in the Mothers March to Madison and enrolled in the UW Milwaukee Day Care Training Program. Located on the south side, where many Latino Milwaukeeans resided, La Causa Day Care Center served those communities. Castro envisioned La Causa as a "bi-lingual, bi-cultural, pre-school center."[67] After it opened, La Causa gained the support of the UW Milwaukee School of Education and received funding from the Work Incentive Program (WIN) to establish it as a training center for five people.[68]

Clementina Castro, a divorced mother of three, opened La Causa because of her passion for making sure children on welfare received a quality education. In her piece in *Welfare Mothers Speak Out*, Castro called out the inadequacy of the public school system, where she claimed students were not being educated at all and that teachers targeted children whose parents were involved with the welfare rights movement. Her experiences represented what many children went through.

> We know the child is not learning. They pass the kids just to get rid of them, especially if they are on welfare. . . . The schools are not teaching. They're too prejudiced. My daughter is nine years old. Her teacher gives her a hard time because I'm in Welfare Rights. Children are absent from school because they don't have any clothing, coats, boots, shoes, anything. I'm not going to send my kids to school if they're going to get sick on the way there, and this keeps them behind. Especially for the last two years when welfare won't give clothing, all my children are home in the winter—it gets down to 15 below in Milwaukee. They don't have anything to wear. This means the child goes down. If the child is on welfare, the school keeps him down, because he didn't have the money to pay for the books. In spite of all of this, some kids try to go to school every day and still the teacher doesn't teach them. The child has to be very smart to get just a little thing.[69]

This angered mothers like Castro and prompted them to join the fight for welfare rights, which was also a fight for quality education for their children. Castro knew that "when a child can't get a good education no matter how he tries and because of that he can't get a job, and even if he has the education he still can't get a job, he has to have some support."[70] While La Causa wouldn't help her three children—they were older than five—it would provide support to other children on welfare.

During its first year of operation La Causa established its training curriculum and gained support from community members who both entered the training program and sent their children to its day care center. Unfortunately, unable to renew outside funding, the center could not provide stipends for its students, and all its staff were considered volunteers. Despite the cutbacks, La Causa staff were committed to its cause, so much so that one worker paid for her training out of her own pocket.[71] By 1973, wholly financially self-sufficient,

La Causa still faced funding difficulties but it remained open four hours a day, Monday through Friday, in an effort to provide some education and care for preschool children whose families received public assistance.

In establishing a relationship with the UW Milwaukee School of Education to obtain day care centers and training programs, welfare rights activists demonstrated their use of militant motherhood as a strategy. In this instance they displayed "mother power" by taking the lead in pressing for quality education for their young children early in their development, before they went to public schools.[72] Mothers joined a citywide coalition of community members who were concerned about early childhood education and acted to address the needs of their children and provide them with a solid educational foundation. Additionally, for mothers who enrolled in either La Causa's or the UW Milwaukee School of Education's day care training program, it also provided them with income—a key component of the welfare movement's stated goals.

Poor People's Intellectual History: *Welfare Mothers Speak Out: We Ain't Gonna Shuffle No More*

In 1972, a year after opening Jolly Juneau and La Causa day care centers, the mother activists of the Milwaukee County Welfare Rights Organization contributed to and published *Welfare Mothers Speak Out: We Ain't Gonna Shuffle No More.*[73] A collaboration between the National Welfare Rights Organization and the Milwaukee chapter, the book dispels myths about public assistance, the welfare rights movement, and the mothers organizing to reform the welfare system from the inside out. Published by W. W. Norton, the book prominently features the stories of MCWRO activist mothers and quotes from mother recipients from across the nation, as well as social scientific research written by editors Thomas Howard Tarantino and Father Dismas Becker that illustrates and critiques the nature of the United States as a welfare state.

Welfare Mothers Speak Out

by the Milwaukee County
Welfare Rights Organization

Introduction by
Dr. George A. Wiley,
Executive Director,
National Welfare
Rights Organization

FIGURE 10. Cover of *Welfare Mothers Speak Out* (W.W. Norton, 1972)

Poor people's intellectual history, including their efforts to articulate and disseminate their own analysis, has been overlooked and silenced in the historical record. However, in the 1960s and 1970s, poor folks wrote manifestos, contributed essays to anthologies, and published their ideas in radical presses. In this way, what the MCWRO did in publishing *Welfare Mothers Speak Out* was audacious, but it was not unique. For example, a group of radical Black women organized by social worker and psychotherapist Pat Robinson had been meeting in Mount Vernon/New Rochelle, New York, since 1960. This diverse group of Black women included mothers, grandmothers, welfare recipients, factory workers, housewives, and women employed in the domestic service industry. Pat Robinson's Group, or the Damned, as they later referred to themselves, originally formed to strategize around addressing rising rates of teenage pregnancy. The group expanded their concerns to include a range of issues that mattered to the members, including childcare, welfare rights, education, and housing, to name a few. They ran a freedom school, operated a day-care, and advocated for reproductive access.[74]

Pat Robinson's Group realized that in addition to organizing, they had to articulate, write, and publish their analyses and critiques, which they did throughout their existence. They co-wrote essays and articles that were published in radical newsletters, anthologies, and eventually their own text, *Lessons from the Damned: Class Struggle in the Black Community*, in which they argued that struggles for Black freedom and liberation had been controlled by aspiring middle-class Black activists who had their own class interests at heart. In the book's introduction, they wrote, "This book covers our struggle over a long span of time—from our first political consciousness as a community of oppressed black people through our growing awareness of our oppression as workers and poor people in a capitalist economic system, and as women and young people oppressed by men and the family."[75] They laid out their critique asserting that any struggle for Black freedom must include a critique of class exploitation. This text, important though it was and continues to be, has not received the activist or scholarly attention it deserves.[76]

While *Lessons from the Damned* and *Welfare Mothers Speak Out* both critiqued class and economic oppression, they did differ. A major difference between *Lessons* and *Welfare Mothers Speak Out* was that the latter was published by W. W. Norton, a major mainstream publishing house, instead of an independent press. This led to challenges, especially relating to editorial processes and authorial

FIGURE 11. Cover of *Lessons from the Damned* (Times Change Press, 1973)

authority. Many of the essays in *Welfare Mothers Speak Out* originated as speeches that the mothers had previously given at demonstrations or protests. Conflict developed between the book's editors, specifically Thomas Howard Tarantino, who managed the publication process for the MCWRO, and the Norton editorial team. Tarantino worked with MCWRO chairwoman Cassie Downer to compile the mothers' contributions as well as additional essays relating to the history of the US as a welfare state, explanations of Nixon's proposed Family Assistance Plan, and breakdowns of welfare myths. Tarantino submitted the manuscript to Norton, who then responded with suggested edits focusing on the essays written by the mothers. Norton editors wanted to change phrasings and language for what they thought would be more suitable for a reading audience. Downer and Tarantino adamantly disagreed and refused to accept any editing of the mothers' contributions. Norton acquiesced.[77]

With *Welfare Mothers Speak Out*, Black mothers continued a tradition of Black women's economic and intellectual organizing rooted in the city and connected to the national movement. In the book, mothers spoke up and out by telling their own personal, many times painful, stories of exploitation and resistance. Storytelling, an intellectual act, was a primary way they vocalized their critiques of poverty and the welfare system.[78] In an era where the dissemination of alternative facts about those on welfare proliferated, the words of mother activists dislodged myths, disrupted stereotypes, and downright rejected the lies circulating in the media about welfare recipients. The foreword of *Welfare Mothers Speak Out* offers a telling description of the book's content, its methods, and its message: "This book combines research conducted by the editors with the words—the knowledge—of the welfare mothers themselves. The research is of secondary importance, but it underlines what the mothers have to say: and what the mothers have to say is that you can't fool the people on the bottom."[79] Five mother activists critiqued the welfare system; they exposed its faults and proposed solutions they thought would improve the plight of all poor people. The insights of Mildred Calvert, Loretta Domencich, Betty Niedzwiecki, Clementina Castro, and Cassie Downer have been included throughout this chapter, and in *Welfare Mothers Speak Out*, each had a chapter where they began by sharing their personal experience receiving public assistance including the mistreatment they received at the hands of welfare department officials, reflected on the moment of awakening they experienced when they learned about the welfare rights movement, and finally provided their ideas about how the system should be transformed. In their own words, these passionate chapters came together to paint an evocative image of mothers' experiences.

These essays were powerful because of the individual stories they contained, but also because of ways in which these individual experiences connected the mothers in the movement. Take for example Cassie Downer and Clementina Castro's comments about the welfare system. Downer noted in her chapter, "The current system stinks. There is too much red tape—bureaucracy—too much money goes into the administration of the welfare and not enough to the people. Welfare recipients aren't even told their legal rights."[80] As a result of bureaucracy and lack of knowledge Downer stated, "There are so many horror stories about people trying to get on welfare that they're beyond telling. People every day coming with no food only to be turned away. People being scared of even coming down and asking for aid, so when they finally do, they're in such bad shape they can't even function."[81]

Castro corroborated Downer's assertion: "In the Latin community, it is very hard to get on welfare because the people don't know what is going to happen. They think their children will be taken away or their husbands will be put in jail with no reason. There are many Latins who could be on welfare but aren't because they don't know their rights. They're afraid."[82] Welfare rights activists saw educating people about their welfare rights as their responsibility. This was one of the main areas around which the Milwaukee group committed its resources, and an idea on which mother activists reflected in their essays.

Other topics mothers explored included a guaranteed adequate income (GAI) and the gendered meanings of work, especially care work. A highly contentious idea that gained media attention in 1966, a guaranteed adequate income was an alternative to the current way the welfare system operated. A GAI would establish the minimum amount needed to live, and any person or family not meeting the minimum would receive cash benefits from the federal government to fill the gap. According to historian Brian Steensland, the movement toward a guaranteed adequate income had long roots, and by the 1960s deindustrialization, automation, and technological change all increased unemployment and poverty, especially among low-skilled and low-income workers, causing economists, lawmakers, and activists to rethink welfare and public assistance.[83] Executive director of the NWRO George Wiley learned about GAI and brought it to the organization, which coincided with President Richard Nixon proposing the Family Assistance Plan (FAP) bill, his version of a guaranteed adequate income plan.[84]

NWRO's ideas regarding the GAI differed from Nixon's FAP. The NWRO argued that in 1969, a family of four needed $5,500 to provide for its basic necessities such as food, housing, clothing, personal care, medical care, transportation, and other expenses related to recreation, reading, and education. Nixon proposed $1,600 for a family of four, with a food stamp allotment of $864.[85]. Nixon's plan provided $500 for the first two family members and $300 for each additional family member. Welfare rights activists and mothers did not understand how Nixon reached the seemingly arbitrary allotment of $1,600. While the FAP passed the House, the bill died during the 1970 session of Congress because the Senate never voted on it.

In 1971, Nixon proposed another version of FAP that increased the guaranteed minimum to $2,400. While the increase seemed like a step toward a positive direction, it would have been more harmful than the first version of FAP. FAP II removed food stamp allotments and did not require states to maintain their current welfare allotments, so states could decrease their contribution to zero and the federal allotment would be all a family received.[86] In some states, FAP II would increase the allotment families received. This was true of states where families already received low welfare allotments, such as states in the South like Alabama, Arkansas, Florida, Georgia, and Mississippi.[87] However, in states where the current state allotment surpassed $2,400, this would mean welfare recipients would lose out. According to Cassie Downer, in contrast to FAP, the NWRO's GAI "would be a national standard of living that the states couldn't play around with, so they couldn't cheat people."[88] In fact, she continued, "it would make it easier for people to know their rights." There was no disagreement about whether the welfare system needed to be reformed; it did. The disagreement was on how. Welfare recipient Mrs. Lee Williams stated, "If this country is going to reform welfare, for crying out loud, reform it so we can live and not die."[89]

The monthly allotment was only one reason why FAP II was so contentious; a work requirement also proved divisive. Nixon suggested that requiring that recipients work would bolster a work ethic, which many erroneously believed recipients lacked.[90] This work requirement became a gendered debate within the welfare rights movement, with male and female welfare rights activists disagreeing on the work requirement.[91] Milwaukee mothers addressed this topic in *Welfare Mothers Speak Out*, challenging prevailing notions about motherhood and work. "Can you imagine it?" declared Betty Glosson,

> A mother of two children, say, aged three and four, would get up in the morning, dress herself and her kids, walk or take a bus to the day-care center, watch, feed, and work with her children between 9 and 5, dress them up again, go home, and take care of them the rest of the day. Between 9 and 5, she would be "working in a day-care center," and the rest of the time she would be just a "mother." How ridiculous.[92]

Welfare rights activist Cassie Downer argued, "A guaranteed adequate income [would] recognize work that is not paid for by society."[93] The work she referred to was that performed by a mother. Downer continued, "I think that the greatest thing that a woman can do is to raise her own children, and our society should recognize it as a job. A person should be paid an adequate income to do that."[94] A guaranteed adequate income recognized mothers' work inside the home and gave them the choice to decide whether they should work outside of home. Welfare rights activist Clementina Castro agreed with Downer. She said, "The mother has got a job all the time, taking care of her children. It's a big job. She has to wash and cook and do everything because she has to manage the house. If a woman can, she wants to have an outside job to help her husband, but she already has a job with the house and the children."[95] During the time of *Welfare Mothers Speak Out*'s publication, the idea of a guaranteed adequate income continued to be deliberated, and mother activists contributed to this debate and others related to the movement.

In addition to providing a platform for mothers to share their experience and analysis, *Welfare Mothers Speak Out* was an educational tool with a call to action. As such, it ends with a three-pronged appeal. First, it encourages readers to take the knowledge they have learned and apply it—demand that their legislators reform the welfare system. Second, it emboldens those who could benefit from public aid to go to their nearest aid office to sign up. Finally, it asks readers to imagine a new economic vision for the country—one where economic prosperity is defined not by capitalism and militarism, but by ensuring that the needs of the most vulnerable have been met. By including and gathering up the stories and critiques articulated by Milwaukee mother activists, *Welfare Mothers Speak Out* shows the connections between economic justice activism and community intellectualism.

Conclusion

Although the welfare rights movement was moving full steam ahead in 1972, the NWRO was declining due to financial troubles. As early as 1969, its expenses exceeded its income and put the organization on a path toward financial difficulty. It could barely pay its operating expenses, let alone taxes. By 1972, the NWRO's executive director, George Wiley, threatened to close the doors of its Washington, DC, office. Due to fundraising efforts, in 1973 the NWRO was able to pay its back taxes and reduce the organization's debt, but it was not enough to keep the organization afloat permanently, and by early 1975, the NWRO had declared bankruptcy and closed its doors.

The MCWRO faced a similar fate, although the exact date of its demise is unknown. As early as 1972, the most pressing item of discussion at Finance Committee meetings was fundraising—applying for grants and soliciting money from wealthy liberal supporters. In January of 1972, Mattie Richardson, the chair of the MCWRO Finance Committee, wrote a letter to the area organizations affiliated with MCWRO, stating bluntly, "We have no money."[96] Richardson explained that the MCWRO was nearly $5,000 in debt—a sum that could be erased if each area group fundraised nearly $600. Richardson told the areas, "Although times look bad for us now because we are out of money and our enemies are ready to laugh at us and say that we cannot do it. . . . I and the Finance committee believe that we can raise our own money. We don't need others to move in and control our lives anymore. We are the greates [sic] and are going to become stronger."[97]

Richardson ended the letter by urging area groups to send representatives to the next Finance Committee meeting. The Finance Committee submitted grant proposals, hosted fundraisers for the MCWRO, and supported the publication of *Welfare Mothers Speak Out*, which W. W. Norton sold for $1.45 a copy. The MCWRO and the NWRO split the royalties from the book. Since the MCWRO was never incorporated in the state of Wisconsin, there is no official record of its dissolution, although activity had ceased by the time the national organization folded in 1975.

After civil rights insurgency rocked the city, welfare rights mothers transformed that insurgency into militant motherhood. They demanded dignity, justice, and the right to be mothers and defend their children—whatever the cost. They marched, protested, argued, raised their voices, and organized on behalf of themselves, their children, and poor people everywhere. They forced "those in power" to listen and sometimes gained concessions that would better their lives. Even when they were unsuccessful, mothers like Mildred Calvert kept on because "the only way changes [would] be made, especially in the welfare system, [was] through poor people, welfare people, organizing and raising a lot of hell."[98]

Although the welfare rights movement fizzled out by the mid-1970s, welfare mothers in Milwaukee did not halt their activism. Some went on to organize in different arenas. For example, Cassie Downer continued by fighting for better children's education. Another activist who participated in welfare rights marches, Betty Thompson, went on to work for Project Equality (PE), the subject of the final chapter of this book. Project Equality was a religious nonprofit organization in Milwaukee established in the 1970s. Like the welfare rights movement, Project Equality's focus was structural change. It attacked the Jim Crow job system by concentrating its energy on compliance. The Black women who ran the Wisconsin office of Project Equality, located in Milwaukee, engaged in the tedious, behind-the-scenes administrative work to hold business accountable to equal employment and affirmative action practices. While PE was not a direct-action organization, the work of its Black women leaders follows the tradition of economic and intellectual activism this book lays out.

CHAPTER 5

"No Longer Marching"

Dismantling the Jim Crow Job System in a Post-Civil Rights Era

Black women fighting for economic justice employed multiple strategies at the same time: they submitted complaints protesting employment discrimination, organized for welfare rights, and helped create new organizations to make fair and equal employment a reality. In 1970, Project Equality was among the new organizations that emerged in Milwaukee. PE began as a project of the Catholic Church and started in Chicago in 1965. Because of its popularity among people of faith, within a few years it had become an interfaith organization. Milwaukee activists brought the organization to the city because of its novel focus: instead of directing attention to the individual experiences of racism workers experienced, PE's goal was to eliminate the deeply entrenched structural and systematic employment discrimination that lay at the core of the corporate world. PE compelled businesses to recognize the implicit and explicit ways they upheld the Jim Crow job system. By interpreting state and federal laws, policies, and procedures, PE held businesses accountable for implementing the changes that would remove barriers to equal employment and make companies compliant with Title VII of the 1964 Civil Rights Act, which prohibits discrimination based on race, color, religion, sex, or national origin. For its more-than-thirty-year existence, the Project Equality Wisconsin (PE-W) office in Milwaukee was run by Black women.

Ensuring businesses complied with federal laws was tedious and painstaking, requiring hours and hours of meetings with company executives and representatives, interviewing workers, reading and critiquing outdated human resources policies, analyzing forms and reports, and helping businesses draft new policies and procedures to eliminate bias and discrimination in the recruitment, hiring, and promotion processes. PE aimed to generate compliance, create accountability, and promote equality—objectives the federal and state employment agencies had but could not fulfill because of the backlog of cases they had to adjudicate. In addition to the day-to-day administrative work, Project Equality workers provided trainings and workshops, sent out a regular newsletter, and held events to educate the public about fair and equitable employment.

Well-known community and civil rights activist Helen Barnhill worked as the first executive director of PE-W from 1970 to 1973. Prior to joining PE-W, Barnhill served as secretary of the Milwaukee Citizens for Equal Opportunity (MCEO), a grassroots organization engaged with several struggles, including fair housing. After her tenure at MCEO, the state hired Barnhill to work for fair housing in its Equal Rights Division, which she did until she started at PE-W. As the first executive director, Barnhill established PE-W as an approachable, cooperative partner that walked beside businesses on the road to equal employment opportunity. Because businesses engaged with PE-W on a voluntary basis, Barnhill spent a lot of her time introducing the organization and its benefits to companies all over the state of Wisconsin. One of the two main benefits included avoiding legal or financial repercussions for failing to comply with federal law. Project Equality helped businesses determine if they were compliant with the federal law and if not, move toward compliance. The other benefit included being listed in Project Equality *Buyer's Guide*, a compendium of companies across the United States committed to Project Equality and to equal employment opportunity. As an interfaith organization, PE's reach was in the millions.

After a three-year tenure, Helen Barnhill left Project Equality to start her own business, prompting the organization to search for its next executive director. In 1974, Betty Thompson became Project Equality's final permanent executive director, a role she remained in until her retirement in 2004. Thompson, a devout Catholic, participated in welfare rights marches and before starting at Project Equality, worked at Northwestern Mutual Life Insurance Company and at the Milwaukee Council on Urban Life. Building upon the foundation Helen Barnhill had laid, Betty Thompson made Project Equality Wisconsin into one of the most successful and longest running of the organization's twenty satellite offices. It became recognized in the city, state, and nation for moving the needle forward toward employment justice.

Although PE-W described itself as nonconfrontational, Barnhill and Thompson did the critical work of exposing the nature of the Jim Crow job system, which businesses and state officials continually erased or denied. Part of this work was bringing to light the false ideas that bolstered racial inequality in the jobs economy. As explained in a previous chapter, some city leaders thought a "culture of poverty" had developed among Black city dwellers, the results of which included an inability to adjust to urban, northern city life.[1] They believed that behaviors of Black people, and not structural discrimination, were the reason Black people could not rise above urban poverty and join the ranks of the American middle class. Employers' belief in these erroneous and destructive ideas meant that they assigned Black workers the hardest and dirtiest jobs while providing few training opportunities and little to no chance of advancement. For a long time, businesses placed the blame on Black workers for their employment difficulties, but Barnhill and Thompson sought to change the narrative surrounding unjust work in the city. Their determined activism reveals community intellectualism, especially through their critique of these damaging ideas and their efforts to hold businesses and employers responsible for their role in sustaining inequality in the workplace.

Black Project Equality workers proposed a society where people of faith took the lead in addressing issues of employment injustice and used their consumer power to make change. Bringing PE into the story of worker rights and economic justice disrupts the narrative that defines economic justice as an exclusively male domain, especially in the urban, northern Milwaukee context. Also, examining the administrative and technical work of Project Equality exposes the intellectual, and in the case of Betty Thompson, feminist, underpinnings of this work. PE-W's Black women executive directors created an educational environment where PE members and businesses could learn the practices of employment equality. These women engaged in community intellectualism as they taught complex labor laws, broke them down into digestible segments, and helped their communities develop actionable steps that would lead to employment justice.

In centering the work of Helen Barnhill and Betty Thompson with PE-W, this chapter shows how entrenched the Jim Crow system was (and continues to be). Like the other chapters before it, this chapter illuminates Black women's efforts to dismantle structural employment discrimination, bit by bit. After examining the development of PE-W and Helen Barnhill and Betty Thomson's respective tenures as executive director of PE-W, this chapter ends by briefly examining the National Interreligious Commission on Civil Rights (NICCR), which Betty Thompson seeded the idea for and helped to create in 1984 while continuing to serve as executive director as PE-W. Project Equality's beginning coincided with deindustrialization and a conservative backlash that made fighting for fair employment an uphill battle in the 1970s. By the 1980s, many former freedom fighters believed the civil rights gains of the 1960s were being eroded on the federal level. Betty Thompson and her fellow activists saw NICCR as a way to reprioritize civil rights and economic justice by holding hearings in cities across the country to bring communities together to listen to the testimonies of working people struggling to survive in urban environments with few job opportunities, continued unequal education, and poor housing. One goal of the commission was to bring awareness; the other goal was to activate local organizations to continue working to better the lives of those in their communities. Taken together, Project Equality and the NICCR illuminate the continuing work needed to achieve civil rights and economic justice in Milwaukee and in the nation.

Launching Project Equality

After decades of civil rights struggle, racial discrimination and intimidation in employment remained entrenched. As a result, the National Catholic Conference for Interracial Justice (NCCIJ), headquartered in Chicago, launched Project Equality in 1965 in two cities, Detroit, Michigan, and St. Louis, Missouri. With a focus on the Jim Crow job system, PE organizers thought that targeting employers was the best way to tackle employment discrimination. Additionally, because federal and state equal employment commissions were backlogged with complaints, PE served as a voluntary nonprofit compliance organization. PE developed a compliance review that determined whether a business or organization had a proactive antidiscrimination, affirmative action employment process. It was not enough to simply have an equal employment clause on an application or job description. Because employment discrimination was structural, companies had to identify concrete steps to rectify economic inequality. Any business that signed on with Project Equality agreed to an annual compliance review and received support from local PE offices to help implement their affirmative action plans.

The national PE office in Chicago typically handled national businesses, with the state offices working with affiliate offices or branches in their cities. An example of the national PE process was the relationship it began with the Christian Church (Disciples of Christ) in 1969. After organizing itself as an official Protestant denomination in 1968, the Christian Church endorsed PE and made a financial pledge to support the organization.[2] Because the Christian Church, headquartered in Indianapolis, Indiana, employed numerous workers and purchased many goods and services in its administrative units, churches, and the seventeen colleges it ran, it decided to move beyond being only a supporter of PE. The denomination enlisted PE to take it through PE's official process for certification as an equal employment opportunity workplace.[3] Similar to what PE would offer to a national business, PE provided direct services to the Christian Church by developing an equal employment opportunity program, ensuring the suppliers of its goods and services also were EEO compliant, and helping the Christian Church make sure its financial investments were financially just as well.[4] According to the denomination, participating in PE's process helped it "translate words into deeds."[5]

Developing and implementing equal employment opportunity plans took much administrative effort. How much effort was required depended on how much work the entity needed to get into affirmative action compliance. With the example of the Christian Church, the national Project Equality office developed a three-year program that would take two years to fully implement. In the final year, PE's role would be reduced. During the first two years, Project Equality staff people would provide direct services by traveling to the headquarters in Indianapolis, Indiana. PE staff would also travel to any national units not in Indiana, if needed. To develop a comprehensive EEO program for the Christian Church, PE determined this would require thirty-two days of work from national PE staff and thirty-two days of work from local PE staff. Of course, these thirty-two days of work were not consecutive and would be scheduled over the course of the two years. Specifically, of the total thirty-two days required of the national PE staff, PE expected that it would take ten workdays to develop the EEO program. The remaining work days would comprise semi-annual reviews of the headquarters and other units to ensure the EEO program was being implemented. In addition to creating a comprehensive EEO program for the denomination, PE also developed a system to monitor the denomination's process for contracting suppliers of goods and services. PE would generate materials specific to the Christian Church set up a program to track information related to suppliers of goods and services, organize and hold meetings to disseminate equal employment information to suppliers, and research the denomination's investments. PE estimated this would take thirty-six work days on the part of PE national staff and fourteen work days on the part of local PE staff. The program that PE laid out for the Christian Church served as a model for PE's work across the country.

The PE program was not a quick fix, and change transpired over years. The goal was that PE would provide businesses the tools they needed to learn first what equal employment opportunity meant and then how to align their workplace policies and procedures. In the model PE set up for the Christian Church, by the third year PE's role had decreased, because by that time PE would have fully trained church staff to do their own compliance reviews, which would then be submitted to PE for evaluation and revision. Continued work resulted in incremental change.

Although Project Equality started out as a Catholic social action program it grew into an interreligious program, and PE leaders purposefully invited the participation of people of faith from Protestant and Jewish religious backgrounds, urging them to use their immense buying power for economic justice. Businesses or organizations that went through the PE program, such as the Christian Church and national airlines, hotels, and restaurant chains, as well as other businesses were then included in PE's *Buyer's Guide*. The *Buyer's Guide* could be described as a compendium, a yellow pages of sorts, of companies across the nation committed to equal employment opportunity. PE encouraged constituents to consult the *Buyer's Guide* first when purchasing goods or services. National businesses certified with the national office, while on the local level, smaller businesses and firms could be included if they affirmed fair employment practices and certified this with a local office. In short, the national popularity and reach of the *Buyer's Guide*, coupled with the buying power of people of faith across the nation, second only to that of the federal government, made it such that no company wanted to be left out of the annual publication. Nationally, thirty million people of faith affiliated with PE through their religious organizations had access to the *Guide*, and by 1970, Project Equality had twenty local offices in urban areas across the nation. The Wisconsin office, with its headquarters in Milwaukee, provided an opening for Black women to take the lead in matters of economic justice. Seeing PE as an extension of civil rights activism in the city, the PE-W board of directors hired experienced civil rights activist Helen I. Barnhill as PE-W's inaugural executive director in 1970.

Laying the Foundation: The First Executive Director of Project Equality Wisconsin, Helen I. Barnhill

Helen I. Barnhill served as Project Equality Wisconsin's first executive director. Considering Barnhill's background provides some insight into her interest in working for civil rights and economic justice, especially through a religious organization. Born on November 10, 1937, to Willie and Faustana Ponds in Ponce de Leon, Florida, Helen Iphigenia Ponds moved with her family to Milwaukee in 1947. With this migration, the Ponds family joined the growing number of African Americans who moved to the city during the second great migration. Like the many Black migrants who settled in Milwaukee, the Ponds family resided on the city's north side. Helen's father, Willie, served as a deacon at Mount Zion Baptist Church, one of the well-known churches in Milwaukee's Bronzeville that had experienced a membership and financial boom due to the prosperity of the city during World War II.[6] Helen attended North Division High School and eventually received a degree from Marquette University. Helen married Ernest Barnhill in her twenties. Together, they had seven children. The marriage did not last, and they divorced in 1967 when Helen was twenty-nine. Helen Barnhill raised her children on her own while actively participating in racial justice causes, which sometimes became her full-time job.

As discussed in previous chapters, Black activists in Milwaukee had been organizing for several decades to push for equal housing and fair employment, especially as the Black population increased. By the 1960s, like many places around the country, this organizing reached a high point. In Milwaukee, the NAACP Youth Council, advised by white Catholic priest Father James Groppi, planned and carried out demonstrations related to fair housing. In addition to the Youth Council, several other groups existed that focused on other areas. For example, Helen Barnhill joined and became executive secretary of a group called the Milwaukee Citizens for Equal Opportunity (MCEO). Organized in November 1960, one of MCEO's original interests included supporting civil rights campaigns in the South. The organization raised money for school integration in New Orleans, Louisiana, and for evicted tenant farmers in Fayette County, Tennessee. In addition to supporting these local southern campaigns, MCEO also circulated a petition to send to President John F. Kennedy to "urge his strongest support to school integration in all states."[7] MCEO was also affiliated with the Foundation for Freedom and Democracy in Community Life, which had been founded in Illinois in 1964.[8] The same year activists organized MCEO in Milwaukee, fair housing advocates in Illinois organized the United Citizens' Committee for Freedom of Residence in Illinois to work on fair housing across the state.

Unable to ignore housing inequality in Milwaukee, MCEO began to focus on fair housing. In cooperation with the local Citizens Committee for Fair Housing Practices, the MCEO circulated "Good Neighbor Pledges" and in 1962 and 1963 published the list of those who had taken the pledge in the major local white paper, the *Milwaukee Journal*. Helen Barnhill actively participated in the organization's free housing referral service and after exposing the difficulties of finding quality, affordable housing, realized that the only way Black residents would be able to find housing on a nondiscriminatory basis was if there was a law in place. As a result, the organization turned its attention to supporting efforts for a state fair housing law.

With Helen Barnhill still in the position of executive secretary, MCEO also supported the activities of the Milwaukee United for School Integration Committee (MUSIC), which led efforts to integrate Milwaukee's public school system. In 1964 and 1965, MUSIC protested school segregation and organized school boycotts.[9] Participating families sent their children to the Freedom School MUSIC organized where students learned Black history in addition to mathematics, science, art, and music.[10] Excerpts of MUSIC's Freedom School curriculum found in the MCEO records, which were compiled and donated to the Wisconsin Historical Society by Helen Barnhill, suggest a relationship between the two organizations and that Helen

Barnhill was, most likely, the connective tissue. In addition to the MCEO, Barnhill had also worked with the Milwaukee Urban League as a counselor. In this position, she assisted working class families with their housing needs.

Barnhill's work with MCEO and the Urban League led to a job as the state coordinator of Housing and Public Accommodations with the Wisconsin Equal Rights Division where she investigated instances of housing discrimination. After the passage of a citywide fair housing ordinance in 1968 as the culmination of protests in the city and Dr. Martin Luther King Jr.'s assassination, Barnhill's work with the Equal Rights Division seemed to be a step in the process of making fair housing a reality in the city and the state. However, after a short time at the state agency, Barnhill thought the agency "changed for the worse."[11] Barnhill noted that the state's conservative legislature made efforts to enact housing equality virtually impossible.[12] Even though Barnhill knew that a conservative majority existed in the Wisconsin state legislature, she did not think these politicians represented the views of the state's population. However, Milwaukee's reputation as the "Selma of the North" tells a different story of the city and the state's readiness for racial equality. Having participated in Milwaukee's civil rights movement, once handling the bail fund for arrested protestors and witnessing the viciousness of counterdemonstrators' response to activists' demands for fair housing, Barnhill knew that the state had a long way to go, and her work with state agency further confirmed this reality.[13] While working for the state, Barnhill saw beyond the façade of the state's liberalism and experienced firsthand politicians' insensitivity to poor people, as evidenced by their response to welfare rights activists described in the previous chapter.[14] Barnhill described the legislature's attitude toward anyone working for equality in the state as "automatically hostile."[15] Unable to make progress or contribute in the way she desired, Barnhill resigned her position with the state.

While Barnhill worked at the Equal Rights Division, she and other activists in the city were considering bringing Project Equality to the state and headquartering it in Milwaukee, because it was Wisconsin's largest city.[16] The city's major newspapers reported Project

Equality's successes. For example, an article described the program in Detroit, noting that in one year alone, 550 people obtained employment, ranging from skilled labor positions to management positions, as a result of the work of PE.[17] The Milwaukee newspapers' reporting of Detroit's success with PE inspired Milwaukee activists to open an office in the state. In April 1970, the Wisconsin office of Project Equality opened with Helen I. Barnhill as its first executive director.[18]

Barnhill laid the foundation for PE-W. Although the executive director answered to a board of directors, she set the agenda for and culture of the local office. The executive director was responsible for guiding the daily activities of the office, representing PE-W on the local, regional, and national level, as well as developing and offering affirmative action training workshops and raising funds. Most importantly, before PE hired a separate position to undertake compliance reviews, the executive director played a large role in determining whether companies were making sufficient progress toward their affirmative action goals. The results of these compliance reviews determined whether companies would be included in the national annual *Buyer's Guide* and the Wisconsin supplement. Compliance reviews took two forms: the desk audit and the site visit. With the desk audit, companies sent Project Equality the necessary documents that would allow the organization to determine whether the company was equal employment opportunity compliant. The many documents included the company's

> affirmative action plan, including goals and timetables; work force report, which breaks down the total number of employees by race, sex, and job level; log of applicants; equal employment opportunity policy statement; list of resources used for hiring; copies of tests used; job application forms; purchasing policy; advertising materials; employee handbooks; union contracts; benefit statements; and any other items the company feels have relevance to their total EEO stance.[19]

If the results of the desk audit uncovered major areas of noncompliance, then a site visit would be scheduled to develop a plan of action. The PE compliance review officer met with the owner of the company if it were a small business, or executive management if it were a larger firm. After the site visit, PE made explicit recommendations and provided the company with a timeline for achieving the recommendations. This back-and-forth process took a long time and generated much paperwork that PE staff painstakingly poured over. Upon committing to PE recommendations, the company could then be listed in the *Buyer's Guide*.

As mentioned earlier, the *Buyer's Guide* was PE's ultimate tool in encouraging people of faith to push for affirmative action through their consumer choices. Samuel Wong, associate executive secretary of the United Methodist Church's Commission on Religion and Race, wrote, "if buyers are intentional about equality, they will examine the employment practices of their suppliers and do business with firms that share their commitment to equal employment practices."[20] Wong continued, "equality is everybody's business," noting that consumers could make their "mission follow [their] money" by writing to their suppliers to request they participate in Project Equality. After participating in the compliance process, they could join the thousands of businesses nationwide in the *Buyer's Guide*, which would then be sent to over two dozen religious denominations representing thirty million members.[21]

On the state and local level, Project Equality staffers developed relationships with religious organizations. Because Project Equality was a nonprofit organization, it had to fundraise its operating costs. It did not charge for any of its services and instead asked religious organizations to make donations to support its work. These funds formed the majority of the state office's operating budget. In the case of Project Equality Wisconsin, much of the responsibility of encouraging religious organizations to support PE fell on the shoulders of the executive director. An example of the work of the fundraising process can be seen in Helen Barnhill's actions to develop a relationship with the Milwaukee YWCA, the organization that was the focus of Chapter 1.

The MYWCA had made some progressive strides in interracial relations in its early history, but by the mid-twentieth century, the organization regressed by forcibly integrating its programs and driving all of its Black staff to resign, leading to a drastic reduction in Black volunteer and community participation. Despite this, some Black women still saw the potential of the MYWCA and continued to serve on its board. This led to the MYWCA membership electing Hazel Maxwell as the first Black woman president of the board of directors in 1968. This was also the same year the local Black press blasted the organization with a headline "YWCA Still Jim Crow" and a scathing article that critiqued the MYWCA's past and present practices as it related to Black Milwaukeeans.[22] Black Y women pushed the MYWCA to be more relevant, spearheading a local conference and connecting the MYWCA to the national Y's history-making 1970 mandate to eliminate racism wherever it existed in the organization. Part of taking this national mandate to heart meant addressing the systematic employment inequality in the organization. As a result, in 1971 the MYWCA began a partnership with Project Equality Wisconsin.

Helen Barnhill attended the January 1971 MYWCA board of directors meeting where she provided an overview of Project Equality, its goals, and how the MYWCA could get involved with the work of the organization, specifically through an annual donation. During the meeting, the MYWCA board of directors voted to donate to Project Equality, but they also saw another opportunity. In a subsequent board of directors meeting, the board decided to enlist the services of PE by inviting the organization to participate in a process they called an Action Audit.[23] The Action Audit was the MYWCA's way of taking stock of how racism had infiltrated the very structure of the organization and developing a plan to eradicate it. The MYWCA enlisted the help of individual and organizational consultants to do this work, including Helen Barnhill in her position as executive director of Project Equality. Participating in the MYWCA's Action Audit meant carrying out PE's desk audit of the MYWCA's employment policy and procedures and helping the organization move toward equal employment. This also meant that PE's executive director would work with the organization to train internal MYWCA auditors who would continue to monitor the organization's progress. This was an ongoing process that continued for several years.[24] The MYWCA board of directors and PE both saw this partnership as a crucial step in aligning the MYWCA with the national Y's One Imperative mandate to eliminate racism.[25] As a result of the Action Audit, the MYWCA stepped up its fundraising in an effort to open a new center on Milwaukee's predominantly Black north side, which Black Y staffers and volunteers had been demanding for several years. Additionally, the diversity of the MYWCA staff and board of directors increased, with the executive director reporting that the organization had hired more people of color. Of the MYWCA's nine professional staff members, nearly half were people of color, including three Black staff members and one Chinese staff member. The board of directors went from one or two Black members to nine Black members and one Native American member.[26] PE continued to work with MYWCA and listed the organization in the Wisconsin supplement of the annual *Buyer's Guide*.

PE and the Madison Public School System

The same year that Helen Barnhill attended the MYWCA board meeting to introduce its members to PE she, along with members of PE-W's board of directors, began to engage the Madison Public School system. It took two years for the school system to sign a one-year contract that would allow PE to begin its work. Unpacking the process that occurred over these two years reveals the work of the local PE-W office and the time it took, even when an organization committed itself to and was not opposed to equal opportunity employment.

Prior to PE-W coming on board, George Shands, a social studies teacher at East High School in Madison, Wisconsin, and also a board member of PE-W, devised a project for his students to investigate the Madison Public School system. They focused their research on MPS policies on hiring, purchasing, and construction contracts, concluded that MPS policies regarding affirmative action could be "strengthened," and contacted the Equal Opportunities Commission. After informing the students that the office was interested but busy working with the City of Madison on its affirmative action programs, the EOC recommended Helen Barnhill and Project Equality. After months of conversations and meetings, in July 1972 the MPS School Board approved the implementation of an affirmative action plan. Several months later, in February of 1973, the board selected Project Equality to develop the program.[27]

In the process of coming to an agreement with Project Equality, the Madison Public School system had to come to terms with the structural discrimination that was exposed by Shands and his students. The agreement between MPS and Project Equality explicitly stated MPS' shortfalls. Although MPS had a generic commitment, via a written policy, to equal opportunity in employment, the policy's implementation had not resulted in "significant numbers of minority and women employees throughout all levels of the school system."[28] PE found this typically to be the case with most businesses and organizations who crafted unspecific policies to comply with the federal legislation but then put no money, resources, or procedures behind policy enforcement. As a result of MPS and PE's partnership, PE suggested policy changes and designed procedures for the implementation of equal opportunity policy. PE also agreed to train MPS employees on equal employment policy and procedure as well as lead workshops on the topic. In terms of the contracts MPS held with external suppliers, PE suggested the school system review the current contracts to determine if the suppliers that MPS hired had equal employment practices.[29] Over the next year, the PE office helped MPS revise its policy, write up procedures, disseminate this knowledge to its staff, and implement an affirmative action program. An early draft of the contract stipulated that PE staff would go to Madison two days per week for the first month for direct work with school officials. After that first month, PE professional staff would spend up to two days a week working with either school officials or with suppliers. After discussion, PE and MPS decided that PE professional staff would come to Madison once a week for the first three months of the contract and then once every other week. In 1975, the funds ran dry and MPS concluded its formal consulting relationship with PE, which meant detailed updates on the school district ceased in PE-W records, although it is clear that MPS remained a PE partner because it continued to be listed in the national *Buyer's Guide*.[30]

FIGURE 12. Helen Barnhill. 1973. Photographer: Joel Barkin ©
Milwaukee Journal Sentinel - USA Today Network

Helen Barnhill worked as PE-W's executive director for three years. Although her time with the organization was short, during those three years she built the reputation of the organization and made it one that both people of faith and businesses trusted. Its reputation as friendly and approachable came from her hard work. In addition to meeting individually with businesses and organizations, as illustrated by the examples above, Barnhill also opened an Employers Information and Complaint Center out of the PE office where company representatives could walk in and get their compliance questions answered.[31] Barnhill's early work helped define PE and its offices as an educational space where businesses and employers could get the training and feedback they needed to do the continual work of making their workplaces fair and equal. This was a learning process in which PE invested human and administrative resources. In the PE newsletter that announced Barnhill's departure, the organization described the tremendous loss the nonprofit organization would feel because of Barnhill's departure.[32] Barnhill left to start her own private equal employment opportunity firm. Recognizing the tremendous need of these services in the city and the state, and desirous of her own economic independence, Barnhill turned to entrepreneurship. True to her commitment to fair employment, Barnhill pledged her firm to equal employment opportunity, and it was listed in the Wisconsin supplement of the national *Buyer's Guide*.

Betty Thompson: Messenger of Employment Opportunity

After Barnhill's departure, previous deputy director John R. Maurice served as executive director and left after one year. PE's board of directors promoted deputy director Betty Jean Thompson to executive director. Although Thompson's path to leading PE-W was anything but predictable, many of her personal life experiences prepared her to be an effective equal employment opportunity messenger.

Betty Jean Thompson was born on January 5, 1939, in Shreveport, Louisiana. Because she moved to Milwaukee, Wisconsin, when she was very young, many thought she was a native-born Milwaukeean. She also grew up on Milwaukee's segregated north side. Often, Thompson described the poverty she experienced as a youngster and the shame she felt living in what she described as "the worst house on the block."[33] Her experiences growing up poor served as the impetus for her life's mission, which she devoted to not only serving others, but also in the struggle for freedom and justice. Thompson believed "that the truest act of courage, the deepest act of humanness is to give of ourselves for others in a totally caring, non-violent struggle for equality and justice."[34] After graduating from North Division High School, Thompson devoted her life to this mission. Thompson's educational, employment, and activist experiences shaped her, and she privileged learning from her community, which influenced her vision of economic justice.

Thompson's decision not to pursue a college degree illuminates the value she placed on knowledge not gained in the pursuit of formal degrees, but that came from her community and her positionality as a poor Black woman growing up in Milwaukee. After her father died when she was seven, Thompson's mother raised her and her five siblings alone. Her mother was Thompson's role model, and she watched her struggle to feed, clothe, and raise six children. This greatly affected Thompson and contributed to her commitment to spend her life working on behalf of the Black community. Thompson never received a degree from a four-year college, and this was something that she adamantly spoke about. In an interview she unapologetically stated, "I didn't really want a college degree. . . . When I went to meetings with people who had degrees, I found that they might know one subject, but when it came to the problems of the community, I knew more than they did."[35] Although Thompson did not attend college, she did eventually obtain a degree from Spencerian Business College, a postsecondary vocational school. She also considered herself an "eternal learner," always enrolling in seminars, classes, and workshops to build her skills, awareness, and knowledge.

Before working at Project Equality, Thompson's previous jobs taught her about employment discrimination firsthand and gave her needed experience working with nonprofit community organizations. For example, at first, Northwestern Mutual Life Insurance Company refused to hire her because of her race. According to the company, they had just hired two other Black employees and as a result were not interested in hiring her, despite her qualifications, ability to do the job, and the open position for which they had posted an announcement. Thompson went to Virginia Huebner, the well-known director of the Equal Rights Division of the Wisconsin Industrial Commission and told her of her experience of blatant employment discrimination. Within a day of talking with Huebner, Thompson had a job at Northwestern Mutual. Other Black workers, however, were not so successful in their employment pursuits and this bothered Thompson. After working in the corporate world, she applied the business skills she gained at Northwestern Mutual to the position she had working on the problem of juvenile delinquency at the Milwaukee Council on Urban Life.

In addition to her educational and employment experiences, Betty Thompson's participation in the welfare rights movement also influenced her ideas about economic justice. While it is unclear whether Betty Thompson took on a formal leadership role in the Milwaukee welfare rights movement, she did participate in welfare rights marches. During these marches, she was exposed to the ideas and strategies of welfare rights activists, which contributed to her vision for economic justice. Welfare rights activists used civil rights and Black feminist pedagogies such as consciousness-raising and personal testimonies to encourage people to become active in the struggle for economic justice. Betty Thompson's educational and employment experiences coupled with her welfare rights activism provided a strong foundation for her ideas about economic justice, ideas that would evolve as she took on the mantle of leadership at Project Equality and as she articulated that economic equality would not come overnight.

After working at PE as deputy director for one year, the board of directors promoted Betty Thompson to executive director of the organization, and in this leadership position, Thompson had the opportunity to put her beliefs about economic justice into practice. It was in this position that she connected her faith tradition, Catholicism, to the social justice imperative she felt for her life. She often referred to Project Equality as her "ministry" and her way of helping to change the world.

As discussed earlier, the work of Project Equality was highly administrative and interactive. The review process and onsite visit consisted of various types of audits. The executive director participated in the onsite visit, during which PE officials met with supervisors, management, and employees to determine what recommendations to make regarding the company's progress toward affirmative action. Thompson described the nature of the site visit: "We do a walk-through, and we randomly stop and talk to employees. Sometimes, we see minority people who have different titles or duties than what we were told. And it's not just about hiring, either. It's about how they relate to their employees."[36] After the site visit, PE would draft a confidential report with its recommended next steps and work closely with the company on implementation. PE undertook the compliance process annually for the seven hundred businesses registered with the organization. Mostly the compliance process entailed PE receiving and analyzing the completed employment forms. Because of the small staff in the Milwaukee office, the office only had the time to visit a dozen or so offices each quarter. In addition to participating in the audit process, which required Thompson to analyze and consider whether a business was affirmative action compliant, Thompson also consistently wrote for PE-W's newsletter.

Teaching the Lessons of Economic Justice: Betty Thompson's Epistolary Reflections

In addition to her other administrative duties, Betty Thompson contributed a regular column to PE-W's quarterly newsletter. Titled "Letter from the Executive Director," the column summarized the activities of the organization, but it did much more. Betty Thompson educated her broad religious public, which included Catholic and Protestant Christians, as well as people of Jewish faith. Although Betty Thompson never publicly identified herself as a feminist, she used feminist pedagogies of consciousness-raising and storytelling in her intellectual work as a writer for PE's newsletter.

In her newsletter column, Thompson sought to raise the religious consciousness of her constituents. This meant encouraging religious folk to connect their spiritual beliefs to justice, particularly economic justice. Thompson was clear about this:

> No longer can we, as religious and as concerned citizens, continue to be concerned only with the spiritual life, and separate ourselves from the political areas in which we live. We must continue to work toward eliminating the injustices and inequities in all forms that in turn contribute to poverty in our country and throughout the world today. One out of six workers in the minority community is without a job today. . . . The jobs denied to so many of the minorities and women could be passports to some of the noble achievements in life—like a home, a stable family, education, health, a basic interest in life, above all, HOPE.[37]

She was careful to not single out any one religious tradition, but she did admonish PE constituents to more actively connect their spirituality with social activism. According to Thompson, PE "has never faced a greater challenge to make the scriptures real than it does today. Its program has never been more relevant nor more challenging."[38] Thompson believed that it was the task of religious communities to "serve as catalytic agent[s] in our fearfully secular society to the end that a positive change" could happen. Indeed, in one letter Thompson adamantly stated,

> YOU and I can make PE the "leaven" which leavens out our society so that life can have meaning and purpose for all citizens, at home and abroad—Jew and Gentile, Catholic, and Protestant, Black, Brown, Red, White, Yellow. Humankind now has the opportunity of our lifetime to make a responsible impact on our Society in the name of our moral commitment. ARE WE ABLE? ARE WE WILLING?[39]

Thompson wanted PE constituents to "recapture the revolutionary spirit and go out into a sometimes-hostile world declaring eternal hostility to poverty, racism, and sexism." Thompson knew that rekindling this revolutionary spirit, which hearkened back to her earlier activism and the freedom movements of the 1960s, could have precarious consequences. Abuse, scorn, and losing a job could be probable outcomes in standing up for truth and justice. In fact, Thompson described herself as being naïve because she "never thought someone would want to murder [her] because [she worked] for civil rights."[40] Despite death threats, Thompson felt that her own personal troubles did not compare to the situation for most Black people in US society who, Thompson stated, "have freedom without finance, and access without assets," which "are tantamount to existence without equity."[41] Thompson tried to persuade religious folk to live out the convictions of their faith.

In her column, Thompson also tried to teach the lesson that although the marches and protests of the civil rights movement had ended, the work continued. In the post–civil rights moment that she lived in, this meant informing people that despite local and national civil rights victories, people of color still faced discrimination and inequality. "Many persons," stated Thompson, "have looked at the success of the Civil Rights Movement and have concluded that the problem has been solved." Thompson "heard it said by many that if minorities are no longer marching, the problems must have been solved."[42] In several of her letters, Thompson consistently reminded her readers that economic justice had not been achieved and it was their spiritual responsibility to continue the fight.

Thompson also articulated her beliefs about racial equality and economic justice, which she made known the moment she became executive director. In the PE newsletter announcing her as the new executive director, she stated, "Employment opportunity for all minorities is one of the principle starting points in the struggle for liberation from oppression."[43] She put this belief into action when she hired a Black mother through the Wisconsin Work Incentive Program (WIN). WIN was a highly controversial federal program and required those who received Aid to Families with Dependent Children (AFDC) to register for training and work opportunities that would, hopefully, decrease their dependency on state support. Through the WIN program, Thompson hired Linda Peterson in 1973 and provided her with on-the-job training. Beginning as the office secretary, by the time Peterson left PE in 1977, she had been promoted to the role of office manager. Betty Thompson's vision for economic justice meant that anyone was employable, and that people could be taught the skills they needed to be successful. While Linda Peterson might have been considered a risk by other employers because of her lack of experience, Betty Thompson saw possibility. In addition to hiring and training Linda Peterson, Thompson also hired and trained two teenagers because even though they did not have the skills to do office work, "she knew they could learn, and she set about to teach them."[44] Thompson felt confident about this method because she remembered her own experience: "At one time I was unqualified, too, to do the things that I was asked to do, but I was not unqualifiable, and I had opportunities to prove that."[45] Thompson used her ministry as a PE worker as a site of revolutionary religious resistance by not only writing about these issues, but also speaking publicly about them and creating spaces of economic possibility for those who had been traditionally excluded.

In addition to teaching plainly about the connections between one's spiritual beliefs and economic justice, Thompson also employed a "feminist politics of emotions" where she publicly acknowledged both the emotional labor required to constantly struggle for economic justice and the emotional toll of continued economic oppression. Megan Boler defines a "feminist politics of emotion"

> as a theory and a practice that invites women to articulate and publicly name their emotions, and to critically and collectively analyze these emotions not as "natural," "private," occurrences but rather as reflecting learned hierarchies and gendered roles. The feminist practices of consciousness-raising and feminist pedagogy powerfully reclaim emotions out of the (patriarchically enforced) private sphere and put emotions on the political and public map. Feminist politics of emotions recognize emotions not only as a site of control, but of political resistance.[46]

Several aspects of Boler's definition resonate with Betty Thompson's intellectual practices. In an environment in which the consequences of bringing emotions into the public sphere were negative and where Black women were typically stereotyped as ever angry, Thompson took a risk writing about her disappointment and frustration at the

FIGURE 13. Project Equality Wisconsin staff in 1978. Left to right: Charlene Faiola, Betty Thompson, and Linda Peterson. Image courtesy of Project Equality of Wisconsin Records, Department of Special Collections and University Archives, Marquette University Libraries

pace of social change. Years after the civil rights movement, "the clock seems to be turning back," she lamented.[47] Thompson also spoke of the pain of her activism. In an interview with journalist Sue Burke, Thompson admitted that "it can be hard . . . to deal with racism every day." "Sometimes," Thompson stated, "I have to laugh to keep from crying."[48] Dealing with racism everyday was even more difficult when it came from fellow believers, but in the executive director position Thompson realized that engaging with religious employers was often harder than engaging with secular employers. Thompson did her best to "accept them where they're at," even though she "didn't realize how far behind many members are."[49] Thompson refused to ignore the role emotions played in the struggle for freedom; dealing with emotions was a crucial aspect of the labor she engaged in as an activist.

In fact, Thompson stated plainly in one of her letters the "need to deal with each person as a unique individual with feelings." In doing so she continued, "PE's job more and more is to try and deal with these feelings by being sensitive, by accepting each person where they are (not where we wish them they were) and further explaining what it means to be in compliance with affirmative action guidelines."[50] But this was often emotionally laborious work. Thompson spoke of the response she often received when presenting about Project Equality from ordinary Catholic lay members. Thompson recalled an experience she had at a church where she was speaking. One of the members "stood up and challenged her about 'nigras' and carried on with stereotyped descriptions and epithets."[51] Thompson responded to these comments by continuing to educate, "by showing what hurts and what works," and by being honest about the emotional toll of the work.

In addition to engaging in a feminist politics of emotions, in her column Thompson also emphasized the importance of recognizing and celebrating difference, an important Black feminist principle. According to Black, lesbian, mother, warrior, poet Audre Lorde, "Change means growth, and growth can be painful. But we sharpen self-definition by exposing the self in work and struggle together with those whom we define as different from ourselves, although sharing the same goals. For Black and white, old and young, lesbian and heterosexual women alike, this can mean new paths to our survival."[52] Thompson put this principle into action on a continual basis, both in her writing and in her role as executive director. For example, planning the annual meeting was typically the responsibility of the executive director. Thompson's stated goal for this event was to "bring people together who might not otherwise come together—people from all religious denominations and ethnic groups, who will dine together, be entertained together and be informed together."[53] Thompson thought people could learn from each other and in turn work together to change society. She noted this when she wrote, "Perhaps we need to emphasize the need for offsetting old practices with new programs of learning. Increased knowledge and personal contact with individuals different from ourselves serve to improve many of the conditions of a racist society."[54] While Thompson was not implying that only individual, personal relationships would change the inherently racist structure of US society, she was noting the importance of engaging on the personal level when trying to change people's minds about difference. The purpose, according to Thompson, of engaging on the individual level, was to "see race, sex, cultural and religious difference in America's society with true perception, awareness, sensitivity, and appreciation."[55] Acknowledging, appreciating, and using difference to make change was an important tool in uniting various people of faith in the struggle for economic justice and societal change.

Addressing the Reversal of Civil Rights Gains: The Impetus for the National Interreligious Commission on Civil Rights

By the early 1980s, Black people who lived in Milwaukee faced a devastating economic situation. Continued migration during the 1950s and 1960s coupled with the decimation of the former Bronzeville neighborhood due to the construction of Highway 43, forced Black Milwaukeeans to spread north and westward. Urban historian Marc Levine summed up the decade: "Without question, the 1980s—when deindustrialization hit Milwaukee with full force and unemployment surged—was a decade nothing short of economically devastating for Milwaukee's inner city."[56] Black people experienced higher levels of unemployment compared to other groups. Levine, however, explains that while unemployment numbers are important to consider, more important to consider was "labor market exclusion," which he defines as "the proportion of the working age population (over 16 years old) that is either unemployed or not in the civilian labor force (in school, not looking for work, disabled, or in prison)." Take, for example, the unemployment rate (percentage of the civilian labor force unemployed) in the Hillside/Lapham neighborhood, which was within the boundaries of the former Bronzeville neighborhood. In 1970, the unemployment rate was 7.6 percent. By 1980, the rate jumped to 23.8 percent because of the loss of manufacturing jobs in the city. When compared to figures for the city of Milwaukee as a whole, one can see quite easily the devastating effects of deindustrialization. In the city of Milwaukee as a whole, the unemployment rate was 4.1 percent in 1970. It grew to 6.9 percent in 1980.[57] While the difference between the unemployment rate for Hillside/Lapham and the city of Milwaukee was stark, the figures for labor market exclusion provide additional context. For the city of Milwaukee, labor market exclusion was 40.7 percent in 1970; it was 41.2 percent for 1980.[58] In the Hillside/Lapham neighborhood, labor market exclusion was 65.3 percent in 1970 and 70.7 percent in 1980.[59] These figures show that even in 1970, residents in this neighborhood faced economic distress due to higher levels of labor market exclusion.

With the country in a recession, the reversal of some of the advances that had come because of the civil rights era, and local Black workers facing unprecedented levels of labor market exclusion, Thompson could either be discouraged or she could continue working for economic justice. Thompson chose to continue by leading the efforts toward the creation of the National Interreligious Commission on Civil Rights (NICCR) in 1984.

Betty Thompson saw the need for a national independent civil rights commission after witnessing the disintegration of the US Commission on Civil Rights under the administration of President Ronald Reagan. In a 1983 newsletter, Betty Thompson wrote, "Minorities and other protected classes can no longer put their trust in a system that continues to sidetrack justice issues and refuses to meet basic human rights."[60] In this statement, Thompson made explicit her distrust in the US Commission on Civil Rights, which was originally created in 1957 as a bipartisan and independent commission tasked with investigating, reporting, and making recommendations on issues related to civil rights. By the early 1980s, President Reagan had succeeded in pushing the commission in a conservative direction. He appointed Clarence Pendleton Jr., who was the first African American chair of the commission but who also opposed affirmative action and used his position as chair to decrease the staff and work of the commission. Several civil rights organizations outwardly criticized Pendleton and the eight-member commission, stating "that a majority of the Civil Rights Commission has become public advocates against the remedies for discrimination."[61] Mainstream newspapers published editorials and articles condemning the disintegration of the commission. The *New York Times* was particularly harsh:

> For a generation, the United States Commission on Civil Rights has served as something like a rooster, trying to waken the nation to racial discrimination and the need to extend equal protection to all citizens. Small and lacking enforcement power, the commission relied on its voice. It gathered and presented solid evidence of discrimination, prodding Presidents and Congress to bring equal opportunity closer to reality. Sadly, however, the commission is now becoming a parrot.[62]

According to the *New York Times* editorial, whereas the Commission had in the past been an independent body, as it was newly constituted, it had begun to "parrot" the conservative views of President Reagan and his administration.

The conservative direction of the US Commission on Civil Rights had a direct impact on the local level and the work of civil rights organizations, and this is what prompted Betty Thompson to spearhead the creation of a new organization to carry out the work of the commission. On January 25, 1984, Thompson brought together Catholic, Protestant, and Jewish leaders, and together they formed the Interreligious Emergency Task Force on Civil Rights with a stated goal "to address its urgent concern regarding the reconstituted United States Civil Rights Commission and deteriorating climate for civil rights in this country."[63] Together, taskforce members convened the National Interreligious Commission on Civil Rights with the following agenda:

> Conduct hearings throughout the United States on the status of civil rights. Develop, based upon the testimony of the hearings, a formal

statement addressing the need for efforts to protect and enhance civil rights in the United States. Reaffirm that the religious leadership of the United States continues to be a strong and active witness in the area of civil rights enforcement.[64]

On March 28, 1984, the NICCR sponsored the first of its local hearings in Milwaukee. Forty people testified to the ways they continued to experience discrimination in their lives. According to Loretta Williams, the NICCR chairperson, "The fact that people can document the injustices we heard about is impressive. . . . Much of the work we have done for about the past 30 years is being eroded."[65] Betty Thompson spoke to the need for hearing the stories of "grassroots people," stating that they "are many times overlooked when national polls and surveys are taken which impact their lives." Often, she continued, "data gathered quickly becomes statistical information aired nationally on the six-o'clock news. All with little or no input from the people the information is about."[66] Even though in the 1980s more Black people served in positions of power within the city government, the vast majority of Black Milwaukeeans struggled. The NICCR was a way to make sure the experiences of local people did not get silenced, erased, or downplayed. After the first hearing in Milwaukee, for which the official records are unavailable, subsequent hearings were held in Indianapolis, Indiana, in September 1984; in Kansas City, Missouri, in May 1986; in Montgomery, Alabama, in October 1986; and in Louisville, Kentucky, in 1988. The testimony and findings from the first four hearings were published in a report: *Dangerous Waters: Testimony, Findings, and Recommendations form the National Interreligious Commission on Civil Rights, Civil Rights Hearings 1984–1986*. The findings from the Louisville hearing were published in *A Tale of Two Cities: The Status of Civil Rights in Louisville* in 1988.[67]

At each of the hearings, residents from each of the cities testified before thirty volunteer commissioners about the problems they faced in "education, health, finance credit, insurance, the criminal justice system, employment, housing, and business development."[68] Testimony from Sister Ann Weller of Kokomo, Indiana, a small town about an hour north of Indianapolis, illuminated the precarious position of many working-class people:

> In most instances our neighborhood is not only not better off than it was four years ago, it is not as well off as it was twenty years ago. Some parents who are nearing fifty years old had maintenance and security jobs, and a few had foreman positions in the early 50s. They retired with thirty years of service and an adequate pension. Now they are supporting their grown children, many of whom have moved back home or due to unemployment found it impossible to leave in the first place.[69]

According to Weller, during the 1950s, some workers found quality work that allowed them to take care of their families and retire. However, this progress was not universal and did not last for even one generation as unemployment and poverty persisted. In her testimony, Veronica Pitts of Louisville explained her thoughts about the difference between being poor and living in poverty:

> Being poor and living in poverty has two different meanings for me. Poor meant wearing what was handed down from the largest to the smallest. Poor meant sharing a bed with two sisters instead of having one by yourself. Poor meant living in an apartment with twelve in four rooms. Yet poor meant working but still struggling. . . . As an adult raising my children in the world where poverty is a reality, I start out the gate three steps behind. Poverty is a work force where the job creates minimum wages and doesn't carry medical benefits. Poverty is illiteracy in a world that continues to advance. Poverty is displacement from an affordable housing system. . . . Poverty is also unemployment. It is also oppression. And poverty is most lethal when it takes over your mind and your life.[70]

For Pitts, living in poverty illuminated structural inequality: persistent inadequate employment, education, housing, and healthcare.

Testimony like Weller's and Pitt's provided direct evidence about the impact of the regression in civil rights, which the NICCR and its local commissioners hoped would prompt more involvement from the religious community. For example, Reverend William Clark, who was the president of the Urban League of Greater Kansas City, felt that the hearing would signal "the resurrection of the interreligious community, its reentry in civil rights where, for the most part it has been a non-participating observer since the death of Martin Luther King Jr.[71] Alvin Brooks, the Kansas City Human Rights director, agreed with Clark. "Hopefully," he said, "this will be the reactivation of the conscience of the broader religious community in a coalition of conscience that will begin to move us beyond where we are now."[72] While the goal of these hearings was to hear the stories of the people most affected by racism and discrimination, commissioners also hoped that hearing the testimonies would encourage the religious community to be at the forefront of the struggle for social justice. This is what Betty Thompson wished for when she conceived of the commission and she stated as much: "I feel this kind of effort by this religious commission is extremely important because people need to be made aware of possible change. . . . Although gains in civil rights are now on the books, efforts are underfoot to change them."[73]

Conclusion

While Betty Thompson continued her work with Project Equality, it is telling that she and others felt the need to create NICCR. The creation of NICCR signified two things. One, that activists saw that they could not rely solely on the state or the national government in the struggle for civil rights and economic justice. The government was not on the side of the people. Second, the creation of NICCR brought activists, in some ways, full circle, back to grassroots organizing as it related to social and economic justice.

When activists created Project Equality in the 1960s, there was the sense that the organization would exist parallel to the state and federal government's equal employment opportunity commissions and that these government organizations were committed to civil rights and equal employment opportunity. By the 1980s, conservatism, according to Project Equality leaders like Betty Thompson, both halted and reversed progress. Since the government was in part responsible for this retrenchment, the logical next step would be to put the focus back on grassroots solutions to economic inequality. Therefore, the NICCR hearings served to hear the problems from the people so that local organizations could respond creatively to their community's needs.

Betty Thompson continued her work with Project Equality into the early 2000s. Nationally, Project Equality continued until 2007, when waning support and interest led the national president and CEO Kirk Perucca to reorganize it into a national diversity summit. Project Equality's longevity as an organization focused on employment justice speaks to the points that employment inequality is both built into the fabric of business and government and continually morphing and reshaping itself. Understanding this idea was crucial to Betty Thompson's work, and she tried to explain to her white audiences how economic inequality manifested and why they were responsible for helping to eradicate it. Thompson's knowledge came from her own personal experiences of employment discrimination, from her participation in the welfare rights movement, and from her previous positions working in community organizations. She transmitted this knowledge in her epistolary contributions to PE's quarterly newsletters and as part of her leadership of the organization.

Project Equality as an equal employment opportunity organization ceased to exist, not because it solved the problem of employment injustice—to the contrary. In the early 2000s, the problem of employment injustice still existed, especially in Milwaukee where the manufacturing industry's demise had decimated working-class possibilities in the city. While Black women had dominated service industries during the city's manufacturing boom, after deindustrialization, Black people generally dominated service industries. While some Black professionals gained managerial or corporate positions, they remained minorities in their workplaces. Project Equality's work did result in more workers of color being hired in some industries, and in some companies, but without continued government commitment, it could only go so far.

Still, telling the story of Project Equality, especially by examining the work of Black women in Wisconsin, illustrates an important aspect of the struggle for employment injustice. PE-W workers began their work with a clear directive to dismantle the Jim Crow job system. Legally, Jim Crow had been outlawed, but in practice, there was much work to do. Helen Barnhill, and then Betty Thompson, did this work. The work continues.

Epilogue

Though PE ended soon after Betty Thompson's tenure as executive director, the economic and employment inequality Black Milwaukeeans faced continued. A report published by the University of Wisconsin–Milwaukee Center for Economic Development compared Milwaukee to other cities in the Frostbelt region of the United States.[1] The report found that between 1970 and 1990, Milwaukee's poverty rate doubled. The report also illustrated the connections between race and poverty, finding that by 1990, the poverty rate for African Americans had reached 41.2 percent, four times the rate experienced by white Milwaukeeans. As Milwaukee lost its industrial base—between 1970 and 2000, 80 percent of manufacturing jobs disappeared—low wage work replaced higher paid industrial jobs. During and after the 1980s, most new job growth occurred in low wage sectors. As a result of this, Milwaukee became one of the fastest growing low-wage cities in the nation, and life for Black Milwaukeeans continued to worsen.[2] By the early 2000s, Milwaukee ranked among the lowest in educational, employment, housing, and health outcomes for Black folks in the country.[3]

Despite the worsening economic conditions for Black people in Milwaukee, most Americans only know of Milwaukee as one of the most racially segregated cities in the nation.[4] Hidden but blatantly obvious is the fact that Milwaukee's racial segregation is and has always been intimately tied to an economic system that keeps Black people trapped in an unending cycle of poverty. Even though Black men joined the industrial labor force by mid-century, they had very little seniority compared to white men, and when manufacturing positions began to disappear, Black men were the first fired. As the economy transitioned to a service economy, low-wage service work employed a disproportionate number of women of color. Black women became over-represented as maids in hotels, cooks and cashiers in fast food establishments, and cleaners in office buildings—wages that, when full-time, barely add up to $20,000 annually.[5] In the 1990s, welfare reform pushed people off welfare, added a work requirement, and did so little to relieve urban poverty that by the early 2000s, nearly half of Milwaukee's Black households lived in extreme poverty.[6] Given the explosive civil rights movement in 1960s Milwaukee, how did life for African Americans get this bad? Current scholarship on Black Milwaukee has addressed this question by stating the obvious—racial and economic inequality persists.[7]

A Usable Past: History Catalyzes Economic Justice Activism

While inequality persists, Black women are revitalizing Milwaukee, particularly Bronzeville, the neighborhood where most Black Milwaukeeans resided before highway construction and incomplete urban renewal projects coupled with an increase in drugs and mass incarceration seriously deteriorated the community. By the 2000s, Black community members in Milwaukee began to remember what life was like during the heyday of the Bronzeville community. Community member and organizer Sharon Adams, who grew up in Bronzeville, described a loss of purpose and hope as unemployment and poverty soared among Black Milwaukeeans. A neighborhood where people once sat on their porches chatting and looking out for one another became a gang, gun, and drug battleground. Ironically, this neighborhood was renamed Lindsay Heights in honor of Bernice Lindsay, the former MYWCA worker and community-change agent considered the "mother of the Black community."

In 2000, Sharon Adams, along with her husband Larry, established the Walnut Way Conservation Corporation (WWCC), a multidimensional organization with a mission "to sustain economically diverse and abundant communities through civic engagement, environmental stewardship, and creating venues for prosperity."[8] After they formed the nonprofit, many in the neighborhood joined forces with the Adams, and together they are transforming Lindsay Heights through the WWCC's eight strategic areas: housing, education, youth & family activities, public safety, health & wellness, healthy food access, life-long learning, and commercial corridors. These strategies represent a holistic focus on the community's needs, an idea that was seeded from neighborhood members' dreams of what a thriving neighborhood could look like and be.

While transforming an entire community takes time, the WWCC has facilitated many changes in Lindsay Heights. Since much of the Lindsay Heights neighborhood was demolished for portions of a highway that never appeared, the WWCC works to turn vacant property into green space and community gardens. These initiatives coincide with their strategic areas relating to health and wellness as well as healthy food access. In addition to transforming vacant lots, the WWCC secured major funding from philanthropic entities and the federal government to rehabilitate older homes in the neighborhood and build new homes. These funds and this commitment to Lindsay Heights made it an area where people would want to live. In addition to its commitment to rebuilding the physical space and resources of Lindsay Heights, the WWCC has also sought to build up the community of residents who call Lindsay Heights their home and live, work, and play there, 25 percent of whom are unemployed and 48 percent of whom live below the poverty line and don't have a high school diploma.[9] In recent years, the WCCC has invested in community wealth building, turning its interest and focus on the physical revitalization of the neighborhood into Blue Skies Landscaping, a business that provides job training and employment for those who have faced employment barriers.[10]

Providing job training and opportunities highlights one area where community intellectualism plays out in the organization. The heart of WWCC's efforts mirrors Black women organizers like Mattie DeWese who started Pressley School of Beauty Culture and Betty Thompson of Project Equality Wisconsin who knew that access to fair and equal opportunity could make a world of difference. This was certainly true for one of Sharon and Larry Adams mentees, Danielle Washington, who recalled how the Adams provided opportunities through summer programs, employment, and participation in WWCC projects that enabled her to develop her interests and her voice. Another young person, X'zayvion McCoy, who interned with WWCC, spoke about the impact the Adams and the organization had on his life and thinking, noting Sharon "and Larry have taught me it's not just about one person—it's about family, friends and the community."[11]

Fueling WWCC's efforts is the knowledge of the past, memories of a thriving Bronzeville full of possibility, and their belief in a present and future where better outcomes are possible. The Walnut Way Conservation Corp is just one example of a modern-day community development effort rooted in social justice—racial, economic, and now, environmental. Run by neighborhood members and developed using the process of community intellectualism, its longstanding existence serves as a model for neighborhoods across the nation.

A final example of Black women's modern-day efforts rooted in economic justice and community intellectualism is the Bronzeville Collective MKE started by the Bronzeville Babes, Lilo Allen and Tiffany Miller, in 2016.[12] The Bronzeville Babes are artist-entrepreneurs who believe in the power of radical collaboration to transform lives and communities. The two artists met while vending their crafts at a festival. They realized that instead of paying booth or table rent individually, they could partner and split the costs, decreasing their expenses and maximizing their profits. After doing this several times, they wanted to make this opportunity available to other Black, Brown, and Queer artist-entrepreneurs, because of the economic barriers these creatives have historically faced. Separately, the two competed in and won two small business incubator competitions, which gave them the funds they needed to launch the collective and open a storefront in 2018 with fellow creators Tomira White and Jasmine Wyatt.[13]

The ethos of Bronzeville Collective is rooted in history, infused with economic justice, and powered by community intellectualism, all of which figures into how they run their business together. With a goal to empower other artist-entrepreneurs, they use a sliding scale to determine commissions. This allows the maker with even the smallest income to vend their crafts in the storefront. Smith and Miller have committed to passing on both the lessons they have learned as they have navigated their business journey and the history of the Bronzeville neighborhood where their showroom is located. They provide resources for emerging artist-entrepreneurs, including business coaching. Additionally, they teach business development to students in the Milwaukee Public School system, infusing these classes with the history of the Bronzeville neighborhood, highlighting Black business leaders like Ardie Halyard, the bank owner from Chapter 3 who also advocated on behalf of working women in the 1950s. Their efforts are an important example of the power of intentional collective action and what happens when everyone's contributions are expected, desired, and celebrated. In the beginning, the Bronzeville Collective was Smith and Miller's brainchild, but through intentional community building and partnerships, it has grown and become a space of radical economic and intellectual possibility.

I end this book with these two contemporary examples not to suggest that it is only the responsibility of Black grassroot organizations to transform their communities, but to highlight a lesson that Black women workers and organizers have taught us through their resistance to economic injustice: when neglected, tossed aside, and presented with seemingly insurmountable obstacles, they continue their struggle, working on multiple fronts. They engage with and urge the participation of members in their communities, encouraging them to use their voices, their stories, their words, their thoughts, and their actions to transform their environments. With their community-focused work, they apply pressure where they can to affect change. As this book ends, the lesson Black women activists teach us is that as long injustice persists, they will be "continually working."

Notes

INTRODUCTION

1. In 1997, historian Tera Hunter published *To 'Joy My Freedom: Southern Black Women's Lives and Labors after the Civil War* (Cambridge, MA: Harvard University Press, 1997). This groundbreaking book put Black working women at the center of the historical narrative and considered their relationship to labor, politics, and culture. Hunter's contribution helped lay the foundation for studying Black working women's lives and labors. This book is a part of the historiographical lineage of *To 'Joy My Freedom*.

2. On migration and African Americans, see Peter Gottlieb, *Making Their Own Way: Southern Blacks' Migration to Pittsburgh, 1916–30* (Urbana: University of Illinois Press, 1987); James N. Gregory, *The Southern Diaspora: How the Great Migrations of Black and White Southerners Transformed America* (Chapel Hill: University of North Carolina Press, 2005); James R. Grossman, *Land of Hope: Chicago, Black Southerners, and the Great Migration* (Chicago: University of Chicago Press, 1989); Darlene Clark Hine, "Black Migration to the Urban Midwest: The Gender Dimension, 1915–1945," in *Hine Sight: Black Women and the Re-construction of American History* (Bloomington: Indiana University Press, 1997); Nicholas Lemann, *The Promised Land: The Great Black Migration and How It Changed America* (New York: A.A. Knopf, 1991); Kimberley L. Phillips, *AlabamaNorth: African-American Migrants, Community, and Working-Class Activism in Cleveland, 1915–45* (Urbana: University of Illinois Press, 1999); Joe William Trotter, *The Great Migration in Historical Perspective: New Dimensions of Race, Class, and Gender* (Bloomington: Indiana University Press, 1991).

3. Paul Geib, "From Mississippi to Milwaukee: A Case Study of the Southern Black Migration to Milwaukee, 1940–1970," *Journal of Negro History* 83, no. 4 (Autumn 1998): 229–48.

4. Sylvia Bell White and Jody LePage, *Sister: An African Life in the Search for Justice* (Madison: University of Wisconsin Press, 2013), 156.

5. Sara Ahmed, *On Being Racism and Diversity in Institutional Life* (Durham, NC: Duke University Press, 2012), 26. My usage of the "concrete wall" metaphor is

informed by Sara Ahmed's use of the "brick wall" in her analysis on diversity workers in the university setting in the early 2000s. Ahmed notes that "the institution can be experienced by practitioners as resistance. One expression that came up in a number of interviews was 'banging your head against a brick wall.' . . . The feeling of doing diversity work is the feeling of coming up against something that does not move, something solid and tangible." My application of the "concrete wall" is in opposition to the metaphor of the glass ceiling, which has become popularized since it first appeared in the 1980s. While those in corporate America have described the inability of women to progress to the upper levels of executive leadership as the glass ceiling effect, the phrase has now been expanded to include people of color and arenas outside of the corporate world, including politics. In its initial usage, the metaphor illuminated the experiences of white women in middle management positions who experienced barriers to executive leadership. It was not meant to apply as a blanket metaphor to all workers experiencing any kind of structural barrier in their jobs.

6. On beauty work as an alternative to menial, low-wage work, see Julia Kirk Blackwelder, *Styling Jim Crow: African American Beauty Training During Segregation* (College Station: Texas A & M University Press, 2003); Tiffany Gill, *Beauty Shop Politics: African American Women's Activism in the Beauty Industry* (Urbana: University of Illinois Press, 2010); Jacqueline Jones, *Labor of Love, Labor of Sorrow: Black Women, Work, and the Family, from Slavery to the Present* (New York: Basic Books, 2010).

7. White and LePage, *Sister*, 155; Robert O. Self, *American Babylon: Race and the Struggle for Postwar Oakland* (Princeton, NJ: Princeton University Press, 2003) 172–73; J. Jones, *Labor of Love*, 148.

8. Charles W. Mills, "White Time: The Chronic Injustice of Ideal Theory," *Du Bois Review: Social Science Research on Race* 11, no. 1 (2014): 27–42.

9. Mills builds on the ideas of George Lipsitz who wrote about the spatial politics of race. Lipsitz shows how racism determines which spaces and places various groups are able to access, leading to inequality and lack of social, economic, political, educational, etc., opportunities. George Lipsitz, *How Racism Takes Place* (Philadelphia, PA: Temple University Press, 2011). Michael Hanchard theorizes racial time as "the inequalities of temporality that result from power relations between racially dominant and subordinate groups . . . producing unequal temporal access to institutions, goods, services, resources, power and knowledge" (qtd in Mills, "White Time," 28). Explaining Hanchard, Mills states that "a racial regime imposes particular dispositions and allocating of time that are differentiated by race: working time, eating time, and sleeping times, free times, consuming times, waiting times and ultimately, of course, living and dying times." "White Time," 28.

10. Brittney Cooper, "The Racial Politics of Time," filmed October 2016 in San Francisco, CA. TEDWomen Video, :50.

11. My reading of the archive for Black women's intellectual history and activism is informed by the growing subfield of African American intellectual history, especially as represented by the following works: Mia Bay et al., *Toward*

an Intellectual History of Black Women (Chapel Hill: University of North Carolina Press, 2015); and Keisha Blain, Christopher Cameron, and Ashley Farmer, eds., *New Perspectives on the Black Intellectual Tradition* (Evanston, IL: Northwestern University Press, 2018).

12. Marisa J. Fuentes, *Dispossessed Lives: Enslaved Women, Violence, and the Archive* (Philadelphia: University of Pennsylvania Press, 2016); Sarah Haley, *No Mercy Here: Gender, Punishment and the Making of Jim Crow Modernity* (Chapel Hill: University of North Carolina Press, 2016); LaShawn Harris, *Sex Workers, Psychics, and Numbers Runners: Black Women in New York City's Underground Economy* (Urbana: University of Illinois Press, 2016); Saidiya Hartman, *Wayward Lives, Beautiful Experiments: Intimate Histories of Riotous Black Girls, Troublesome Women, and Queer Radicals* (New York: W.W. Norton, 2019).

13. Lila Abu Lughod theorizes resistance as a diagnostic of power. See, Lila Abu Lughod, "The Romance of Resistance: Tracing Transformation of Power through Bedouin Women," *American Ethnologist* 17, no. 1: 41–55.

14. Grappling with the scholarship of George Lipsitz, Barbara Ransby, and Ula Taylor, specifically their biographical treatments of Ivory Perry, Ella Baker, and Amy Jacques Garvey, contributed to my ability to notice the pattern of community intellectualism. George Lipsitz, *A Life in the Struggle: Ivory Perry and the Culture of Opposition* (Philadelphia, PA: Temple University Press, 1995); Barbara Ransby, *Ella Baker and the Black Freedom Movement: A Radical Democratic Vision* (Chapel Hill: University of North Carolina Press, 2003); Ula Yvette Taylor, *The Veiled Garvey: The Life and Times of Amy Jacques Garvey* (Chapel Hill: University of North Carolina Press, 2003).

15. Antonio Gramsci, Quintin Hoare, and Geoffrey Nowell-Smith, *Selections from the Prison Notebooks of Antonio Gramsci* (New York: International Publishers, 1971).

16. Aimee Carillo Rowe, "Romancing the Organic Intellectual: On the Queerness of Academic Activism," *American Quarterly* 64, no. 4 (December 2012): 800. Rowe critiques how "organic intellectual" is taken up in the academic context, especially how intellectual production has the potential to alienate one from one's home community. Although Rowe focuses on the academy, portions of her critique of Gramsci are relevant for this study.

17. Rowe, "Romancing the Organic," 800.

18. Stuart Hall's critique of applying Gramscian thought to Black studies is relevant here. Specifically, Hall writes, "in relation specifically to racism, [Gramsci's] original contribution cannot be simply transferred wholesale from the existing context of his work. Gramsci did not write about race, ethnicity or racism in their contemporary meanings or manifestations. Nor did he analyze in depth the colonial experience or imperialism, out of which so many of the characteristic 'racist' experiences and relationships in the modern world have developed. His principal preoccupation was with his native Italy; and behind that, the problems of socialist construction in Western and Eastern Europe, the failure of revolutions to occur in the developed capitalist societies of the 'West,' the threat posed by the rise of fascism in the inter-war period, the role of the party in the construction

of hegemony." Stuart Hall, "Gramsci's Relevance for Studies of Race and Ethnicity," in *Stuart Hall: Critical Dialogues in Cultural Studies*, eds. David Morley and Kuan-Hsing Chen, 411–41 (New York: Routledge, 1996), 415.

19. See, for example, Thabiti Asulkile, "J. A. Rogers: The Scholarship of an Organic Intellectual," *Black Scholar* 36, no. 2-3 (June 2006): 35–50; Grace Lee Boggs, "The Audacity of the Organic Intellectual," *Souls* 13, no. 3 (July 2011): 353–55; Lipsitz, *A Life in the Struggle*; Ransby, *Ella Baker*.

20. Additionally, the masculinist intellectual environment in which Gramsci produced his ideas cannot be ignored. The norms of this environment meant that while the production of Gramsci's political theories depended on the emotional, physical, and intellectual assistance of Tatiana Schultz, his sister-in-law, and Giulia Gramsci, his wife, neither Gramsci nor the colleagues who took the credit for circulating his ideas took these contributions seriously. Instead, characterizations of Giulia Gramsci's postpartum health and mental struggles eclipsed her early involvement in Gramsci's ideological development. Also minimized were Tatiana Schutz's labors on Gramsci's behalf. Of the five hundred letters that we have records of Gramsci writing while imprisoned, over half were to Tatiana Schutz. In these letters they discussed personal matters as well as political ideas. Additionally, it was Tatiana Schutz who safeguarded Gramsci's journals and smuggled them out of Italy. Despite all of this, extended analyses of these women's lives or thought are extremely limited. The production of Gramscian thought has, over time, ignored, nearly erased, and silenced the women without whom it would have been impossible. Taking the historical context in which Gramsci is writing into consideration, one cannot ignore the ways misogyny might be encoded within the development of the idea and how it gets practiced. See Teresa Chataway, "Giulia Gramsci: Democracy and 'the Sexual Question,'" *Australian Journal of Political Science* 30, no. 1 (1995): 120–36; Renate Holub, *Antonio Gramsci: Beyond Marxism and Postmodernism* (New York: Routledge, 2012), 191–203; and Jane Slaughter, "Gramsci's Place in Women's History," *Journal of Modern Italian Studies* 16, no. 2 (2011): 256–72.

21. See Beverly Guy-Sheftall, *Words of Fire: An Anthology of African-American Feminist Thought* (New York: New Press, 1995); Honorée Fanonne Jeffers, *The Age of Phillis.* (Middletown, CT: Wesleyan University Press, 2020); Martha S. Jones, *All Bound Up Together: The Woman Question in African American Public Culture, 1830–1900* (Chapel Hill: University of North Carolina Press, 2009); Nell Irvin Painter, *Sojourner Truth: A Life, a Symbol* (New York: W.W. Norton, 1997); Jane Rhodes, *Mary Ann Shadd Cary: The Black Press and Protest in the Nineteenth Century* (Bloomington: Indiana University Press, 1999).

22. See Mia Bay, *To Tell the Truth Freely: The Life of Ida B. Wells* (New York: Farrar, Straus and Giroux, 2010); Nannie Helen Burroughs, *Nannie Helen Burroughs: A Documentary Portrait of an Early Civil Rights Pioneer, 1900–1959* (Notre Dame, IN: University of Notre Dame Press, 2019); Bettye Collier-Thomas, *Jesus, Jobs, and Justice: African American Women and Religion* (New York: Knopf Doubleday, 2010); Anna Julia Cooper, *A Voice from the South* (Xenia, OH: Aldine Printing House, 1892); Brittney C. Cooper, *Beyond Respectability:*

The Intellectual Thought of Race Women (Urbana: University of Illinois Press, 2017); Paula J. Giddings, *Ida: A Sword among Lions: Ida B. Wells and the Campaign against Lynching* (New York: HarperCollins, 2009); Evelyn Brooks Higginbotham, *Righteous Discontent: The Women's Movement in the Black Baptist Church, 1880–1920* (Cambridge, MA: Harvard University Press, 1994); Richard Knapp and Charles Weldon Wadelington, *Charlotte Hawkins Brown and Palmer Memorial Institute: What One Young African American Woman Could Do* (Chapel Hill: University of North Carolina Press, 1999); Vivian M. May, *Anna Julia Cooper, Visionary Black Feminist: A Critical Introduction* (New York: Taylor & Francis, 2012); Alison M. Parker, *Unceasing Militant: The Life of Mary Church Terrell* (Chapel Hill: University of North Carolina Press, 2020); Ida B. Wells, *Crusade for Justice: The Autobiography of Ida B. Wells*, 2nd ed. (Chicago: University of Chicago Press, 2020).

23. Eliza Potter, *A Hairdresser's Experience in High Life*, ed. Xiomara Santamarina (Chapel Hill: University of North Carolina Press, 2009). See also Nikki Marie Taylor, *Frontiers of Freedom: Cincinnati's Black Community, 1802–1868* (Athens: Ohio University Press, 2005).

24. Elsa Barkley Brown, "Womanist Consciousness: Maggie Lena Walker and the Independent Order of Saint Luke," *Signs: Journal of Women in Culture and Society* 14, no. 3 (Spring 1989): 610–33; Gertrude Woodruff Marlowe, *A Right Worthy Grand Mission: Maggie Lena Walker and the Quest for Black Economic Empowerment.* (Washington, DC: Howard University Press, 2003); Shennette Garrett-Scott, *Banking on Freedom: Black Women in U.S. Finance before the New Deal* (New York: Columbia University Press, 2019).

25. Burroughs, *Nannie Helen Burroughs.*

26. Tyrone McKinley Freeman, *Madam C. J. Walker's Gospel of Giving: Black Women's Philanthropy during Jim Crow* (Urbana: University of Illinois Press, 2020).

27. While *Continually Working* does not focus on the lives of rural Black Midwesterners, see, for example, the following: Dave Baron, *Pembroke: A Rural, Black Community on the Illinois Dunes* (Carbondale: Southern Illinois University Press, 2016); Zachary Cooper, *Black Settlers in Rural Wisconsin* (Madison: Wisconsin Historical Society, 1994); Stephen Vincent, *Southern Seed, Northern Soil: African-American Farm Communities in the Midwest, 1765–1900* (Bloomington: Indiana University Press, 1999).

28. For Chicago, see Davarian Baldwin, *Chicago's New Negroes: Modernity, the Great Migration, and Black Urban Life* (Chapel Hill: University of North Carolina Press, 2007); St. Claire Drake and Horace Cayton, *Black Metropolis: A Study of Negro Life in a Northern City* (Chicago: University of Chicago Press, 2015); Adam Green and Wayne Miller, *Selling the Race: Culture, Community, and Black Chicago, 1940–1955*, Historical Studies of Urban America (Chicago: University of Chicago Press, 2007); Christopher Reed, *Black Chicago's First Century: 1833–1900* (Columbia: University of Missouri Press, 2005). For Detroit, see Beth Tompkins Bates, *The Making of Black Detroit in the Age of Henry Ford* (Durham: University of North Carolina Press, 2012); Herb Boyd, *Black Detroit: A People's History of Self-Determination* (New York: Amistad, 2017); Tiya Miles, *The Dawn of Detroit: A Chronicle of Slavery and Freedom in*

the City of the Straits (New York: New Press, 2019); Heather Ann Thompson, *Whose Detroit?: Politics, Labor, and Race in a Modern American City* (Ithaca, NY: Cornell University Press, 2017).

29. Joe Trotter, Jr., *Black Milwaukee: The Making of an Urban Industrial Proletariat*, 2nd ed. (Urbana: University of Illinois Press, 2007).

30. Rhonda Y. Williams, "Black Milwaukee, Women, and Gender." *Journal of Urban History* 33, no. 4 (May 2007): 551–56.

31. Jeanne Theoharis and Komozi Woodard, *Freedom North: Black Freedom Struggles outside the South, 1940–1980* (New York: Palgrave Macmillan, 2003). Also see other texts that examine the Black freedom struggle outside of the south: Martha Biondi, *To Stand and Fight: The Struggle for Civil Rights in Postwar New York City* (Cambridge, MA: Harvard University Press, 2006); Matthew Countryman, *Up South: Civil Rights and Black Power in Philadelphia* (Philadelphia: University of Pennsylvania Press, 2005); Patrick Jones, *Selma of the North: Civil Rights Insurgency in Milwaukee* (Cambridge, MA: Harvard University Press, 2009); Nancy MacLean, *Freedom Is Not Enough: The Opening of the American Work Place* (Cambridge, MA: Harvard University Press, 2008); Self, *American Babylon*; Thomas J. Sugrue, *The Origins of the Urban Crisis: Race and Inequality in Postwar Detroit: With a New Preface by the Author* (Princeton, NJ: Princeton University Press, 2005); Thomas J. Sugrue, *Sweet Land of Liberty: The Forgotten Struggle for Civil Rights in the North* (New York: Random House, 2008).

32. Brian Purnell and Jeanne Theoharis with Komozi Woodard, *The Strange Careers of Jim Crow North: Segregation and Struggle outside of the South, 1940–1980* (New York: New York University Press, 2019).

33. Jack Dougherty, *More Than One Struggle: The Evolution of Black School Reform in Milwaukee* (Durham: University of North Carolina Press, 2004).

34. Jones, *Selma of the North*.

35. Some examples include Sugrue, *Origins of the Urban Crisis*; Thompson, *Whose Detroit?*; Trotter, *Black Milwaukee*.

36. Clarence Lang, "Locating the Civil Rights Movement: An Essay on the Deep South, Midwest, and Border South in Black Freedom Studies," *Journal of Social History* 47, no. 2 (2013): 371–400; Keona K. Ervin, *Gateway to Equality: Black Women and the Struggle for Economic Justice in St. Louis* (Lexington: University Press of Kentucky, 2017).

37. On Black beauty work see Blackwelder, *Styling Jim Crow*; Gill, *Beauty Shop Politics*; on Black women in finance see Garrett-Scott, *Banking on Freedom*.

38. Michael Ezra, ed., *The Economic Civil Rights Movement: African Americans and the Struggle for Economic Power* (New York: Routledge, 2013).

39. Lisa Levenstein, *A Movement without Marches: African American Women and the Politics of Poverty in Postwar Philadelphia* (Chapel Hill: University of North Carolina Press, 2009); Rhonda Y. Williams, *The Politics of Public Housing: Black Women's Struggles against Urban Inequality* (Oxford: Oxford University Press, 2005).

40. See Felicia Kornbluh, *The Battle for Welfare Rights: Politics and Poverty in Modern America* (Philadelphia: University of Pennsylvania Press, 2007);

Premilla Nadasen, *Welfare Warriors: The Welfare Rights Movement in the United States* (New York: Routledge, 2004); and Annelise Orleck, *Storming Caesar's Palace: How Black Mothers Fought Their Own War on Poverty* (New York: Beacon Press, 2006).

41. Barkley Brown, "Womanist Consciousness."
42. Bay et al, *Toward an Intellectual History.*
43. Keisha Blain, *Set the World on Fire: Black Nationalist Women and the Global Struggle for Freedom* (Philadelphia: University of Pennsylvania Press, 2018). For additional connections between Black women's internationalism and intellectual activism, See also, Tiffany N. Florvil, *Mobilizing Black Germany: Afro-German Women and the Making of a Transnational Movement* (Urbana: University of Illinois Press, 2021).
44. 1910 Census: Volume 3. Population, Reports by States, with Statistics for Counties, Cities, and Other Civil Divisions: Nebraska-Wyoming, Alaska, Hawaii, and Porto Pico (1913), 1096.
45. 1920 Census: Volume 3. Population, Composition and Characteristics of the Population by States (1922), 1131.
46. 1930 Census: Volume 3. Population, Reports by States (1932), 1333.
47. Geib, "From Mississippi to Milwaukee," 231.
48. Geib, "From Mississippi to Milwaukee," 231.
49. Genevieve McBride, "The Progress of 'Race Men' and 'Colored Women' in the Black Press in Wisconsin, 1892–1985," in *The Black Press in the Middle West: 1865–1985*, ed. Henry Lewis Suggs, 325–46 (Westport, CT: Greenwood Press, 1996); Trotter, *Black Milwaukee*, 12–13.
50. J. Jones, *Labor of Love*, 131–62.
51. Paul Geenen, *Milwaukee's Bronzeville 1900–1950* (Charleston, SC: Arcadia Publishing, 2006) 7.
52. Grand Boulevard was later named South Parkway Boulevard and is now Martin Luther King Jr. Drive.
53. William Albert Vick, "From Walnut Street to No Street: Milwaukee's Afro-American Businesses, 1945–1967" (master's thesis, University of Wisconsin–Milwaukee, 1993).
54. Vick, "From Walnut Street," 65–90; Trotter, *Black Milwaukee*, 202. For other works that examine the history of African Americans and the game of policy see: Ann Fabian, "Gambling on the Color Line," in *Card Sharps, Dream Books, and Bucket Shops: Gambling in 19th-Century America* (Ithaca, NY: Cornell University Press, 1990), 108–52; Harris, *Sex Workers*; Rufus Schatzberg and Robert J. Kelly, *African-American Organized Crime: A Social History* (New York: Garland, 1996); Victoria W. Wolcott, *Remaking Respectability: African American Women in Interwar Detroit* (Chapel Hill: University of North Carolina Press, 2001).
55. Vick, "From Walnut Street," 65–90.
56. Trotter, *Black Milwaukee*, 128–31.
57. For a history of the Black press in Milwaukee, see Genevieve G. McBride and Stephen R. Byers, "The First Mayor of Black Milwaukee: J. Anthony Josey,"

Wisconsin Magazine of History 91, no. 2 (Winter 2007–2008): 2–15; McBride, "Progress of 'Race Men.'"

58. Vick, "From Walnut Street," 5.

59. Douglas Booth, "Municipal Socialism and City Government Reform: 'The Milwaukee Experience,' 1910–1940," *Journal of Urban History* 12, no. 1 (November 1985): 51–74; John M. McCarthy, *Making Milwaukee Mightier: Planning and the Politics of Growth, 1910–1960* (Dekalb: Northern Illinois University Press, 2009); Richard William Judd, *Socialist Cities: Municipal Politics and the Grassroots of American Socialism* (Albany: State University of New York Press, 1989); Margo J. Anderson and Victor Greene, eds. *Perspectives on Milwaukee's Past* (Urbana: University of Illinois Press, 2009).

60. Sally M. Miller, "For White Men Only: The Socialist Party of America and Issues of Gender, Ethnicity and Race." *Journal of the Gilded Age and Progressive Era* 2, no. 3 (2003): 283–302; Trotter, *Black Milwaukee*, 55; Berger, co-founder with Eugene Debs of the Socialist Party, was the first Socialist to be elected to Congress where he represented Wisconsin in the US House of Representatives from 1911–1913.

61. Sally M. Miller, ed. *Race, Ethnicity, and Gender in Early Twentieth-Century American Socialism* (New York: Garland, 1996).

62. "Letter to the Honorable Daniel W. Hoan, Mayor from Leon M. Gurda, Inspector of Buildings, May 19, 1937," (Daniel Hoan Papers, Milwaukee County Historical Society, "Housing, 1935–1939," Box 18, Folder 451A).

63. Ivory Abena Black, *Black Bronzeville: A Milwaukee Lifestyle, a Historical Overview*, rev. (Milwaukee: Publishers Book Group, 2006) 19.

64. Many cities developed urban redevelopment plans throughout the 1950s and 1960s that removed "slums" and "blighted areas," replacing them with highways and other "improvements." Many of these urban redevelopment or "urban renewal" plans destroyed thriving African American communities. For more on this see Eric Avila, *The Folklore of the Freeway: Race and Revolt in the Modernist City* (Minneapolis: University of Minnesota Press, 2014); Clarence Lang, *Grassroots at the Gateway: Class Politics and Black Freedom Struggle in St. Louis, 1936–75* (Ann Arbor: University of Michigan Press, 2009); Self, *American Babylon*; Sugrue, *Origins of the Urban Crisis*; Sugrue, *Sweet Land of Liberty*.

65. "YWCA Still Jim Crow," *Milwaukee Courier*, October 26, 1968.

66. Mary Evelyn Williams, letter to State Board of Health, Cosmetology Division, September 17, 1947, Wisconsin Cosmetology Examining Board, Beauty School Correspondence and Reports, series 889, box 2, folder 7 "Pressley Beauty School, 1946–1949," Wisconsin Historical Society.

CHAPTER 1

1. "Milwaukee Negro YWCA Staff Quits when 'Lily-White' Program Starts," *Chicago Defender*, April 12, 1950.

2. See Stephanie Shaw, *What a Woman Ought to Be and to Do: Black Professional Women Workers during the Jim Crow Era* (Chicago: University of Chicago

Press, 1996). This book examines Black professional women, positing that their work as social workers, teachers, nurses, and librarians was shaped by their upbringing and their desire to contribute to African American racial uplift. Also see Collier-Thomas, *Jesus, Jobs and Justice*; and Judith Weisenfeld, *African American Women and Christian Activism: New York's Black YWCA,1905–1945* (Cambridge, MA: Harvard University Press, 1997).

3. Dorothea Browder, "A 'Christian Solution of the Labor Situation': How Working Women Reshaped the YWCA's Religious Mission and Politics," *Journal of Women's History* 19, no. 2 (2007): 85–110.

4. Trotter, *Black Milwaukee*, 45.

5. Trotter, *Black Milwaukee*, 136.

6. For more on African American women's Christian activism, especially through the YWCA, see Betty Livingston Adams, *Black Women's Christian Activism: Seeking Social Justice in a Northern Suburb* (New York: New York University Press, 2018); Margaret Ann Spratt and Nina Mjagkij, eds. *Men and Women Adrift: The YMCA and the YWCA in the City* (New York: New York University Press, 1997); Weisenfeld, *African American Women*.

7. Gerda Lerner ed., *Black Women in White America: A Documentary History* (New York: Vintage Books, 1992), 478.

8. Lerner, 478; Dorothea Browder, "Working Out Their Economic Problems Together: World War I, Working Women and the Civil Rights in the YWCA," *Journal of the Gilded Age and Progressive Era* 14, no. 2 (April 2015): 243–65.

9. Emphasis in original. Bowles, qtd. in Lerner, *Black Women in White America*, 485.

10. Bowles, qtd. in Lerner, *Black Women in White America*, 486.

11. Lerner, *Black Women in White America*, 486

12. "YWCA Worker Here," *Wisconsin Enterprise Blade*, September 8, 1928.

13. Marilyn Gardner, "Jane Addams Inspired Milwaukeean's Work: Mrs. Lindsay Wins Service Award, Traces Career, Own Life," *Milwaukee Journal*, April 3, 1959.

14. For more information on free Black communities in Indiana, see Cheryl Janifer LaRoche, *Free Black Communities and the Underground Railroad: The Geography of Resistance* (Urbana: University of Illinois Press, 2014).

15. For an early study on Cabin Creek, see Penny A. Ralston, "The Cabin Creek Settlement: The Historical Study of a Black Community in Randolph County, Indiana," honors program paper, Ball State University, 1971.

16. "Trained Journalist for Negro Press: A Good Example," *Negro Star* (Wichita, Kansas) 14, no. 25, October 13, 1922. The *Negro Star* picked up the story from the Associated Negro Press which circulated Black news stories around the country.

17. Jane Addams, "The *Subjective* Necessity for Social Settlements," in *The Jane Addams Reader*, ed. Jean Bethke Elshtain, 14–28 (New York: Basic Books, 2002).

18. "Historical Sketch," *Phillis Wheatley YWCA Collection, 1897–1955*, Collections M 494 OM 300, Indianapolis Historical Society, Indianapolis, IN.

19. On Black professional women during the Jim Crow era, see Shaw, *What a Woman Ought to Be*.

20. Bernice Lindsay, "Colored Work Department 1949–1950," Box 37, Annual Reports 1949–1950 Folder, Madison Manuscript Collection M89-247, State Historical Society of Wisconsin, Madison, WI.

21. While Lindsay had to answer to Eva Eubanks, who eventually answered to the all-white board of directors, evidence suggests that Lindsay's relationship with Eubanks was not antagonistic. Bernice Lindsay, "Colored Work Department 1949–1950," Box 37, Annual Reports 1949–1950 Folder, Madison Manuscript Collection M89-247, Wisconsin Historical Society, Madison, WI.

22. For more on discriminatory housing practices and the role the federal government and banks played in propping up these practices, see Richard Rothstein, *The Color of Law: A Forgotten History of How Our Government Segregated America* (New York: Liveright, 2017); Keeanga-Yamahtta Taylor, *Race for Profit: How Banks and the Real Estate Industry Undermined Black Homeownership* (Chapel Hill: University of North Carolina Press, 2019).

23. Earle H. Gray, "Milwaukee, WISC," *Chicago Defender*, February 20, 1943, 24.

24. Nana Reed, "Teenage Program Annual Report, 1944–1945," Annual Reports 1944–1945 folder, box 37, Madison Manuscript Collection M89-247, Wisconsin Historical Society, Madison, WI MYWCA Records.

25. "Colored Work Department Annual Report 1944–1945," Annual Reports 1944–1945 folder, MYWCA Records.

26. "Colored Work Department Annual Report 1944–1945," Annual Reports 1944–1945 folder, MYWCA Records.

27. Bernice Copeland, "Colored Work Department Annual Report," No date, Annual Reports 1940–1942 folder, Box 37, Madison Manuscript Collection M89-247, Wisconsin Historical Society.

28. Copeland, "Colored Work Department Annual Report," MYWCA Records.

29. Copeland, "Colored Work Department Annual Report," MYWCA Records.

30. Bernice Lindsay, "Colored Work Department 1949–1950," Annual Reports 1949–1950 folder, MYWCA Records.

31. Bernice Lindsay, "Colored Work Department 1949–1950," Annual Reports 1949–1950 folder, MYWCA Records.

32. "Colored Work Department 1949–1950," Annual Reports 1949–1950 folder, MYWCA Records.

33. Lindsay, "Colored Work Department 1949–1950," Annual Reports 1949–1950 folder, MYWCA Records.

34. Historians have explored the difficulties that African American women faced at Ys across the country, particularly as the Y began implementing the Interracial Charter, which sought to integrate local chapters. See Nancy Robertson, *Christian Sisterhood, Race Relations, and the YWCA, 1906–46* (Urbana: University of Illinois Press, 2007), and Weisenfeld, *African American Women.*

35. Jeanne Hopkins, "Young Adult Report, June 1950," Annual Reports 1949–1950 folder, MYWCA Records.

36. "Colored Work Department Annual Report," No date, Annual Reports 1940–1942 folder, MYWCA Records.

37. "Colored Work Department 1948–1949," Annual Reports 1948–1949 folder, MYWCA Records.

38. During her tenure at the MYWCA Nana Reed got married and thus will be referred to from now on as Nana Reed Baker. Nana Reed Baker, Teenage Department Report, June 1950, Annual Reports 1949–1950 folder, MYWCA Records.
39. Baker, Teenage Department Report, June 1950, MYWCA Records.
40. Baker, Teenage Department Report, June 1950, MYWCA Records.
41. Baker, Teenage Department Report, June 1950, MYWCA Records.
42. MYWCA Personnel Committee Meeting Minutes, June 9, 1950, Annual Reports 1949–1950 folder, MYWCA Records.
43. MYWCA Personnel Committee Meeting Minutes, June 9, 1950, MYWCA Records.
44. MYWCA Personnel Committee Meeting Minutes, June 9, 1950, MYWCA Records.
45. "Letter to Bernice Lindsay from Margaret Hill, May 9, 1950," "Colored Work Department 1949–1950," Annual Reports 1949–1950 folder, MYWCA Records, .
46. Letter to Personnel Committee c/o Mrs. C. Burnham Hill from Bernice Lindsay May 24, 1950," "Colored Work Department 1949–1950," Annual Reports 1949–1950 folder, MYWCA Records.
47. Letter to Personnel Committee c/o Mrs. C. Burnham Hill from Bernice Lindsay May 24, 1950, MYWCA Records.
48. "Letter to Bernice Lindsay from Margaret Hill, June 9, 1950" "Colored Work Department 1949–1950," Annual Reports 1949–1950 folder, MYWCA Records.
49. "Milwaukee Negro YWCA Staff Quits When 'Lily-White' Program Starts," *Chicago Defender*, August 12, 1950.

CHAPTER 2

1. Mary Evelyn Williams, letter to State Board of Health, Cosmetology Division, September 17, 1947, Wisconsin Cosmetology Examining Board, Beauty School Correspondence and Reports, series 889, box 2, folder 7 "Pressley Beauty School, 1946–1949," Wisconsin Historical Society. All the records from Pressley Beauty School are from the collection, box, and folder referenced in this footnote; hereafter Pressley Beauty School Records.
2. E. H. Jorris, MD, Assistant State Health Officer, letter to Mary Evelyn Williams, September 19, 1947, Pressley Beauty School Records.
3. US Census Bureau, 1950 Census, Population, Vol. 2: Characteristics of the Population. Part 49: Wisconsin, Tables 74 (pp. 49-174) and 77 (pp. 49-189) (Washington, DC: US Government Printing Office, 1952), https://www.census.gov/library/publications/1953/dec/population-vol-02.html.
4. Trotter, *Black Milwaukee*, 123–28.
5. Laws Relating to the Regulation of Beauty Parlor Shops Together with Amendment to the State Barber Law Affecting Beauty Parlors, Wisconsin State Board of Health, 1919.
6. Gill, *Beauty Shop Politics*, 69.
7. Gill, *Beauty Shop Politics*, 72.

8. Leah B. Nelson, departmental correspondence to Mrs. Marion Groth, , February 5, 1945, Pressley Beauty School Records.

9. Leah B. Nelson, departmental correspondence to Mrs. Marion Groth, Subject: Colored Girl's licenses, Pressley Beauty School Records. Marion Groth, Supervisor, Cosmetology Division, letter to Mrs. Leah Nelson, Re: Colored Situation, Pressley Beauty School Records.

10. Leah B. Nelson, departmental correspondence to Mrs. Marion Groth, Subject: Colored Girl's licenses, Pressley Beauty School Records.

11. Marion Groth, Supervisor, Cosmetology Division, letter to Mrs. Leah Nelson, Re: Colored Situation, Pressley Beauty School Records.

12. Blackwelder, *Styling Jim Crow*, 31. Illinois did not institute segregated training for beauticians although there were separate licensing examinations for Black and white beauticians. "Beauty School Founder Buried," *Washington Afro-American*, June 5, 1956.

13. "Enroll Now, Pressley School of Beauty Culture," *Milwaukee Sentinel*, June 10, 1944.

14. Blackwelder, *Styling Jim Crow*, 8.

15. Juliet E. K. Walker, *The History of Black Business in America: Capitalism, Race, Entrepreneurship* (New York: Twayne, 1998).

16. Blackwelder, *Styling Jim Crow*, 3.

17. Gill, *Beauty Shop Politics*, 44–45; Freeman, *Madam C. J. Walker's Gospel*.

18. Blackwelder, *Styling Jim Crow*, 3.

19. Marion Groth, Supervisor, Cosmetology Division, letter to Mrs. Mattie DeWese Pressley, School of Beauty Culture, December 17, 1947,Pressley Beauty School Records.

20. Flora Simms, letter to Marion Groth, June 19, 1948,Pressley Beauty School Records.

21. James D. Anderson, *The Education of Blacks in the South, 1890–1935* (Chapel Hill: University of North Carolina Press, 1988), 187–88.

22. Blackwelder, *Styling Jim Crow*, 8, 82.

23. Mary Evelyn Williams, letter to State Board of Health, Cosmetology Division, September 17, 1947, Pressley Beauty School Records.

24. Hazel Kratsch, departmental correspondence to Marion Groth, Subject: Pressley Beauty School, Pressley Beauty School Records.

25. Kratsch, departmental correspondence to Groth, Pressley Beauty School Records.

26. See Deborah Gray White, *Too Heavy a Load: Black Women in Defense of Themselves, 1894–1994* (New York: W.W. Norton, 1999, 155; and Gill, *Beauty Shop Politics*, 73.

27. White, *Too Heavy*, 155.

28. Leah B. Nelson, departmental correspondence to Mrs. Marion Groth, February 5, 1945, Pressley Beauty School Records.

29. Emphasis in original. Leah B. Nelson, departmental correspondence to Mrs. Marion Groth, April 14, 1945, Pressley Beauty School Records.

30. Hazel Kratsch, departmental correspondence to Mrs. Marion Groth, October 28, 1947, Pressley Beauty School Records.

31. Hazel Kratsch, departmental correspondence to Mrs. Marion Groth, March 30, 1948, Pressley Beauty School Records.
32. Hazel Kratsch, departmental correspondence to Mrs. Marion Groth, April 6, 1948, Pressley Beauty School Records.
33. Hazel Kratsch, departmental correspondence to Mrs. Marion Groth, September 22, 1948, Pressley Beauty School Records.
34. Marion Groth, Supervisor Cosmetology Division, letter to Mrs. Mattie DeWese, April 23, 1948; Mattie DeWese, letter to Mrs., Marion Groth, July 12, 1948; Mattie DeWese, letter to Mrs. Groth, January 18, 1949, Pressley Beauty School Records.
35. E. H. Jorris, MD, Assistant State Health Officer, letter to Mrs. Mattie DeWese, Pressley Beauty School, April 2, 1949, Pressley Beauty School Records.
36. For more on the connections between professionalization, the politics of respectability, and Black women's labor, see Darlene Clark Hine, *Black Women in White: Racial Conflict and Cooperation in the Nursing Profession, 1890–1950*, Blacks in the Diaspora (Bloomington: Indiana University Press, 1989); Shaw, *What a Woman Ought to Be*; Wolcott, *Remaking Respectability*.
37. "Chapter 159," Rules of the Wisconsin State Board of Health Governing the Sanitary Regulation of Beauty Parlors (adopted in 1939), Pressley Beauty School Records.
38. Hazel Kratsch, departmental correspondence to Marion Groth, Subject: Pressley Beauty School, October 28, 1947, Pressley Beauty School Records.
39. Hazel Kratsch, departmental correspondence to Marion Groth, Subject: Pressley Beauty School, March 30, 1948, Pressley Beauty School Records.
40. Hazel Kratsch, departmental correspondence to Marion Groth, Subject: Pressley Beauty School, March 1948, Pressley Beauty School Records.
41. Hazel Kratsch, departmental correspondence to office, Subject: Pressley Beauty School, September 20, 1949, Pressley Beauty School Records.
42. "Beauty School Founder Buried," *Baltimore Afro-American*, June 5, 1956.
43. Pressley graduating class photo, printed in the *Milwaukee Courier*, February 11–17, 1973, supplement.
44. "Children's Service Group Has First Annual Dinner," *Chicago Defender*, December 28, 1940.
45. "Beauticians Sponsor Post-Yule Party," *Chicago Defender*, January 18, 1941.
46. Blackwelder, *Styling Jim Crow*, 34–63.
47. Gill, *Beauty Shop Politics*, 73.
48. Gill, *Beauty Shop Politics*, 72.
49. Alpha Chi PI Omega Sorority and Fraternity, Constitution and Bylaws, Marjorie Stewart Joyner Collection, Vivian Harsh Collection of Afro-American History and Literature, Woodson Regional Library, Chicago Public Library (hereafter, Joyner Collection).)
50. Alpha Chi PI Omega Sorority and Fraternity, National Convention March 2–8, 1952, Miami Florida and Haiti Program Booklet, Joyner Collection.
51. "94 Beauticians Return from Four-Day Goodwill Tour of Haiti," *Chicago Defender*, March 22, 1952.
52. Gill, *Beauty Shop Politics*, 87–91.

53. Gill, *Beauty Shop Politics*, 89.
54. "Payne Calypso Group Here on April 4," *Milwaukee Defender*, March 28, 1957.
55. "The Defender Salutes National Beauty Week," *Milwaukee Defender*, April 11, 1957.
56. Post Convention Notes, Newsletter, June 15, 1965, Alpha Chi Pi Omega Sorority and Fraternity—United Beauty School Owners and Teachers Association, Joyner Collection.
57. Post Convention Notes, Joyner Collection.
58. Post Convention Notes, Joyner Collection.

CHAPTER 3

1. *Hazel Williamson v. Globe Union, Inc.*, Hearing Number 1963-2, December 19, 1963, Decision of the Wisconsin Industrial Commission, Fair Employment Practices Division Records, Box 2, Folder 14, Wisconsin Historical Society.
2. The complaints analyzed in this chapter are a small sample of the more than five hundred complaints included in the Industrial Commission Equal Rights Division records of cases filed between 1945 and 1993. This chapter focuses on complaints filed between the 1950s and 1970s. Cases that the MNAACP and MUL took to the Industrial Commission during these years can be found in the Industrial Commission records, but there were some cases that these organizations handled without involving the IC. The records of the MNAACP and MUL are not exhaustive, are often incomplete, and usually omit an official outcome. Although imperfect, these complaint records often include the narrative of what happened, either written by the Black woman worker herself or transcribed by a MNAACP or MUL staff member.
3. White and LePage, *Sister*, 145.
4. White and LePage, *Sister*, 158
5. White and LePage, *Sister*, 156.
6. White and LePage, *Sister*, 157.
7. White and LePage, *Sister*, 160.
8. White and LePage, *Sister*, 163.
9. J. Jones, *Labor of Love*.
10. Branch, Enobong Branch, *Opportunity Denied: Limiting Black Women to Devalued Work* (New Brunswick, NJ: Rutgers University Press, 2011), 71–96.
11. For a history of the emergence of cities like Milwaukee in the industrial Midwest, see J. C. Teaford, *Cities of the Heartland: The Rise and Fall of the Industrial Midwest* (Bloomington: Indiana University Press, 1993).
12. Geib, "From Mississippi to Milwaukee," 242; 1940 Census of Population: Volume 2. Characteristics of the Population. Sex, Age, Race, Nativity, Citizenship, Country of Birth of Foreign-born White, School Attendance, Years of School Completed, Employment Status, Class of Worker, Major Occupation Group, and Industry Group, Part 7 (1943), 681; 1950 Census, of Population:, Volume Vol. 2: Characteristics of the Population,. Part 49:

Wisconsin, Tables 74 (pp. 49–174) and 77 (pp. 49–189) (Washington, DC: US Government Printing Office, 1952), https://www.census.gov/library/publications/1953/dec/population-vol-02.html; US Census Bureau, 1960 Census, Population, Vol. 1: Characteristics of the Population. Part 51: Wisconsin, Tables 121 (pp. 51–386) and 122 (pp. 51–401) (Washington, DC: US Government Printing Office, 1961), https://www.census.gov/library/publications/1961/dec/population-vol-01.html.

13. US Census Bureau, 1950 Census, Population, Vol. 2: Characteristics of the Population. Part 49: Wisconsin, Tables 74 (pp. 49–174) and 77 (pp. 49–189) (Washington, DC: US Government Printing Office, 1952), https://www.census.gov/library/publications/1953/dec/population-vol-02.html; US Census Bureau, 1960 Census, Population, Vol. 1: Characteristics of the Population. Part 51: Wisconsin, Tables 121 (pp. 51–386) and 122 (pp. 51–401) (Washington, DC: US Government Printing Office, 1961), https://www.census.gov/library/publications/1961/dec/population-vol-01.html.

14. William F. Thompson, *The History of Wisconsin: Continuity and Change*, vol. VI (Madison: State Historical Society of Wisconsin, 1988), 363.

15. For more on Vel Phillips, see P. Jones, *Selma of the North* and Phillips's papers, which are available at the State Historical Society of Wisconsin.

16. For a detailed history on the FEPC in the Midwest, see Andrew Edmund Kersten, *Race, Jobs and the War: The FEPC in the Midwest, 1941–1946* (Urbana: University of Illinois Press, 2000).

17. For a history on the role of labor on the March on Washington movement, see: William P. Jones, *The March on Washington: Jobs, Freedom, and the Forgotten History of Civil Rights* (New York: Norton, 2013).

18. Thompson, *History of Wisconsin*, 329–30; "Biography/History of the Equal Rights Division of the Wisconsin Department of Industry, Labor and Human Relations, and of its predecessor, the Equal Opportunities Division of the Wisconsin Industrial Commission," Manuscript Series 1744, State Historical Society of Wisconsin, Madison, WI.

19. "Biography/History of the Equal Rights Division of the Wisconsin Department of Industry," Wisconsin Historical Society.

20. "State Criticized in Negro Jobs," *Milwaukee Journal*, April 16, 1964.

21. "High Court Decision Bars Negros from Local 8 Bricklayers," *Milwaukee Defender*, April 11, 1957; "Court Decision Re-emphasizes Need for Strong FEPC Law in Wisconsin, Congressman Henry S. Reuss Says." *Milwaukee Defender*, May 2, 1957

22. "Coggs Introduces Bill in Assembly." *Milwaukee Defender*, April 18, 1957.

23. "F. E. P. Law with Teeth Enacted: Coggs Worked Hard for 'Law with Teeth.'" *Milwaukee Defender*, June 6, 1957

24. Black Women Oral History Project. Interviews, 1976–1981. Ardie Clark Halyard. OH-31. Schlesinger Library, Radcliffe Institute, Harvard University, Cambridge, MA.

25. NAACP Milwaukee Branch 1950 Program, Box 5, Folder 11, Milwaukee NAACP Papers. Milwaukee Mss. EP, State Historical Society of Wisconsin, Madison, WI (hereafter MNAACP Papers).

26. Ardie Halyard, Report on the Conference with Hon. Frank P. Zeidler, Mayor, and Dr. E. R. Krumbeigel, Commissioner of Health City of Milwaukee, May 8, 1952, pg. 2. Box 5, Folder 9, MNAACP Papers.

27. E. R. Krumbeigel, MD to The Honorable Frank P. Zeidler, May 28, 1952, Box 5, Folder 9, MNAACP. Papers.

28. Resolution, June 15, 1952, Box 5, Folder 9, MNAACP Papers.

29. Ardie Halyard to Hon. Mayor Frank P. Zeidler August 26, 1952, Box 5, Folder 9, MNAACP Papers.

30. Ardie Halyard to Hon. Mayor Frank P. Zeidler August 26, 1952, Box 5, Folder 9, MNAACP Papers.

31. PROBLEM RE: HOSPITALS, Milwaukee NAACP, Box 1, Folder 11, MNAACP Papers; "Milwaukee, Wisconsin, April 12, 1954, Daisy Thompson and Rosetta Thompson," Box 5, Folder 9, MNAACP Papers.

32. PROBLEM RE: HOSPITALS, MNAACP Papers; "Milwaukee, Wisconsin, April 12, 1954," MNAACP Papers.

33. PROBLEM RE: HOSPITALS, MNAACP Papers; "Milwaukee, Wisconsin, April 12, 1954," MNAACP Papers.

34. PROBLEM RE: HOSPITALS, MNAACP Papers; "Milwaukee, Wisconsin, April 12, 1954," MNAACP Papers.

35. Kersten, *Race, Jobs*, 72.

36. Trotter, *Black Milwaukee*, 171.

37. Trotter, *Black Milwaukee*, 171.

38. Frenchie Bell's story, including all quotes, are from "Testimony as given on November 5, 1952," Industrial Commission, Colonial Tanning Company, Frenchie Bell, Box 1, Series 1744, Wisconsin Equal Rights Division, Case Files, Employer Files and General Correspondence, Wisconsin Historical Society, Madison, WI.

39. *Edris Washington vs. Bernard Goldstein*, January 8, 1958, Box 17, Folder 8, Milwaukee Urban League Records, Wisconsin Historical Society, Madison, WI.

40. While historian of Black women's history Darlene Clark Hine theorized that a culture of dissemblance made Black women less likely to share these types of experiences, historian Danielle McGuire posits that some Black women eschewed the culture of dissemblance, many times at great cost. See Hine, "Rape and the Inner Lives of Black Women: Thoughts on the Culture of Dissemblance," in *Hine Sight: Black Women and the Re-Construction of American History* (Bloomington: Indiana University Press, 1997), 37–47; Danielle McGuire, *At the Dark End of the Street: Black Women, Rape, and Resistance—A New History of the Civil Rights Movement from Rosa Parks to the Rise of Black Power* (New York: Vintage Books, 2011).

41. Plan of Cooperation Between the Milwaukee Urban League and the Fair Employment Practices Division of the Wisconsin Industrial Commission, July 23, 1963, Box 2 Wisconsin Equal Rights Division, General Correspondence and Subject File 1954–1970, Series 1746, Wisconsin Historical Society.

42. "State Criticized in Negro Jobs," *Milwaukee Journal*, April 16, 1964.

43. Corneff Taylor, "Employment Practices on National and Local Level," *Milwaukee Defender*, June 6, 1957.

44. "Court Decision Re-Emphasizes Need for Strong FEPC Law in Wisconsin, Congressman Henry S. Reuss Says," *Milwaukee Defender*, May 2, 1957.
45. Sylvia Bell married O. C. White in the 1950s, but they divorced after a few years. White and Lepage, *Sister*, 147.
46. White and LePage, *Sister*, 182.
47. White and LePage, *Sister*, 176; P. Jones, *Selma of the North*, 33.
48. White and LePage, 188–89; P. Jones, *Selma of the North*, 36–39.
49. Reverend T. T. Lovelace, quoted in P. Jones, *Selma of the North*, 36.
50. White and Lepage, *Sister*, 196
51. Jones, *Selma of the North*, 6.
52. Peter B. Levy, *The Great Uprising: Race Riots in Urban America during the 1960s* (Cambridge: Cambridge University Press, 2018).
53. Paula Pfeffer, A. *Phillip Randolph, Pioneer of the Civil Rights Movement* (Baton Rouge: Louisiana State University Press, 1996), 210.
54. P. Jones, *Selma of the North*, 42.
55. On SNCC and the sit-in movement, see Iwan W. Morgan and Philip Davies, *From Sit-ins to SNCC: The Student Civil Rights Movement in the 1960s* (Gainesville: University Press of Florida, 2012); Clayborne Carson, *In Struggle: SNCC and the Black Awakening of the 1960s, with a New Introduction and Epilogue by the Author* (Cambridge, MA: Harvard University Press, 1995).
56. P. Jones, *Selma of the North*, 46–47.
57. P. Jones, *Selma of the North*, 47.
58. Industrial Commission of the Wisconsin Equal Opportunities Division, Statement of Employment Complaint, Anna Mae Finney and Bobbie Chappel vs. Kromer Cap Company, September 7, 1967, Equal Rights Division of the Wisconsin Industrial Commission, Box 9, Wisconsin Historical Society, Madison, WI (hereafter Equal Rights Division).
59. Finney and Chappel vs. Kromer Cap Company, Meeting with Respondent, September 13, 1967, Equal Rights Division.
60. Letter to Wisconsin Industrial Commission from Richard Grossman, President Kromer Cap Company, September 15, 1967, Equal Rights Division.
61. Initial Determination, Anna Mae Finney and Bobbie Chappel vs. Kromer Cap Company, October 4, 1967, Equal Rights Division.
62. Tula Connell, "1950s Milwaukee: Race, Class and a City Divided," *Labor Studies Journal* 42, no. 1 (2017): 27–51; Ervin, *Gateway to Equality*. For more on African Americans, unions, and Wisconsin, see Naomi R. Williams, "Sustaining Labor Politics in Hard Times: Race, Labor, and Coalition Building in Racine, Wisconsin," *Labor* 18, no. 2 (2021): 41–63.
63. See Steve Estes, *I Am a Man!: Race, Manhood, and the Civil Rights Movement* (Chapel Hill: University of North Carolina Press, 2005).

CHAPTER 4

1. Bernice Buresh, "Marchers to Pressure Legislators," *Milwaukee Sentinel*, September 29, 1969.

2. Mac Walton, "Welfare Marchers Seize Capitol," *Soul City Times*, October 4, 1969

3. Historians who study the welfare rights movement have rightly referenced *Welfare Mothers Speak Out* as a crucial text that explores the development and growth of the movement and have used the book to show how welfare rights activists connected their movement to the wider Black freedom struggles. For overviews of the welfare rights movement from a national perspective, see Nadasen, *Welfare Warriors*; Kornbluh, *Battle for Welfare Rights*; Premilla Nadasen, *Rethinking the Welfare Rights Movement* (New York: Taylor and Francis, 2012); Felicia Kornbluh and Gwendolyn Mink, *Ensuring Poverty: Welfare Reform in Feminist Perspective* (Philadelphia: University of Pennsylvania Press, 2018).

4. "United Welfare Recipients," Box 0115; "Northside Welfare Recipients," Box 98; and "Nat Turner Welfare Mothers," Box 0113, Non-Stock Corporations, 1889–1993, State Historical Society of Wisconsin, Madison, WI.

5. "Union Benefica Hispana," Box 0115, Non-Stock Corporations, 1889–1993, Wisconsin Historical Society.

6. "Welfare Mothers Organize," *Greater Milwaukee Star*, November 2, 1968.

7. "Welfare Mothers Want Christmas grants," *Soul City Times*, December 7, 1968.

8. Gregory Stanford, "In the Eye of the Welfare Storm," *Soul City Times*, December 14, 1968.

9. Gregory Stanford, "A Lesson in the Power of Organization," *Soul City Times*, December 25, 1968.

10. Historian Felicia Ann Kornbluh writes that the Milwaukee sit-in has been described as "the most dramatic confrontation over a state budget cut" in the history of the welfare rights movement. Kornbluh, *Battle for Welfare Rights*, 141.

11. "Groppi's Folly," *Milwaukee Sentinel*, October 1, 1969.

12. Mildred Calvert, "Welfare Rights and the Welfare System," in MCWRO (Milwaukee County Welfare Rights Organization), *Welfare Mothers Speak Out: We Ain't Gonna Shuffle Anymore*, ed. Thomas Howard Tarantino and Reverend Dismas Becker (New York: W.W. Norton, 1972), 29.

13. Calvert, "Welfare Rights," 29.

14. Milwaukee County Welfare Rights Organization local area groups, Box 1, Folder 9, Dismas Becker Papers Milwaukee Mss. 9, University of Wisconsin Milwaukee Libraries, Archives Division.

15. "Welfare Recipients Question Organizer," *Milwaukee Sentinel*, November 26, 1969. This is the only news article that references a dispute between the Nat Turner Welfare Mothers and Bruce Thomas, an NWRO staff member who came from Washington, DC, to help organize the Milwaukee Country organization. According to the article, Nat Turner Welfare Mothers' leader Corinne Lawson expressed displeasure and questioned Bruce Thomas's authority in organizing Milwaukee mothers. Evidence of this dispute could not be corroborated, and records of the Nat Turner Welfare Mothers group are not available.

16. Calvert, "Welfare Rights," 29. Mari Boor Tonn, "Militant Motherhood: Labor's Mary Harris 'Mother' Jones," *Quarterly Journal of Speech* 82, no. 1 (1996):

1–21. Tonn's essay on labor activist Mary Harris "Mother" Jones informs my understanding of militant motherhood. Tonn described Jones' activism as militant motherhood because she used a persona and ideology of symbolic motherhood to make gains in the labor movement. Tonn's rhetorical analysis revealed that, "Jones's militant maternal persona took form through her use of personal experience and person provocation, narrative, and inductive structures, intimate and familial terms of address and ad hominem attacks, empathy and shaming, and opportunities for audience imitation, including enactment and dialogic dialectics" (3). Specifically, "militancy and defense demand assertive, even aggressive modes of presentation" (5). The work of historians of the welfare rights movement Annelise Orleck, Premilla Nadasen, and Felicia Kornbluh describes the militancy of the mother activists by referring to them as "warriors" who, in the example of the Nevada mothers, "stormed Caesar's Palace." Orleck, *Storming Caesar's Palace*; Nadasen, *Welfare Warriors*; Kornbluh, *Battle for Welfare Rights*.

17. For freedom songs and the civil rights movement, see Reiland Rabaka, *Civil Rights Music: The Soundtracks of the Civil Rights Movement* (New York: Lexington Books, 2016); Kerran L. Sanger, *When the Spirit Says Sing!: The Role of Freedom Songs in the Civil Rights Movement* (New York: Taylor and Francis, 1995); Craig H. Werner, *A Change Is Gonna Come: Music, Race and the Soul of America* (Ann Arbor: University of Michigan Press, 2006).

18. MCWRO, *Welfare Mothers Speak Out*, 16.

19. Betty Niedzwiecki, "At War with the War on Poverty," in MCWRO, *Welfare Mothers Speak Out*, 40.

20. Betty Niedzwiecki, "At War with the War on Poverty," in MCWRO, *Welfare Mothers Speak Out*, 40–45.

21. Betty Niedzwiecki, "At War with the War on Poverty," in MCWRO, *Welfare Mothers Speak Out*, 42.

22. Betty Niedzwiecki, "At War with the War on Poverty," in MCWRO, *Welfare Mothers Speak Out*, 42.

23. Jones, *Selma of the North*, 109–42; Erica Metcalfe, "'Future Political Actors': The Milwaukee NAACP Youth Council's Early Fight for Identity," *Wisconsin Historical Society* 95, no. 1 (2011): 16–25.

24. Jones, *Selma of the North*, 109–42.

25. Jones, *Selma of the North*, 223.

26. Jones, *Selma of the North*, 223.

27. Jones, *Selma of the North*, 226. Masculinist uplift as civil rights strategy was not unique to Milwaukee. See Estes, *I Am a Man!*, 7–8.

28. Jones, *Selma of the North*, 225.

29. Calvert, "Welfare Rights," 26. That Calvert's children would be crucial in her decision to participate is not unusual. Charles Payne writes about the leadership and involvement of children in civil rights activism in his seminal work on organizing in Mississippi. Charles Payne, *I've Got the Light of Freedom: The Organizing Tradition and the Mississippi Freedom Struggle* (Berkeley: University of California Press, 2007), 22–23.

30. Daniel Patrick Moynihan and the United States Department of Labor, *The Negro Family: The Case for National Action* (Washington, DC: US Government Printing Office, 1965).
31. MCWRO, *Welfare Mothers Speak Out*, 81.
32. Rosie Hudson, quoted in *Welfare Mothers Speak Out*, 81.
33. MCWRO, *Welfare Mothers Speak Out*, 83.
34. MCWRO, *Welfare Mothers Speak Out*, 82.
35. Anne Henderson, quoted in *Welfare Mothers Speak Out*, 83.
36. MCWRO, *Welfare Mothers Speak Out*, 72.
37. "Mother's Hopes Hang on Thread of Welfare," *Milwaukee Journal*, September 29, 1969.
38. "Mother's Hopes Hang on Thread of Welfare," *Milwaukee Journal*, September 29, 1969.
39. MCWRO, *Welfare Mothers Speak Out*, 89.
40. MCWRO, *Welfare Mothers Speak Out*, 89.
41. "First Annual Welfare Rights Dance" Program Booklet, Milwaukee County Welfare Rights Fundraising and Clothing Drives 1971–1972, Programs, Pamphlets, Correspondence, Dismas Becker Papers, Mss. 9, State Historical Society of Wisconsin; "Milwaukee's Poor Prod Stores in Clothing Fight," *New York Times*, February 2, 1970; "Downtown: A Prime Target," *Milwaukee Journal*, January 27, 1970. For example, welfare rights activists in New York City also waged a "multifaceted campaign to join the affluent society," by trying to get credit at local department stores, urging the welfare department to disburse funds directly to recipients, instead of schools, to purchase their children's educational supplies and challenging the utility company for "unequal treatment of welfare families." Kornbluh, *Battle for Welfare Rights*, 116.
42. "Downtown: A Prime Target," *Milwaukee Journal*, January 27, 1970.
43. "Welfare Mothers Reject Used Garb," *Milwaukee Sentinel*, January 29, 1970.
44. "Welfare Mothers Reject."
45. "Milwaukee's Poor Prod Stores in Clothing Fight," *New York Times*, February 2, 1970.
46. "Welfare Mothers Reject."
47. "Welfare Mothers Reject."
48. "Welfare Mothers Reject."
49. "Milwaukee's Poor Prod Stores."
50. "Welfare March Planned Saturday," *Milwaukee Sentinel*, January 30, 1970.
51. Steering Committee Meeting, January 3, 1971, Milwaukee County Welfare Rights Organization, Dismas Becker Papers, Box 1, Folder 8. State Historical Society of Wisconsin.
52. Proposal for Emergency Funds, 1971, Milwaukee County Welfare Rights Fundraising and Clothing Drives 1971–1972, Programs, Pamphlets, Correspondence, Dismas Becker Papers, Mss. 9, Box 1, Folder 9, State Historical Society of Wisconsin.
53. "1 Vote Spells Defeat for Funds for Welfare," *Milwaukee Journal*, March 10, 1971.
54. Wisconsin Welfare Rights Organization, Community Development, Training and Advocacy Program, February 1971, Box 1, Folder 18, Dismas Becker Papers,

Milwaukee Mss. 9, University of Wisconsin Milwaukee Libraries, Archives Division.

55. Ibid. While this does not add up neatly to 100 percent, these are the stats the Wisconsin WRO noted in a proposal they drafted in 1971.

56. Community Relations–Social Development Commission in Milwaukee County, Special Purpose Reserve Fund, Applicant for a Day Care Training Center, Box 6 Folder 1, UWM Archival Collection 5 University of Wisconsin Milwaukee School or Education Records, University of Wisconsin–Milwaukee Libraries, Archives Department.

57. For more on the Head Start program a site of the Black freedom struggle, see Crystal Sanders, *A Chance for Change: Head Start and Mississippi's Black Freedom Struggle* (Chapel Hill: University of North Carolina Press, 2016).

58. Maris A. Vinovskis, *Birth of Head Start: Preschool Education Policies in the Kennedy and Johnson Administrations* (Chicago: University of Chicago Press, 2008), 87–118.

59. Community Board, Community Education Centers for Young Children, Membership List, Box 4, Folder 33, UWM Archival Collection 5, University of Wisconsin Milwaukee School of Education Records, University of Wisconsin–Milwaukee Libraries, Archives Department (hereafter UW-M Archives).

60. Business Organization Client Data Report, Nellie Thomas, Day Care Center, Box 11, Folder 8 Milwaukee Mss. EZ Milwaukee Urban League Records, 1919–1979, UW-M Archives.

61. Community Relations–Social Development Commission in Milwaukee County, Special Purpose Reserve Fund, Applicant for a Day Care Training Center, Box 6 Folder 1, UWM Archival Collection 5, University of Wisconsin Milwaukee School of Education Records, UW-M Archives.

62. Community Relations–Social Development Commission in Milwaukee County, UW-M Archives.

63. Community Relations–Social Development Commission in Milwaukee County, UW-M Archives.

64. Community Relations–Social Development Commission in Milwaukee County, UW-M Archives.

65. Milwaukee Country Welfare Rights Organization, Bread and Justice Day Care Training Program, and Proposal for Emergency Funding, Box 1, Folder 9, Dismas Becker Papers, Milwaukee Mss. 9, UW-M Archives.

66. First Annual Milwaukee County Welfare Rights Dance Program Booklet, Fundraising and Clothing Drives, 1971–1972, Dismas Becker Papers, Milwaukee, Mss. 9, Box 1, Folder 7, State Historical Society of Wisconsin.

67. La Causa Day Care Center, August 21, 197, Box 6, Folder 10, UWM Archival Collection 5, University of Wisconsin Milwaukee School of Education Records, UW-M Archives.

68. Established in 1967, WIN was a federal program designed to reduce welfare dependency by increasing employment training and opportunities for welfare recipients.

69. Clementina Castro, "Spanish-Speaking People in Welfare System," in MCWRO, *Welfare Mothers Speak Out*, 71.

70. Castro, "Spanish-Speaking People," 71.
71. La Causa Day Care Center, August 21, 1973, Box 6, Folder 10, UWM Archival Collection 5, University of Wisconsin Milwaukee School of Education Records, UW-M Archives.
72. First Annual Milwaukee County Welfare Rights Dance Program Booklet, Fundraising and Clothing Drives, 1971–1972," Dismas Becker Papers, Milwaukee, Mss. 9, Box 1, Folder 7, State Historical Society of Wisconsin.
73. MCWRO, *Welfare Mothers Speak Out.*
74. Rosalyn Baxandall, "Re-Visioning the Women's Liberation Movement's Narrative: Early Second Wave African American Feminists," *Feminist Studies* 27, no. 1 (Spring 2001): 225–45.
75. Damned, *Lessons from the Damned: Class Struggle in the Black Community* (Washington, NJ: Times Change Press, 1973), 8.
76. In the early 2000s, more scholars considered the meaning and impact of *Lessons from the Damned*, but it is still relatively unknown. See Baxandall, "Re-Visioning," and Robin D. G. Kelley, *Freedom Dreams: The Black Radical Imagination* (Boston: Beacon Press, 2002) 135–56.
77. Letter to Thomas Howard Tarantino from Georgia Griggs, October 15, 1971, George Wiley Papers, Box 33: Folder 20, Part 1, Mss. 324, Audio 544A, PH 5025, PH 5026, VCA 247–VCA 253, Original Collection, 1949–1975, State Historical Society of Wisconsin.
78. Premilla Nadasen, *Household Workers Unite: The Untold Story of African American Women Who Built a Movement* (Boston: Beacon Press, 2015), 3. In *Household Workers Unite*, Premilla Nadasen examines how domestic workers who organized in the 1960s and 1970s also used storytelling as a form of activism, which became "a strategic way to make sense of the past as well as the present and to overturn assumptions about domestic workers."
79. MWRO, *Welfare Mothers Speak Out*, 9.
80. Cassie B. Downer, "Guaranteed Adequate Income Now," in MCWRO, *Welfare Mothers Speak Out*, 133.
81. Downer, "Guaranteed Adequate Income," in MCWRO *Welfare Mothers Speak Out*, 134.
82. Castro, "Spanish-Speaking People," in MCWRO, *Welfare Mothers Speak Out*, 67.
83. Brian Steensland, *The Failed Welfare Revolution: America's Struggle over Guaranteed Income Policy* (Princeton, NJ: Princeton University Press, 2008), 34.
84. Steensland, *The Failed Welfare Revolution*, 58.
85. MCWRO, *Welfare Mothers Speak Out*, 126.
86. MCWRO, *Welfare Mothers Speak Out*, 115.
87. MCWRO, *Welfare Mothers Speak Out*, 116.
88. Downer, "Guaranteed Adequate, Income," in MCWRO, *Welfare Mothers Speak Out*, 135.
89. MCWRO, *Welfare Mothers Speak Out*, 131.
90. Nadasen, *Rethinking the Welfare Rights Movement*, 81–82.
91. Nadasen, *Rethinking the Welfare Rights Movement*, 74–77.
92. Betty Glosson, quoted in *Welfare Mothers Speak Out*, 116–17.

93. Downer, "Guaranteed Adequate Income," in MCWRO, *Welfare Mothers Speak Out*, 135. Downer, quoted in *Welfare Mothers Speak Out*, 135.
94. Downer, "Guaranteed Adequate Income," 135–36.
95. Castro, "Spanish Speaking People," 68–69.
96. Mattie Richardson, Chairman, Finance Committee, January 17, 1972, Letter, Box 1, Folder 5, Dismas Becker Papers, Milwaukee Mss. 9, UW-M Archives.
97. Mattie Richardson, Chairman, Finance Committee, UW-M Archives.
98. Mildred Calvert, "Welfare Rights and the Welfare System," in MCWRO, *Welfare Mothers Speak Out*, 30.

CHAPTER 5

1. See Brian Purnell and Jeanne Theoharis, with Komozi Woodard, introduction to *Strange Careers of the Jim Crow North* (New York: NYU Press). Also, in his work on the civil rights movement in Brooklyn, Brian Purnell examines the impact of the culture of poverty discourse on the social, economic and political status of people of color in the 1950s and 1960s. See Brian Purnell, *Fighting Jim Crow in the County of Kings: The Congress of Racial Equality in Brooklyn* (Lexington: University of Kentucky Press, 2015), 25–26.
2. Lester G. McAlister and William E. Tucker, *Journey in Faith: A History of the Christian Church (Disciples of Christ)* (St. Louis, MO: Chalice Press, 1975).
3. Project Equality Program Manual, Project Equality, Inc. Records, 1971–2007, pg. 5 (hereafter Project Equality Records, Marquette University).
4. Project Equality Program Manual, pg. 6, Project Equality Records, Marquette University.
5. Project Equality Program Manual, pg. 6, Project Equality Records, Marquette University.
6. Trotter, *Black Milwaukee*, 209.
7. Finding Aid for the Record of the Milwaukee Citizens for Equal Opportunity, 1960–1966, Milwaukee Micro 16 and Micro 670, State Historical Society of Wisconsin, http://digital.library.wisc.edu/1711.dl/wiarchives.uw-whs-micro670.
8. Records of the United Citizens' Committee for Freedom of Residence in Illinois, Manuscript Collection 11, State Historical Society of Wisconsin.
9. See Dougherty, *More Than One Struggle*, 104–30.
10. Freedom School Program of Activities for Intermediate Grades, Records of the Milwaukee United School Integration Committee, Curricula and Lessons for Freedom School, Box 1, Folder 2, State Historical Society of Wisconsin, 2.
11. "Helen Barnhill Resigns Post," *Milwaukee Star*, February 14, 1970; "Equal Opportunity for Women Is Talk Subject," *Milwaukee Star*, February 28, 1970.
12. "Helen Barnhill Resigns Post."
13. Ron Marose, "Rights Activists Renew Ties, Remember Struggles," *Milwaukee Sentinel*, April 29, 1974, pt. 1, pg. 5.
14. "Helen Barnhill Resigns Post."
15. "Helen Barnhill Resigns Post."

16. Notes from the Early History of Project Equality of Wisconsin, Project Equality of Wisconsin, Inc. Records, 1969–2004, Box 1, Folder 9, History Folder, 1984, Marquette Archives (hereafter Project Equality of Wisc., Marquette Archives).

17. "Project Equality; Detroit," *Milwaukee Star*, January 11, 1969.

18. "Project Equality Gains State Support," *Milwaukee Star*, May 2, 1970.

19. "What Is a Compliance Review?" *Project Equality of Wisconsin Inc Newsletter*, vol 10, February/March 1975, p. 3, series 5, box 4, folder 3, Project Equality Records, Marquette Archives.

20. Samuel Wong, Guest Editorial, *Project Equality of Wisconsin Inc Newsletter*, vol. 26, April 1978, p. 4 Series 1, Box 2, Folder 1, Project Equality of Wisc., Marquette Archives.

21. "Project Equality: Low-Key Approach to Effecting Change," *Business Journal*, April 16, 1994, 9.

22. "YWCA Still Jim Crow," *Milwaukee Courier*, October 26, 1968.

23. MYWCA Board of Directors Meeting Minutes, March 1971, Manuscript Collection M89-247, Box 2, State Historical Society of Wisconsin.

24. *Project Equality of Wisconsin Inc Newsletter*, vol 2, July 1972, Project Equality of Wisc., Marquette Archives.

25. *Project Equality of Wisconsin Inc Newsletter*, vol 2, July 1972, Project Equality of Wisc., Marquette Archives. While the MY was listed as a supporter of PE in the 1971 Wisconsin supplement to the annual *Buyer's Guide*, evidence of the result of the MYWCA's audit could not be located in PE's records.

26. Paula Brookmire, "Director Hopes YY Can Translate Service to Action," *Milwaukee Journal*, November 26, 1972.

27. *Project Equality of Wisconsin Inc Newsletter*, vol. 4, April 1973, Project Equality of Wisc., Marquette Archives; "Firms Dealing with City Schools May Be Checked," *Wisconsin State Journal*, July 7, 1971.

28. Madison Public School System and Project Equality of Wisconsin, Inc. Agreement, March 5, 1973, Series 4, Employment Audit Files, Folder 5, Project Equality Records, Marquette University.

29. Background on MPS PE Partnership, Project Equality Records, Marquette University.

30. John V. Odom, letter to Betty J. Thompson, Madison Public Schools Affirmative Action Coordinator, January 18, 1975, Marquette Archives.

31. *Project Equality of Wisconsin Inc Newsletter*, vol. 2, July 1972, Project Equality of Wisc., Marquette Archives.

32. *Project Equality of Wisconsin Inc Newsletter*, vol. 4, April 1973, Project Equality of Wisc., Marquette Archives.

33. "Memoirs: Betty J. Thompson," in *Wisconsin Annual Conference The United Methodist Church: 2004 Yearbook and Journal*, vol. 1, ed. Kevin Rice Myers, 236–48 (Sun Prairie, WI: Wisconsin Annual Conference, 2004), 247. https://www.wisconsinumc.org/files/wifiles/documents/secretary/2004/Volume1/14.Memoirs2004.pdf.

34. Project Equality, Biography of Betty J. Thompson, Series 1, Box 1, Folder 6, Project Equality of Wisc., Marquette Archives.

35. Betty Jean Thompson, quoted in Dorothy Austin, "A Woman with a Mission—Project Equality," *Milwaukee Sentinel*, March 31, 1977.

36. Thompson, quoted in Ernst Franzen, "Project Equality Marks 25th Anniversary," *Milwaukee Sentinel*, April 16, 1994.

37. Betty Thompson, "Letter from the Executive Director," *Project Equality of Wisconsin Inc Newsletter*, vol. 10, February/March 1975, series 5, box 4, folder 3, Project Equality Records, Marquette University.

38. Thompson, "Letter from the Executive Director," *Project Equality of Wisconsin Inc Newsletter*, vol. 31, May, 1979, series 5, box 4, folder 3, Project Equality Records, Marquette University.

39. Thompson, "Letter from the Executive Director," *Project Equality of Wisconsin Inc Newsletter*, vol. 36, Winter 1980, series 5, box 4, folder 3, Project Equality Records, Marquette University.

40. Betty Thompson, quoted in Sue Burke, "Project Equality Fights Discrimination at Cash Register," *Wisconsin Light*, August 12, 1988–September 8, 1999.

41. Thompson, "Letter from the Executive Director," *Project Equality of Wisconsin Inc Newsletter*, vol. 37, Spring 1980, series 5, box 4, folder 3, Project Equality Records, Marquette University.

42. Thompson, "Letter from the Executive Director," *Project Equality of Wisconsin Inc Newsletter*, vol. 29, December 1978, series 5, box 4, folder 3, Project Equality Records, Marquette University.

43. *Project Equality of Wisconsin Inc Newsletter*, vol. 7, August 1974, series 5, box 4, folder 3, Project Equality Records, Marquette University.

44. Dorothy Austin, "A Woman with a Mission—Project Equality," *Milwaukee Sentinel*, March 31, 1977.

45. Thompson, quoted in Austin, "A Woman with a Mission."

46. Megan Boler, *Feeling Power: Emotions and Education* (New York: Routledge, 1999), 112.

47. Thompson, quoted in Burke, "Project Equality Fights"; see also Patricia Hill Collins, *Black Sexual Politics: African Americans, Gender, and the New Racism* (New York: Routledge, 2004).

48. Thompson, quoted in Burke, "Project Equality Fights."

49. Thompson, quoted in Burke, "Project Equality Fights."

50. Thompson, "Letter from the Executive Director," *Project Equality of Wisconsin Inc Newsletter*, vol. 22, June/July 1977, series 5, box 4, folder 3, Project Equality Records, Marquette University.

51. Thompson, quoted in Burke, "Project Equality Fights."

52. Audre Lorde, "Age, Race, Class, and Sex: Women Redefining Difference," *Sister Outsider: Essays and Speeches* (Trumansburg, NY: Crossing Press, 1984), 123.

53. Thompson, "Letter from the Executive Director," *Project Equality of Wisconsin Inc Newsletter*, vol. 8, October 1974, series 5, box 4, folder 3, Project Equality Records, Marquette University.

54. Thompson, "Letter from the Executive Director," *Project Equality of Wisconsin Inc Newsletter*, vol.17, August 1976, series 5, box 4, folder 3, Project Equality Records, Marquette University.

55. Thompson, "Letter from the Executive Director," *Project Equality of Wisconsin Inc Newsletter*, vol. 17, August 1976, series 5, box 4, folder 3, Project Equality Records, Marquette University.

56. Marc Levine, *The Economic State of Milwaukee's Inner City 1970–2000* (Milwaukee: University of Wisconsin–Milwaukee, Center for Economic Development, 2002), 24.

57. The Hillside/Lapham neighborhood is within the boundaries of the former Bronzeville neighborhood. Hillside Terrace was the housing project Bernice Lindsay advocated for in the 1940s, as discussed in Chapter 1. Levine, *Economic State*, 15

58. Levine, *Economic State*, 17.

59. Levine, *Economic State*, 18.

60. Thompson, "Letter from the Executive Director," *Project Equality of Wisconsin Inc Newsletter*, vol. 45, Winter, 1983, series 5, box 4, folder 3, Project Equality Records, Marquette University.

61. Peterson, Bill, "Civil Rights Commission Boycotted by Groups; Pendleton Labeled Administration 'Lackey,'" *Washington Post*, March 7, 1985.

62. "The Civil Rights Commission as Parrot," *New York Times*, January 25, 1984.

63. Susan Lindberg and Betty Thompson, "For Your Information," Project Equality of Wisconsin Update, vol. 12, February 1984. series 5, box 4, folder 3, Project Equality Records, Marquette University.

64. "Wisconsin Update," June 1986.

65. Loretta Williams, quoted in Mary Beth Murphy, "Erosion of Civil Rights Seen," *Milwaukee Sentinel*, April 2, 1984.

66. Thompson, "Letter from the Executive Director," *Project Equality Wisconsin Update*, vol. 12, June 1984, series 5, box 4, folder 3, Project Equality Records, Marquette University.

67. Sheila Collins and Kenyon C. Burke, eds., *Dangerous Waters: Testimony, Findings, and Recommendations form the National Interreligious Commission on Civil Rights, Civil Rights Hearings 1984–1986* (New York: Division of Church and Society, Nation Council of Churches, Churches of Christ in the USA, 1988); National Interreligious Commission on Civil Rights, *A Tale of Two Cities: The Status of Civil Rights in Louisville, Louisville Hearing, March 24, 1988* (Louisville, KY: Kentuckiana Interfaith Community, 1988).

68. Helen Gray, "Hearings Bring Home to Clergy Needs of Minorities and the Poor," *Kansas City Times*, May 10, 1986.

69. Weller, quoted in Collins and Burke, *Dangerous Waters*, 9.

70. Veronica Pitts, quoted in National Interreligious Commission on Civil Rights, Louisville Hearing, March 24, 1988, National Interreligious Commission on Civil Rights, *A Tale of Two Cities*, 26.

71. Clark, quoted in Gray, "Hearings Bring Home."

72. Brooks, quoted in Gray, "Hearings Bring Home."

73. Thompson, quoted in Gray, "Hearings Bring Home."

EPILOGUE

1. Marc Levine, *The Economic State of Milwaukee: The City and the Region* (Milwaukee: University of Wisconsin–Milwaukee, Center for Economic Development, 1998).

2. Marc Levine, *The Crisis of Low Wages in Milwaukee: Wage Polarization in Metropolitan Labor Market 1970–1990* (Milwaukee: University of Wisconsin–Milwaukee, Center for Economic Development, 1994); Jane Collins and Victoria Mayer, *Both Hands Tied: Welfare Reform and the Race to the Bottom in the Low Wage Labor Market* (Chicago: University of Chicago Press, 2010), 35–36.

3. Marc Levine, *The State of Black Milwaukee in National Perspective: Racial Inequality in the Nation's 50 Largest Metropolitan Areas* (Milwaukee: University of Wisconsin–Milwaukee, Center of Economic Development Publications, 2020).

4. John R. Logan and Brian Stults, *The Persistence of Segregation in the Metropolis: New Findings from the 2010 Census*, Census Brief prepared for Project US2010, March 24, 2011, http://www.s4.brown.edu/us2010/Data/Report/report2.pdf. Of fifty metropolitan areas with the highest African American populations, Milwaukee was among the top ten, number two, for the highest levels of segregation. The only city that was more segregated than Milwaukee was Detroit, Michigan. This same study noted that over the past three decades, there has been very little change in the persistence of Black-white segregation in Milwaukee. 5, 10.

5. Collins and Mayer, *Both Hands Tied*, 38.

6. UWM Center of Economic Development, "The Challenges Facing Milwaukee's Inner City: Statistical Snapshots," (PowerPoint slides), slideserv.com, uploaded Sept. 14, 2012, https://www.slideserve.com/waldron/the-economic-challenges-facing-milwaukee-s-inner-city.

7. See also Matthew Desmond, *Evicted: Poverty and Profit in the American City* (New York: Crown Publishers, 2016).

8. Walnut Way Conservation Corp, "Our History," https://www.walnutway.org/about/our-history, accessed December 29, 2022.

9. Georgia Pabst, "Lindsay Heights Steps into a New Area," *Milwaukee Journal Sentinel*, November 1, 2008.

10. Blue Skies Landscaping, https://www.walnutway.org/programs/blue-skies-landscaping-program.

11. Cathy Free, "They Realized a Crack House Was across the Street. Here's How This Couple Turned around Their Wisconsin Neighborhood." *Washington Post*, October 10, 2019.

12. "Bronzeville Collective Inspires Entrepreneurship in Historic Neighborhood." WISN Channel 12, https://www.wisn.com/article/milwaukee-bronzeville-collective-inspires-entrepreneurship-in-historic-neighborhood/39176444, Feb. 22, 2022; Lilo Allen and Tiffany Miller, conversation with author, February 10, 2022.

13. Angelica Euseary, "'When You Walk into the Bronzeville Collective, You Can See Yourself.' Collaborative Storefront Features over 25 Local Brands, Focusing on Creatives of Color." Madison 365, Aug. 16, 2021, https:// madison365.com/when-you-walk-into-the-bronzeville-collective-you-can-see-yourself-collaborative-storefront-features-over-25-local-brands-focusing-on-creatives-of-color.

References

PRIMARY SOURCES

Wisconsin Historical Society

Ardie Halyard Papers
Dismas Becker Papers (Milwaukee County Welfare Rights Organization)
Documenting the Midwestern Origins of the Women's Movement Oral History
    Project
Milwaukee National Association for the Advancement of Colored People Papers
Milwaukee Urban League Papers
Milwaukee Young Women's Christian Association Records
George Wiley Papers
Wisconsin Equal Rights Division
Wisconsin State Department of Health, Cosmetology Division
Wisconsin State Department of Savings and Loan Records
United States Census, 1910–1970
UW Milwaukee School of Education
Women of Wisconsin Labor Oral History Project

Other Repositories

Black Women's Oral History Project, Schlesinger Library
Daniel Hoan Papers, Milwaukee County Historical Society
Indianapolis Young Women's Christian Association Records, Indianapolis
    Historical Society
Marjorie Stewart Joyner Collection, Vivian Harsh Collection of Afro-American
    History and Literature, Woodson Regional Library, Chicago Public Library
Project Equality Papers, Marquette University, Department of Special
    Collections and University Archives Library and Special Collections
University of Wisconsin Milwaukee Libraries, Archives Department
Frank Zeidler Mayoral Papers, Milwaukee Public Library

Periodicals

Wisconsin Enterprise Blade*
Milwaukee Defender*
Milwaukee Globe*
Milwaukee Courier*
Soul City Times*
Milwaukee Courier*
Greater Milwaukee Star*
Chicago Defender*
Milwaukee Journal
Milwaukee Sentinel
*African-American periodicals

SECONDARY SOURCES

Abu-Lughod, Lila. "The Romance of Resistance: Tracing Transformation of Power through Bedouin Women." *American Ethnologist* 17, no. 1: 41–55.

Adams, Betty Livingston. *Black Women's Christian Activism: Seeking Social Justice in a Northern Suburb.* New York: New York University Press, 2018.

Addams, Jane. "The Subjective Necessity for Social Settlements." In *The Jane Addams Reader*, edited by Jean Bethke Elshtain, 14–28. New York: Basic Books, 2002.

Ahmed, Sara. *On Being: Racism and Diversity in Institutional Life.* Durham, NC: Duke University Press, 2012.

Anderson, James D. *The Education of Blacks in the South, 1860–1935.* Chapel Hill: University of North Carolina Press, 1988.

Anderson, Margo J., and Victor Greene, eds. *Perspectives on Milwaukee's Past.* Urbana: University of Illinois Press, 2009.

Asulkile, Thabiti. "J. A. Rogers: The Scholarship of an Organic Intellectual," *Black Scholar* 36, no. 2–3 (June 2006): 35–50.

Avila, Eric. *The Folklore of the Freeway: Race and Revolt in the Modernist City.* Minneapolis: University of Minnesota Press, 2014.

Baldwin, Davarian. *Chicago's New Negroes: Modernity, the Great Migration, and Black Urban Life,* Chapel Hill: University of North Carolina Press, 2007.

Barkley Brown, Elsa. "Womanist Consciousness: Maggie Lena Walker and the Independent Order of Saint Luke," *Signs: Journal of Women in Culture and Society* 14, no. 3 (Spring 1989): 610–33.

Baron, Dave. *Pembroke: A Rural, Black Community on the Illinois Dunes.* Carbondale: Southern Illinois University Press, 2016.

Bates, Beth Tompkins. *The Making of Black Detroit in the Age of Henry Ford.* Chapel Hill: University of North Carolina Press, 2012.

Baxandall, Rosalyn. "Re-Visioning the Women's Liberation Movement's Narrative: Early Second Wave African American Feminists," *Feminist Studies* 27, no. 1 (Spring 2001): 225–45.

Bay, Mia. *To Tell the Truth Freely: The Life of Ida B. Wells.* New York: Farrar, Straus and Giroux, 2010.

Bay, Mia, Farah J. Griffin, Martha S. Jones, and Barbara D. Savage. *Toward an Intellectual History of Black Women*. Chapel Hill: University of North Carolina Press, 2015.

Biondi, Martha. *To Stand and Fight: The Struggle for Civil Rights in Postwar New York City*. Cambridge, MA: Harvard University Press, 2006.

Black, Ivory Abena. *Black Bronzeville: A Milwaukee Lifestyle, a Historical Overview*, rev. Milwaukee: Publishers Book Group, 2006.

Blackwelder, Julia Kirk. *Styling Jim Crow: African American Beauty Training during Segregation*. College Station: Texas A&M University Press, 2003.

Blain, Keisha. *Set the World on Fire: Black Nationalist Women and the Global Struggle for Freedom*. Philadelphia: University of Pennsylvania Press, 2018.

Blain, Keisha, Christopher Cameron, and Ashley Farmer, eds. *New Perspectives on the Black Intellectual Tradition*. Evanston: Northwestern University Press, 2018.

Boggs, Grace Lee. "The Audacity of the Organic Intellectual," *Souls* 13, no. 3 (July 2011): 353–55.

Boler, Megan. *Feeling Power: Emotions and Education*. New York: Routledge, 1999.

Booth, Douglas. "Municipal Socialism and City Government Reform: 'The Milwaukee Experience,' 1910–1940," *Journal of Urban History* 12, no. 1 (November 1985): 51–74.

Boyd, Herb. *Black Detroit: A People's History of Self-Determination*. New York: Amistad, 2017.

Branch, Enobong. *Opportunity Denied: Limiting Black Women to Devalued Work*. New Brunswick, NJ: Rutgers University Press, 2011.

Brown, Leslie. *Upbuilding Black Durham: Gender, Class, and Black Community Development in the Jim Crow South*. Chapel Hill: University of North Carolina Press, 2008.

Browder, Dorothea. "A 'Christian Solution of the Labor Situation': How Working Women Reshaped the YWCA's Religious Mission and Politics." *Journal of Women's History* 19, no. 2 (2007): 85–110.

———. "Working Out Their Economic Problems Together: World War I, Working Women and the Civil Rights in the YWCA." *Journal of the Gilded Age and Progressive Era* 14, no. 2 (April 2015): 243–65.

Burroughs, Nannie Helen. *Nannie Helen Burroughs: A Documentary Portrait of an Early Civil Rights Pioneer, 1900–1959*. Notre Dame, IN: University of Notre Dame Press, 2019.

Calvert, Mildred. "Welfare Rights and the Welfare System." In MCWRO, *Welfare Mothers Speak Out*, 25–30.

Carby, Hazel V. *Race Men: The W. E. B. Du Bois Lectures*. Cambridge: Harvard University Press, 1998.

Carson, Clayborne. *In Struggle: SNCC and the Black Awakening of the 1960s, with a New Introduction and Epilogue by the Author*. Cambridge, MA: Harvard University Press, 1995.

Castro, Clementina. "Spanish Speaking People and the Welfare System." In MCWRO, *Welfare Mothers Speak Out*, 66–71.

Chataway, Teresa. "Giulia Gramsci: Democracy and 'the Sexual Question,'" *Australian Journal of Political Science* 30, no. 1 (1995): 120–36.

Cohen, Lizabeth. *A Consumers' Republic: The Politics of Mass Consumption in Postwar America*. New York: Knopf, 2003.

Collier-Thomas, Bettye. *Jesus, Jobs, and Justice: African American Women and Religion*. New York: Knopf Doubleday, 2010.

Collins, Jane, and Victoria Mayer, *Both Hands Tied: Welfare Reform and the Race to the Bottom in the Low Wage Labor Market*. Chicago: University of Chicago Press, 2010.

Collins, Patricia Hill. *Black Sexual Politics: African Americans, Gender, and the New Racism*. New York: Routledge, 2004.

Collins, Sheila, and Kenyon C. Burke, eds. *Dangerous Waters: Testimony, Findings, and Recommendations form the National Interreligious Commission on Civil Rights, Civil Rights Hearings 1984–1986*. New York: Division of Church and Society, Nation Council of Churches, Churches of Christ in the USA, 1988.

Connell, Tula. "1950s Milwaukee: Race, Class and a City Divided," *Labor Studies Journal* 42, no. 1 (2017): 27–51.

Cooper, Anna Julia. *A Voice from the South*. Xenia, OH: Aldine Printing House, 1892.

Cooper, Brittney C. *Beyond Respectability: The Intellectual Thought of Race Women*. Urbana: University of Illinois Press, 2017.

———. "The Racial Politics of Time," Filmed October 2016 in San Francisco, CA. TEDWomen Video. https://www.ted.com/talks/brittney_cooper_the_racial_politics_of_time.

Cooper, Zachary. *Black Settlers in Rural Wisconsin*. Madison: Wisconsin Historical Society, 1994.

Countryman, Matthew. *Up South: Civil Rights and Black Power in Philadelphia*. Philadelphia: University of Pennsylvania Press, 2005.

Damned. *Lessons from the Damned: Class Struggle in the Black Community*. Washington, NJ: Times Change Press, 1973.

Desmond, Matthew. *Evicted: Poverty and Profit in the American City*. New York: Crown Publishers, 2016.

Dougherty, Jack. *More Than One Struggle: The Evolution of Black School Reform in Milwaukee*. Durham: University of North Carolina Press, 2004.

Drake, St. Claire, and Horace Cayton. *Black Metropolis: A Study of Negro Life in a Northern City*. Chicago: University of Chicago Press, 2015.

Downer, Cassie B. "Guaranteed Adequate Income Now." In MCWRO, *Welfare Mothers Speak Out*, 132–36.

Ervin, Keona K. *Gateway to Equality: Black Women and the Struggle for Economic Justice in St. Louis*. Lexington: University Press of Kentucky, 2017.

Estes, Steve. *I Am A Man!: Race, Manhood, and the Civil Rights Movement*. Chapel Hill: University of North Carolina Press, 2005.

Ezra, Michael, ed. *The Economic Civil Rights Movement: African Americans and the Struggle for Economic Power*. New York: Routledge, 2013.

Fabian, Ann. "Gambling on the Color Line" in *Card Sharps, Dream Books, and Bucket Shops: Gambling in 19th Century America*, 108–52. Ithaca, NY: Cornell University, Press, 1990.

Florvil, Tiffany N. *Mobilizing Black Germany: Afro-German Women and the Making of a Transnational Movement*. Urbana: University of Illinois Press, 2020.

Freeman, Tyrone McKinley. *Madam C. J. Walker's Gospel of Giving: Black Women's Philanthropy during Jim Crow*. Urbana: University of Illinois Press, 2020.

Fuentes, Marisa J. *Dispossessed Lives: Enslaved Women, Violence, and the Archive*. Philadelphia: University of Pennsylvania Press, 2016.

Gaines, Kevin. *Uplifting the Race: Black Leadership, Politics, and Culture in the Twentieth Century*. Chapel Hill: University of North Carolina Press, 1996.

Garrett-Scott, Shennette. *Banking on Freedom: Black Women in U.S. Finance before the New Deal*. New York: Columbia University Press, 2019.

Gates Jr., Henry Louis, and Gene Andrew Jarrett, *The New Negro: Readings of Race, Representation, and African American Culture, 1892–1938*. Princeton: Princeton University Press, 2007.

Geenen, Paul. *Milwaukee's Bronzeville 1900–1950*. Charleston, SC: Arcadia Publishing,

Geib, Paul. "From Mississippi to Milwaukee: A Case Study of the Southern Black Migration to Milwaukee, 1940–1970." *Journal of Negro History* 83, no. 4 (Autumn 1998): 229–48.

Giddings, Paula. *When and Where I Enter: The Impact of Black Women on Race and Sex in America*. New York: W. Morrow, 1984.

Giddings, Paula. *Ida: A Sword among Lions: Ida B. Wells and the Campaign against Lynching*. New York: HarperCollins, 2009.

Gill, Tiffany. *Beauty Shop Politics: African American Women's Activism in the Beauty Industry*. Urbana: University of Illinois Press, 2010.

Gottlieb, Peter. *Making Their Own Way: Southern Blacks' Migration to Pittsburgh, 1916–30*. Urbana: University of Illinois Press, 1987.

Gramsci, Antonio, Quintin Hoare, and Geoffrey Nowell-Smith, *Selections from the Prison Notebooks of Antonio Gramsci*. New York: International Publishers, 1971.

Green, Adam, and Wayne Miller, *Selling the Race: Culture, Community, and Black Chicago, 1940–1955*. Historical Studies of Urban America. Chicago: University of Chicago Press, 2007.

Gregory, James N. *The Southern Diaspora: How the Great Migrations of Black and White Southerners Transformed America*. Chapel Hill: University of North Carolina Press, 2005.

Grossman, James R. *Land of Hope: Chicago, Black Southerners, and the Great Migration*. Chicago: University of Chicago Press, 1989.

Guy-Sheftall, Beverly. *Words of Fire: An Anthology of African-American Feminist Thought*. New York: New Press, 1995.

Haley, Sarah. *No Mercy Here: Gender, Punishment and the Making of Jim Crow Modernity*. Chapel Hill: University of North Carolina Press, 2016.

Hall, Stuart. "Gramsci's Relevance for Studies of Race and Ethnicity." In *Stuart Hall: Critical Dialogues in Cultural Studies*, edited by David Morley and Kuan-Hsing Chen, 411–41. New York: Routledge, 1996.

Harris, LaShawn. *Sex Workers, Psychics, and Numbers Runners: Black Women in New York City's Underground Economy*. Urbana: University of Illinois Press, 2016).

Hartman, Saidiya. *Wayward Lives, Beautiful Experiments: Intimate Histories of Riotous Black Girls, Troublesome Women, and Queer Radicals*. New York: W.W. Norton, 2019.

Higginbotham, Evelyn Brooks. *Righteous Discontent: The Women's Movement in the Black Baptist Church, 1880–1920.* Cambridge, MA: Harvard University Press, 1994.

Hine, Darlene Clark. *Black Women in White: Racial Conflict and Cooperation in the Nursing Profession, 1890–1950.* Bloomington: Indiana University Press, 1989.

———. *Hine Sight: Black Women and the Re-construction of American History.* Bloomington: Indiana University Press, 1997.

Holub, Renate. *Antonio Gramsci: Beyond Marxism and Postmodernism.* New York: Routledge, 2012.

Hunter, Tera. *To 'Joy My Freedom: Southern Black Women's Lives and Labors after the Civil War.* Cambridge, MA: Harvard University Press, 1997.

Jeffers, Honorée Fanonne. *The Age of Phillis.* Middletown, CT: Wesleyan University Press, 2020.

Jones, Jacqueline. *Labor of Love, Labor of Sorrow: Black Women, Work and the Family, from Slavery to the Present.* New York: Basic Books, 2010.

Jones, Martha S. *All Bound Up Together: The Woman Question in African American Public Culture, 1830–1900.* Chapel Hill: University of North Carolina Press, 2009.

Jones, Patrick. *The Selma of the North: Civil Rights Insurgency in Milwaukee.* Cambridge, MA: Harvard University Press, 2009.

Jones, William P. *The March on Washington: Jobs, Freedom, and the Forgotten History of Civil Rights.* New York: Norton, 2013.

Judd, Richard William. *Socialist Cities: Municipal Politics and the Grassroots of American Socialism.* Albany: State University of New York Press, 1989.

Kelley, Robin D.G. *Freedom Dreams: The Black Radical Imagination.* Boston: Beacon Press, 2002.

Kersten, Andrew Edmund. *Race, Jobs and the War: The FEPC in the Midwest, 1941–1946.* Urbana: University of Illinois Press, 2000.

Kesslar-Harris, Alice. *In Pursuit of Equity: Women, Men, and the Quest for Economic Citizenship in 20th Century America.* Oxford: Oxford University Press, 2001.

Knapp, Richard, and Charles Weldon Wadelington. *Charlotte Hawkins Brown and Palmer Memorial Institute: What One Young African American Woman Could Do.* Chapel Hill: University of North Carolina Press, 1999.

Kornbluh, Felicia. *The Battle for Welfare Rights: Politics and Poverty in Modern America.* Philadelphia: University of Pennsylvania Press, 2007.

Kornbluh, Felicia, and Gwendolyn Mink, *Ensuring Poverty: Welfare Reform in Feminist Perspective.* Philadelphia: University of Pennsylvania Press, 2018.

Lang, Clarence. *Grassroots at the Gateway: Class Politics and Black Freedom Struggle in St. Louis, 1936–75.* Ann Arbor: University of Michigan Press, 2009.

———. "Locating the Civil Rights Movement: An Essay on the Deep South, Midwest, and Border South in Black Freedom Studies." *Journal of Social History* 47, no. 2 (2013): 371–400.

LaRoche, Cheryl Janifer. *Free Black Communities and the Underground Railroad: The Geography of Resistance.* Urbana: University of Illinois Press, 2014.

Lemann, Nicholas. *The Promised Land: The Great Black Migration and How It Changed America.* New York: A.A. Knopf, 1991.

Lerner, Gerda, ed. *Black Women in White America: A Documentary History.* New York: Vintage Books, 1992.

Levenstein, Lisa. *A Movement without Marches: African American Women and the Politics of Poverty in Postwar Philadelphia.* Chapel Hill: University of North Carolina Press, 2009.

Levine, Marc. *The Crisis of Low Wages in Milwaukee: Wage Polarization in Metropolitan Labor Market 1970–1990.* Milwaukee: University of Wisconsin–Milwaukee, Center for Economic Development, 1994.

———. *The Economic State of Milwaukee: The City and the Region.* Milwaukee: University of Wisconsin–Milwaukee, Center for Economic Development, 1998.

———. *The Economic State of Milwaukee's Inner City 1970–2000.* Milwaukee: University of Wisconsin–Milwaukee, Center for Economic Development, 2002.

———. *The State of Black Milwaukee in National Perspective: Racial Inequality in the Nation's 50 Largest Metropolitan Areas.* Milwaukee: University of Wisconsin–Milwaukee, Center of Economic Development Publications, 2020.

Levy, Peter B. *The Great Uprising: Race Riots in Urban America during the 1960s.* Cambridge: Cambridge University Press, 2018.

Lipsitz, George. *A Life in the Struggle: Ivory Perry and the Culture of Opposition.* Philadelphia, PA: Temple University Press, 1995.

———. *How Racism Takes Place.* Philadelphia, PA: Temple University Press, 2011.

Logan, John R., and Brian Stults. *The Persistence of Segregation in the Metropolis: New Findings from the 2010 Census.* Census Brief prepared for Project US2010, March 24, 2011. http://www.s4.brown.edu/us2010/Data/Report/report2.pdf.

Lorde, Audre. "Age, Race, Class, and Sex: Women Redefining Difference." In *Sister Outsider: Essays and Speeches.* Trumansburg, NY: Crossing Press, 1984.

MacLean, Nancy. *Freedom Is Not Enough: The Opening of the American Workplace.* Cambridge, MA: Harvard University Press, 2008.

Marlowe, Gertrude Woodruff. *A Right Worthy Grand Mission: Maggie Lena Walker and the Quest for Black Economic Empowerment.* Washington, DC: Howard University Press, 2003.

Mason, David L. "Home Ownership is Colorblind: The Role of African American Savings and Loans in Home Finance, 1880–1980," *Business and Economic History Online*, vol. 8 (2010).

Mather, Mark. "U.S. Children in Single-Mother Families," Population Reference Bureau, May 2010.

May, Vivian M. *Anna Julia Cooper, Visionary Black Feminist: A Critical Introduction.* New York: Taylor & Francis, 2012.

McAlister, Lester G., and William E. Tucker. *Journey in Faith: A History of the Christian Church (Disciples of Christ).* St. Louis, MO: Chalice Press, 1975.

McBride, Genevieve. "The Progress of 'Race Men' and 'Colored Women' in the Black Press in Wisconsin, 1892–1985." In *The Black Press in the Middle West, 1865–1985,* edited by Henry Lewis Suggs, 325–46. Westport, CT: Greenwood Press, 1996.

McBride, Genevieve and Stephen R. Byers, "The First Mayor of Black Milwaukee: J. Anthony Josey." *Wisconsin Magazine of History* 91, no. 2 (Winter 2007–2008): 2–15.

McCarthy, John M. *Making Milwaukee Mightier: Planning and the Politics of Growth, 1910–1960*. Dekalb: Northern Illinois University Press, 2009.

McGuire, Danielle. *At the Dark End of the Street: Black Women, Rape, and Resistance—A New History of the Civil Rights Movement from Rosa Parks to the Rise of Black Power*. New York: Vintage Books, 2011.

MCWRO (Milwaukee County Welfare Rights Organization). *Welfare Mothers Speak Out: We Ain't Gonna Shuffle No More*. Edited by Thomas Howard Tarantino and Reverend Dismas Becker. New York: W.W. Norton, 1972.

"Memoirs: Betty J. Thompson." In *Wisconsin Annual Conference The United Methodist Church: 2004 Yearbook and Journal*, vol. 1, edited by Kevin Rice Myers, 236–48. Sun Prairie, WI: Wisconsin Annual Conference, 2004. https://www.wisconsinumc.org/files/wifiles/documents/secretary/2004/Volume1/14.Memoirs2004.pdf.

Metcalfe, Erica. "'Future Political Actors': The Milwaukee NAACP Youth Council's Early Fight for Identity," *Wisconsin Historical Society* 95, no. 1 (2011): 16–25.

Miles, Tiya. *The Dawn of Detroit: A Chronicle of Slavery and Freedom in the City of the Straits*. New York: New Press, 2019.

Mills, Charles W. "White Time: The Chronic Injustice of Ideal Theory." *Du Bois Review: Social Science Research on Race* 11, no. 1 (2014): 27–42.

Miller, Sally M. "For White Men Only: The Socialist Party of America and Issues of Gender, Ethnicity and Race." *Journal of the Gilded Age and Progressive Era* 2, no. 3 (2003): 283–302.

Miller, Sally M., ed. *Race, Ethnicity, and Gender in Early Twentieth-Century American Socialism*. New York: Garland, 1996.

Morgan, Iwan W., and Philip Davies, *From Sit-ins to SNCC: The Student Civil Rights Movement in the 1960s*. Gainesville: University Press of Florida, 2012.

Moynihan, Daniel Patrick, and the United States Department of Labor. *The Negro Family: The Case for National Action*. Washington, DC: US Government Printing Office, 1965.

Nadasen, Premilla. *Welfare Warriors: The Welfare Rights Movement in the United States*. New York: Routledge, 2004.

———. *Rethinking the Welfare Rights Movement*. New York: Routledge, 2012.

———. *Household Workers Unite: The Untold Story of African American Women Who Built a Movement*. Boston: Beacon Press, 2015.

National Interreligious Commission on Civil Rights. *A Tale of Two Cities: The Status of Civil Rights in Louisville, Louisville Hearing, March 24, 1988*. Louisville, KY: Kentuckiana Interfaith Community, 1988.

Niedzwiecki, Betty. "At War with the War on Poverty." In MCWRO, *Welfare Mothers Speak Out*, 40–45.

Orleck, Annelise. *Storming Caesar's Palace: How Black Mothers Fought Their Own War on Poverty*. New York: Beacon Press, 2006.

Painter, Nell Irvin. *Sojourner Truth: A Life, a Symbol*. New York: W.W. Norton, 1997.

Parker, Alison M. *Unceasing Militant: The Life of Mary Church Terrell*. Chapel Hill: University of North Carolina Press, 2020.

Payne, Charles M. *I've Got the Light of Freedom: The Organizing Tradition and the Mississippi Freedom Struggle*. Berkeley: University of California Press, 1995.

Peiss, Kathy. *Hope in a Jar: The Making of America's Beauty Culture.* New York: Henry Holt, 1998.

Pfeffer, Paula. *A. Phillip Randolph, Pioneer of the Civil Rights Movement.* Baton Rouge: Louisiana State University Press, 1996.

Phillips, Kimberly. *AlabamaNorth: African American Migrants, Community and Working Class Activism in Cleveland, 1915–1945.* Urbana: University of Illinois Press, 1999.

Potter, Eliza. *A Hairdresser's Experience in High Life.* Edited by Xiomara Santamarina. Chapel Hill: University of North Carolina Press, 2009.

Purnell, Brian. *Fighting Jim Crow in the County of Kings: The Congress of Racial Equality in Brooklyn.* Lexington: University of Kentucky Press, 2015.

Purnell, Brian, and Jeanne Theoharis, with Komozi Woodard. *The Strange Careers of Jim Crow North: Segregation and Struggle outside of the South, 1940–1980.* New York: New York University Press, 2019.

Rabaka, Reiland. *Civil Rights Music: The Soundtracks of the Civil Rights Movement.* New York: Lexington Books, 2016.

Ralston, Penny A. "The Cabin Creek Settlement: The Historical Study of a Black Community in Randolph County, Indiana." Honors program paper, Ball State University, 1971.

Ransby, Barbara. *Ella Baker and the Black Freedom Movement: A Radical Democratic Vision.* Chapel Hill: University of North Carolina Press, 2003.

Reed, Christopher. *Black Chicago's First Century: 1833–1900.* Columbia: University of Missouri Press, 2005.

———. *Rise of Chicago's Black Metropolis, 1920–1929.* Urbana: University of Illinois Press, 2011.

Rhodes, Jane. *Mary Ann Shadd Cary: The Black Press and Protest in the Nineteenth Century.* Bloomington: Indiana University Press, 1999.

Robertson, Nancy. *Christian Sisterhood, Race Relations, and the YWCA, 1906–46.* Urbana: University of Illinois Press, 2007.

Robnett, Belinda. *How Long? How Long? African American Women in the Struggle for Civil Rights.* New York: Oxford University Press, 1997.

Roth, Benita. *Separate Roads to Feminism: Black, Chicana, and White Feminist Movements in America's Second Wave.* Cambridge, UK: Cambridge University Press, 2004.

Rothstein, Richard. *The Color of Law: A Forgotten History of How Our Government Segregated America.* New York: Liveright, 2017.

Rowe, Aimee Carillo. "Romancing the Organic Intellectual: On the Queerness of Academic Activism." *American Quarterly* 64, no. 4 (December 2012): 799–804.

Sacks, Karen Brodkin. "Gender and Grassroots Leadership." In *Women and the Politics of Empowerment,* edited by Ann Bookman and Sandra Morgan, 77–94. Philadelphia, PA: Temple University Press, 1988.

Sanders, Crystal. *A Chance for Change: Head Start and Mississippi's Black Freedom Struggle.* Chapel Hill: University of North Carolina Press, 2016.

Sanger, Kerran L. *When the Spirit Says Sing!: The Role of Freedom Songs in the Civil Rights Movement.* New York: Taylor and Francis, 1995.

Schatzberg, Rufus, and Robert J. Kelly. *African-American Organized Crime: A Social History*. New York: Garland, 1996.

Self, Robert O. *American Babylon: Race and the Struggle for Postwar Oakland*. Princeton, NJ: Princeton University Press, 2003.

Shaw, Stephanie. *What a Woman Ought to Be and to Do: Black Professional Women Workers during the Jim Crow Era*. Chicago: University of Chicago Press, 1996.

Slaughter, Jane. "Gramsci's Place in Women's History." *Journal of Modern Italian Studies* 16, no. 2 (2011): 256–72.

Spratt, Margaret Ann, and Nina Mjagkij, eds. *Men and Women Adrift: The YMCA and the YWCA in the City*. New York: New York University Press, 1997.

Steensland, Brian. *The Failed Welfare Revolution: America's Struggle over Guaranteed Income Policy*. Princeton, NJ: Princeton University Press, 2008.

Sugrue, Thomas J. *The Origins of the Urban Crisis: Race and Inequality in Postwar Detroit*. Princeton, NJ: Princeton University Press, 2005.

Sugrue, Thomas J. *Sweet Land of Liberty: The Forgotten Struggle for Civil Rights in the North*. New York: Random House, 2008.

Summers, Martin. *Manliness and Its Discontents: The Black Middle Class and the Transformation of Masculinity, 1900–1930*. Chapel Hill: University of North Carolina Press, 2004.

Taylor, Keeanga-Yamahtta. *Race for Profit: How Banks and the Real Estate Industry Undermined Black Homeownership*. Chapel Hill: University of North Carolina Press, 2019.

Taylor, Nikki Marie. *Frontiers of Freedom: Cincinnati's Black Community, 1802–1868*. Athens: Ohio University Press, 2005.

Taylor, Ula Yvette. *The Veiled Garvey: The Life and Times of Amy Jacques Garvey*. Chapel Hill: University of North Carolina Press, 2003.

Teaford, J. C. *Cities of the Heartland: The Rise and Fall of the Industrial Midwest*. Bloomington: Indiana University Press, 1993.

Theoharis, Jeanne, and Komozi Woodard. *Freedom North: Black Freedom Struggles outside the South, 1940–1980*. New York: Palgrave Macmillan, 2003.

Thompson, Heather Ann. *Whose Detroit?: Politics, Labor, and Race in a Modern American City*. Ithaca, NY: Cornell University Press, 2017.

Thompson, William F. *The History of Wisconsin: Continuity and Change*, vol. 6. Madison: State Historical Society of Wisconsin, 1988.

Tonn, Mari Boor. "Militant Motherhood: Labor's Mary Harris 'Mother' Jones," *Quarterly Journal of Speech* 82, no. 1 (1996): 1–21.

Trotter, Joe William. *The Great Migration in Historical Perspective: New Dimensions of Race, Class, and Gender*. Bloomington: Indiana University Press, 1991.

———. *Black Milwaukee: The Making of an Industrial Proletariat*, 2nd ed. Urbana: University of Illinois Press, 2007.

UWM Center of Economic Development, "The Challenges Facing Milwaukee's Inner City: Statistical Snapshots," (PowerPoint slides), slideserv.com, uploaded Sept. 14, 2012, https://www.slideserve.com/waldron/the-economic-challenges-facing-milwaukee-s-inner-city.

Vick, William Albert. "From Walnut Street to No Street: Milwaukee's Afro-American Businesses, 1945–1967." Master's thesis, University of Wisconsin-Milwaukee, 1993.

Vincent, Stephen. *Southern Seed, Northern Soil: African-American Farm Communities in the Midwest, 1765–1900.* Bloomington: Indiana University Press, 1999.

Vinovskis, Maris A. *Birth of Head Start: Preschool Education Policies in the Kennedy and Johnson Administrations.* Chicago: University of Chicago Press, 2008.

Walker, Juliet E. K. *The History of Black Business in America; Capitalism, Race, Entrepreneurship.* New York: Twayne Publishers, 1998.

Weisenfeld, Judith. *African American Women and Christian Activism: New York's Black YWCA, 1905–1945.* Cambridge, MA: Harvard University Press, 1997.

Wells, Ida B. *Crusade for Justice: The Autobiography of Ida B. Wells,* 2nd ed. Chicago: University of Chicago Press, 2020.

Werner, Craig H. *A Change Is Gonna Come: Music, Race and the Soul of America.* Ann Arbor: University of Michigan Press, 2006.

White, Sylvia Bell, and Jody LePage. *Sister: An African Life in the Search for Justice.* Madison: University of Wisconsin Press, 2013.

White, Deborah Gray. *Too Heavy a Load: Black Women in Defense of Themselves, 1894–1994.* New York: W.W. Norton, 1999.

White House Economic Council, "Jobs and Economic Security for America's Women." October 2010.

Williams, Naomi R. "Sustaining Labor Politics in Hard Times: Race, Labor, and Coalition Building in Racine, Wisconsin." *Labor* 18, no. 2 (2021): 41–63.

Williams, Rhonda Y. *The Politics of Public Housing: Black Women's Struggles against Urban Inequality.* Oxford: Oxford University Press, 2005.

———. "Black Milwaukee, Women, and Gender." *Journal of Urban History* 33, no. 4 (May 2007): 551–56.

Wolcott, Victoria W. *Remaking Respectability: African American Women in Interwar Detroit.* Chapel Hill: University of North Carolina Press, 2001.

Index

Numbers in *italic* refer to images or tables.

Woodard, Komozi, 9–10
Work Incentive Program (WIN), 133,
    167–68
Wyatt, Jasmine, 182

Young Men's Christian Association
    (YMCA), 16–17

Young Women's Christian Association
    (YWCA), 30–32, 33. *See also*
    Milwaukee Young Women's
    Christian Association (MYWCA)
Y-Teens, 38–39

Zeidler, Frank, 92–95

CPSIA information can be obtained
at www.ICGtesting.com
Printed in the USA
LVHW101517290323
742924LV00003B/328

9 780826 505576